SECRETS
of
THE BUTCHER

SECRETS
of
THE BUTCHER

HOW TO SELECT, CUT, PREPARE, AND COOK EVERY TYPE OF MEAT

ARTHUR LE CAISNE

Illustrations by Jean Grosson

Translated by Stephanie Williamson
by arrangement with Cambridge Publishing Management Limited

BLACK DOG
& LEVENTHAL
PUBLISHERS
NEW YORK

Black Dog & Leventhal Publishers
Hachette Book Group
1290 Avenue of the Americas
New York, NY 10104

www.hachettebookgroup.com

www.blackdogandleventhal.com

First English-language edition: May 2018

Black Dog & Leventhal Publishers is an imprint of Hachette Books, a division of Hachette Book Group.
The Black Dog & Leventhal Publishers name and logo are trademarks of Hachette Book Group, Inc.

The publisher is not responsible for websites (or their content) that are not owned by the publisher.

The Hachette Speakers Bureau provides a wide range of authors for speaking events. To find out more, go to
www.HachetteSpeakersBureau.com or call (866) 376-6591.

Library of Congress Control Number: 2017959409

ISBNs: 978-0-316-48066-6 (paper over board); 978-0-316-48065-9 (ebook)

Printed in China

1010

10 9 8 7 6 5 4 3 2 1

CONTENTS

BEFORE THROWING MYSELF INTO THIS PROJECT . . .

I had to create some solid bases, like the foundations or the load-bearing walls of a house. I looked for and found scientific studies. I read books, lots of them. I also met a lot of people—farmers, renowned professionals in the meat industry, restaurant owners. But these exchanges were always a little mundane and nothing very interesting came from them. I felt frustrated. This wasn't working . . .

And then, one day, I went to meet a butcher and a farmer, the first in Sens and the second near Beaune, both in France. Actually, that's not entirely correct. They're not a butcher and a farmer. They are Jean Denaux and Fred Ménager. Jean and Fred (I'm lucky enough to call them by their first names today) are the leading authorities in their professions, both in France and abroad. Perhaps you don't know them, because the media really isn't their thing. They're known for producing meat and poultry of a rare quality. It's practically haute couture!

I met Jean Denaux first. Jean is the French specialist in meat maturation. In fact, he's such an expert that he doesn't talk of "maturation" but of "refinement." He works his meat in the same way one would refine an award-winning cheese or a vintage wine.

We spent a long time sharing stories. I wrote down everything he said to me. I was blown away by his approach to his work and his scientific knowledge. I watched him explain it to me, with piercing blue eyes and slender, outstretched hands. I felt such an intensity in him, such intelligence, that it was almost unsettling.

Then, I went to see Fred Ménager. Fred is the best source of information when it comes to poultry.

We spent the afternoon together as he introduced me to his poultry: ancient breeds, some of which had been virtually extinct, which he helped bring back. I discovered a charming guy, incredibly clever with an unimaginable amount of knowledge. He had a love for his animals and a level of integrity I'd never seen in any other farmer. And again, I filled pages and pages with rare and precious information.

In fact, it was on that day that this book really began. I had just found what I was looking for: a mix of intelligence, knowledge, passion, vision, and shared experiences.

Thank you Jean, thank you Fred, for this memorable day, and for everything you willingly shared with me thereafter.

The Animals

THE BEST BEEF CATTLE BREEDS

It's not so much the muscle that gives beef its taste but the fat inside or around the muscle. Each breed develops its own particular fat, and for this to happen, the animals' food, climate, and environment are crucial. The attention given to them by the farmer is also very important, because beef cattle are highly sensitive to stress.

THE BEST OF THE BEST

THE MATSUSAKA

It's not exactly a breed: it's a wagyu, from the Kuroge Washu breed (Japanese Black, see p 16). The calves, solely females that will remain unbred, are purchased at auction in the Tajima Valley, right next to Osaka, and raised in the Matsusaka region in the center of southwest Japan. The animals are raised in pairs and fattened with cereal grains such as rice straw, barley, and beer residues. Music is played to them to help them stay calm and avoid stress. The temperate climate and the cleanliness of their water play a big role in giving the beef its specific flavor. It's the quality of the fat that earns Matsusaka beef its renown: instead of the meat being marbled with fat, it's the fat that is marbled with meat. Tasting this meat is a unique experience. It's incredibly, indescribably succulent and the fat literally melts in your mouth. Try it once in your life and you'll remember it forever. **Cow:** 1543 lb **Carcass:** 881 lb

THE RUBIA GALLEGA

This breed from Galicia, on the coast of northwest Spain, is a cousin of the Blonde d'Aquitaine. It can often be found in France under the name Blonde de Galice. Formerly considered to be a dual-purpose breed (meant to produce both milk and meat), it's raised for much longer than Anglo-Saxon breeds—between eight and fifteen years. The first breed standards were established in 1933, but selection had begun well before. The Rubia Gallega enjoys lush grass, rich in iodine thanks to the sea spray and mild, temperate weather. It's subjected to absolutely no stress and is left outside all year round. This animal develops a substantial and very tasty amount of fat inside and around the muscles. The flavors are quite distinct: spiced, rich and salty. The fat, which almost crystallizes, has an admirably good length on the palate. The Matsusaka and the Rubia Gallega have been classed numerous times as the best meats in the world. **Bull:** 1984 to 2425 lb **Cow:** 1433 to 1543 lb **Cow carcass:** 837 lb

THE BEST

THE ABERDEEN ANGUS

Don't mistake the American Black Angus, raised in the United States in feed lots and overfed protein supplements and antibiotics, for the original breed, which takes its name from the counties of Aberdeenshire and Angus in northeast Scotland. This breed is mainly fed on good, lush grass. It's of medium build, sturdy, extremely fast-growing, and makes for a very delicate, flavorful meat with sumptuous fat and marbling.

Bull: 1736 to 2204 lb **Cow:** 1433 to 1543 lb
Cow carcass: 749 to 837 lb

THE RED ANGUS

The red coloring of the Red Angus is probably due to several crosses with the Longhorn in the eighteenth century. When the first Aberdeen Angus Herdbook was created in Scotland in 1862, the red coloring was accepted. It was only banned in the United States in 1917 to ensure a pure black breed. The Red Angus Association was born in the United States in 1954. The Red and the Aberdeen Angus have the same physical characteristics.

Bull: 1763 to 2204 lb **Cow:** 1433 to 1543 lb
Cow carcass: 749 to 837 lb

THE TEXAS LONGHORN

This breed is a descendant of the cattle brought to Mexico by the conquistadors. When the northern territories of Mexico were annexed by the United States, crossbreeding with English breeds took place in Texas, which is where the name "Texas Longhorn" comes from. The breed began to die out before being saved from extinction by the American government in 1927. A purebred meat breed, its meat is relatively coarse-grained and contains little fat.

Bull: 1763 to 2204 lb **Cow:** 881 to 1543 lb
Cow carcass: 551 to 771 lb

THE LONGHORN

Originating from the north of England, this is the oldest 100 percent English breed. Well known for the length and shape of its horns, the Longhorn dominated British farming until it virtually disappeared in the 1980s. It isn't related to the Texas Longhorn, which is of Spanish origin. This purebred, robust beef breed makes for flavorful meat with a good meat/fat ratio and length on the palate.

Bull: 1984 to 2204 lb **Cow:** 1212 to 1653 lb
Cow carcass: 683 to 925 lb

11

THE BEST BEEF CATTLE BREEDS

THE SANTA GERTRUDIS

The Santa Gertrudis was created in Texas in 1910 by crossing Brahmans and Shorthorns. Officially recognized in 1940 by the United States Department of Agriculture, it became the first breed to have been created in the United States. Very muscular and capable of traveling long distances in search for food, this breed is particularly adapted to disadvantaged areas. Its meat has little intramuscular fat, but is quite tender.
Bull: 1653 to 1984 lb **Cow:** 1322 to 1653 lb
Cow carcass: 771 to 992 lb

THE HEREFORD

An English breed from the county of Herefordshire in the west of England near Wales, the Hereford is a purebred meat cow, which formerly had a triple purpose: milk, meat, and animal power. Of medium build, with horns or without (the Polled Hereford), this breed is robust, resilient, and very fast-growing. The finishing phase takes place at around eighteen months. Its meat is very flavorful, with a good-quality fat inside and around the muscle.
Bull: 1763 to 2425 lb **Cow:** 1433 to 1653 lb
Cow carcass: 793 to 903 lb

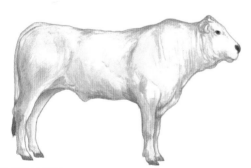

THE CHIANINA

From the Chiana Valley in Tuscany, this breed is most likely the oldest in the world: over 2,000 years old. It's also the biggest: just under 6 feet (180 cm) at the withers! The Chianina was a dairy breed before becoming the source of meat for *bistecca alla fiorentina*, the Florentine-style T-bone steak. The meat is lean and very tasty, with aromatic notes.
Bull: 2425 to 2866 lb **Cow:** 1763 to 2203 lb
Cow carcass: 970 to 1212 lb

THE GALLOWAY

Originally from the province of Galloway in Scotland, this is one of the oldest British breeds. The Galloway is robust enough to live on the Scottish moors, which are battered by wind and rain. It's easy to raise, heavy, but of small stature. It has a long, curly coat, which, similar to the Belted Galloway, has a large white belt across the middle. Its meat is tender, tasty, and lean.
Bull: 1763 to 2204 lb **Cow:** 1102 to 1543 lb
Cow carcass: 661 to 881 lb

THE HIGHLAND

The Highland is originally from . . . the Highlands, in northwest Scotland. The region is covered in hills and mountains and the moors offer poor pastures. This is the only breed of cow capable of living in such a remote region. Small in stature, the Highland is protected by a long winter coat, which it sheds in the summer. Its dark red meat has a large amount of extra-muscular fat, good marbling, and gamy flavors.
Bull: 1763 to 2204 lb **Cow:** 1102 to 1322 lb
Cow carcass: 595 to 727 lb

THE SHORTHORN

Don't mistake the Beef Shorthorn, a meat breed, for the Dairy Shorthorn, a milk breed. Previously known as the Durham, this breed is originally from northeast England. Its color varies from red to white, but it's sometimes mottled with both colors. The variation without the horns is called the Polled Shorthorn. This breed is very fast-growing and makes for a well-marbled meat with a magnificent subcutaneous fat.
Bull: 1984 to 2425 lb **Cow:** 1322 to 1543 lb
Cow carcass: 727 to 859 lb

THE BAZADAISE

Thought to be the oldest French breed, it was allegedly born from a cross between the Ibérico and Aquitaine breeds. Used in the Bordeaux region for farm work, it almost died out after the Second World War. Saved from extinction by several breeders, it's still quite a rare breed. The dark red, marbled meat is often compared to the Angus or the Longhorn. Unfortunately, it's still quite difficult to find.
Bull: 1763 to 2204 lb **Cow:** 1433 to 1653 lb
Cow carcass: 749 to 903 lb

THE BRAHMAN

Born of various crosses between several descendants of the Indian Bos indicus or zebu cattle, the Brahman (or Brahma) has a large hump on its shoulders and neck as well as a dewlap, which allows it to cool itself down with ease. Of medium build, its meat can be quite tough: slow-cooking methods such as braising and boiling are the most well-suited.
Bull: 1763 to 2425 lb **Cow:** 1102 to 1543 lb
Cow carcass: 661 to 881 lb

THE BEST BEEF CATTLE BREEDS

THE AUBRAC

Here's a breed from the southeast area of the Massif Central in France; alpine, robust, and of medium height. It doesn't mind the variation in the quality of the fodder it eats, which is subject to the changing seasons. In the spring and the summer, it finds the food that makes its meat so rich: lush grass composed of a number of different plants that can be found nowhere else, which give it its aromatic, venison-like flavors.

Bull: 1873 to 2425 lb **Cow:** 1212 to 1653 lb
Cow carcass: 683 to 925 lb

THE CHAROLAIS

The Charolais, from the French department of Saône-et-Loire, is a large, muscular animal and one of the first suckling cow breeds in France. It can now be found just about everywhere due to its ability to adapt. The bulls are regularly used to improve other breeds. Its attributes are registered under the French AOC Boeuf de Charolles label, which is a designation of origin. These attributes include: marbling; juiciness; consistency in texture, and grassy, gamy flavors.

Bull: 2204 to 3086 lb **Cow:** 1543 to 1984 lb
Cow carcass: 837 to 1102 lb

THE SIMMENTAL

A crossbreed that produces both milk and meat, the Simmental is originally from the Simme Valley in Switzerland. Part of the big Pies Rouge family, it's a powerful animal that can adapt to all climates and eats an average-quality fodder. It can be found in France as the Simmental Française. Calves, steers, and young bulls are highly sought-after. The meat has good marbling and consistency and is rich in flavor.

Bull: 2204 to 2755 lb **Cow:** 1543 to 1763 lb
Cow carcass: 837 to 970 lb

THE LIMOUSIN

Originating from the west of the Massif Central in the middle of southern France, the Limousin was originally an animal renowned for the quality of its meat. This robust breed is perfectly adapted to suit the local conditions: a hilly landscape and wide temperature variations. It's a breed loved by butchers because the carcass yields a lot of meat. The meat is quite lean with a fine grain.

Bull: 1984 to 2425 lb **Cow:** 1433 to 1763 lb
Cow carcass: 881 to 992 lb

WAGYU

"The best meat in the world," is what they call it. This beef, which can have more fat than it does flesh, is reminiscent of foie gras. Forget everything you thought you knew about meat. Wagyu is something completely different . . .

Let's make one thing perfectly clear: contrary to what you might read, wagyu is not a breed. It's a Japanese cow, that's all. *Wa* means "Japan" and also "the spirit of peace and harmony that reigns there," and *gyu* means "cow." Incidentally, several Japanese breeds are wagyus.

WHY IS IT THE BEST OF THE BEST?

In France, they love fattened goose or duck liver because it results in an exceptional product. In Japan, they raise cows for the same reasons; an extraordinary meat, unbelievably tender, with a fat that melts in the mouth like candy, its flavors buttery, floral, and slightly sweet. It's insanely delicious!

A BIT OF HISTORY

The wagyu's ancestors were supposedly imported from Korea in 400 BC for their endurance. The bodies of these cows are capable of generating a lot of intramuscular fat. It's this fat that gives them the energy necessary for physical labor.

After a period of national isolation from 1635 to 1853, during which time all food originating from four-legged animals was banned for religious reasons, and because animals were essential to agriculture, the Japanese began to raise wagyus for the quality of their meat. Starting in 1864, European cows were introduced to create crossbreeds and increase wagyu numbers.

FARMING

Purchased at auction when they are only calves, the heifers (except the Japanese Shorthorn) are raised in stables, often in pairs, and fed cereal grains (corn, barley, wheat bran, rice straw, etc.), rice concentrate, rice silage, and most of all, beer residues. Beer residues are the barley grain husks, leftover starch and insoluble protein that remain after the beer-brewing process—all without antibiotics, of course.

In contrast to western beef, quality wagyus present more fat than meat. It's the quantity and quality of this fat that makes wagyu so unique.

The animals are fussed over, petted, and gently rubbed. In short, they're given so much love that they fatten without feeling any stress. Slaughter takes place between twenty-six and thirty months, depending on the animal.

CLASSIFICATION

After slaughter, the carcasses are graded by external inspectors. The evaluation is based on two criteria: the quality of the meat and the carcass yield (the quantity of the meat in relation to the weight of the animal).

For the quality of the meat, the color, shine, firmness, and grain are judged. The color and the shine of the fat, as well as the fat deposits, are also assessed.

The grading ranges from 1 to 5, 5 being the highest grade. The carcass yield is graded from C to A, A being the highest grade. Carcass rating depends on two criteria. A5 is the highest grade and C1 the lowest.

WAGYU

THE BREEDS

Wagyu is composed of four (and only four) breeds:

THE JAPANESE BLACK (KUROGE WASHU)

This former dairy breed is now the most common breed and represents almost 90 percent of wagyus. Raised just about everywhere in Japan, the Kuroge Washu presents very white strips of intramuscular fat.

THE JAPANESE POLLED (MUKAKU WASHU)

Born from a cross between the traditional Kuroge Washu and the Aberdeen Angus, the Mukaku Washu is raised primarily in the prefecture of Yamaguchi in southwest Japan. This breed is smaller than the others.

THE JAPANESE BROWN OR JAPANESE RED (KATSUMOU WASHU)

Found only in the prefectures of Kumamoto and Kochi in far southwest Japan, the Katsumou Washu, born from a cross between the Akaushi and the Simmental, is known for its good meat/fat ratio.

THE JAPANESE SHORTHORN (NIHON TANKAKU WASHU)

Born from a cross between the Nanbu and the American Shorthorn at the end of the nineteenth century, the Nihon Tankaku Washu is the least-bred breed. It feeds on pastures and its marbling is much less present.

THE BEST WAGYUS

The best wagyus are Japanese Blacks that are born in the Tajima Valley, near Osaka. The calves are raised in the Matsusaka, Ohmi, or Kobe regions. The cleanliness of the water they consume as well as the specifics of the food gives their meat different characteristics depending on the regions and labels of origin.

THE MATSUSAKA

Renowned for being the best wagyu, it has a very fine marbling, a fat that melts as soon as it meets your mouth, and an unrivaled tenderness. Matsusaka can be eaten less-cooked than the other wagyus and even raw, as sashimi. It's rare to find, even in Japan.

THE OHMI

This wagyu is known as the first to be raised for its meat. Its fat marbling is also very fine and slightly sweet. It's said that when eating beef was banned, thin slices marinated in miso were given to the governor under the guise of a medicinal cure.

THE KOBE

The port of Kobe opened after the period of national isolation of 1853, allowing foreigners to taste wagyu for the first time and give it its reputation. Although it's a little less delicate than the Matsusaka and the Ohmi, it's still incredibly good.

Other good-quality wagyus exist: the Yonezawa, the Iwate Shorthorn, the Itachigyu, the Kazusa, the Kyoto, the Miyazakigyu, and the Akaushi.

WAGYU OUTSIDE OF JAPAN

For a long time, Japanese wagyu was illegal to export. Today, only a small number of carcasses are exported to Europe every month.

For almost twenty years, the United States, Australia, and Chile have developed cattle breeding programs by crossing Japanese Blacks to produce wagyus. Breeding farms can also now be found in France, the United Kingdom, and even in Sweden, but the quality of the animals produced is nothing compared with that of the Japanese wagyus.

Basically, creating a wagyu outside of Japan is like making Normandy camembert in the United States, champagne in Australia, Parma ham in Germany . . . it looks similar, but it's not the real thing.

HOW DO YOU COOK IT?

Wagyu is first and foremost raised to correspond to the tastes and cooking traditions of Japan. The slices must be thin to allow them to melt in the mouth without having to chew. Although providing the same weight in meat as dicing would, this type of cut creates a larger surface area, allowing for a more intense experience of the extent of the flavors and aromas.

COOKING JAPANESE WAGYU

Sukiyaki: the meat is cooked in a cast iron dish called a *sukiyaki-nabe*, caramelized with sugar, soaked in sake, loosened with soy sauce, and dipped in raw, beaten egg after cooking. Both crispy and melt-in-the-mouth, this is without a doubt the best way to cook wagyu. But please, don't mistake sukiyaki for a Japanese meat fondue! True sukiyaki, when made in its hometown, Osaka, is cooked without a broth.

On the grill: cut into thin slices, the meat grills on small Korean charcoal barbecues. During cooking, the surplus fat drops down onto the coals. The meat browns and stays tender, even when well-cooked.

Shabu-shabu: very thin slices of meat are cooked in a light broth. It's then seasoned with ponzu, an acidic, citrus based sauce, or with goma dare, a sweet-and-sour, sesame-based sauce.

Gyudon: the meat is cooked in a broth seasoned with mirin, shoyu, and onion. It's served on a bowl of rice and the broth is poured on top, followed by a poached egg and sansho (Szechwan pepper).

Seiro-mushi: vegetables and slices of wagyu are placed in a bamboo basket and steam-cooked. As it cooks, the meat's fat melts slightly and gives some of its flavor to the vegetables.

OTHER COOKING METHODS

Teppanyaki: a kind of Japanese griddle on which a thin slice of meat is cooked directly, then diced smaller and smaller as it cooks to avoid thick chunks and to ensure all parts are equally cooked.

Broiling or panfrying: honestly, this isn't the best way to appreciate wagyu, because the meat doesn't develop as much flavor and the fattiness becomes the dominant texture.

A BRIEF HISTORY OF BEEF

Have you heard of the Bos primigenius?
It's the scientific name for the aurochs, ancestor of our cattle,
which has changed a lot since its beginnings.

FROM AUROCH TO MODERN-DAY CATTLE

The aurochs was an impressive animal measuring 6½ feet (2 meters) at the withers. A wild creature with immense horns, it's thought to have appeared 2 million years ago in India. It migrated towards the Middle East, then to Asia, Europe, and North Africa. It was already being hunted in prehistoric times.

Domestication of the aurochs began between 8,000 and 10,000 years ago in southeast Turkey, on the one hand with the Bos taurus (without a hump), which presumably led to modern cattle, and on the other hand in the Indo-Pakistani region, with the Asian version (with a hump), which is supposedly the ancestor of the zebu. The aurochs was first raised for its physical force and milk. When aurochs populations emigrated to Europe, the crossbreeding that took place there between wild and domesticated aurochs slowly modified the species.

Depending on which qualities were sought, breeders developed breeds that allowed them to respond to precise regional production needs: butter in Normandy, cheese in Franche-Comté, milk in Flanders, and meat in Charolais.

MEAT BREEDS

From the sixteenth century onward, the English developed their agriculture and the farming of cattle for meat. By the end of the eighteenth century, the Shorthorn, exported to Europe as well as North and South America, was the progenitor of numerous British and continental breeds.

In France, experiments ended in failure. Only the Centre region and the South succeeded in developing meat breeds, but the cattle were essentially raised for physical work and milk and then slaughtered for their meat. During this time, English farming developed considerably and produced animals with a very high-quality meat.

THE FRENCH "EUREKA!" MOMENT

At the end of the twentieth century, French breeders finally began to safeguard ancient breeds from extinction, resulting in great public enthusiasm. Breeds such as the Bazadaise, the Corsicana and the Fin Gras du Mézenc provided great-quality meat and attracted connoisseurs.

BEEF

THE COW FAMILY

If your capacity to differentiate cattle is limited to identifying a cow in the pasture, you're in need of a little diagram.

CALF

When born into the world, a baby cow is a calf, and remains one for its first six months of life, be it male of female.

It's when it grows up that the nature of its sex becomes important. Its weight depends mostly on its breed.

If it's female

If it's male

HEIFER

Before being able to frolic with the males and as long she hasn't had babies, the female is a heifer. Generally, she stays this way until she turns three and is already big and beautiful. Heifers from Anglo-Saxon breeds are absolutely delicious.

BULL-CALF

This one is stuffed like a goose to fatten him up fast. He becomes the stewing or braising beef.

BULL

He spends the vast majority of his life taking and giving pleasure to his female counterparts. He can sire up to thirty calves per year; a superman! Once he's finished mating he isn't worth a penny. He's exhausted and his meat is as tough as leather.

STEER

If his testicles have been removed the male becomes a steer and his growth slows. His muscle mass evens out, as does his fat. He has a more distinctive taste than the cow and a higher amount of fat.

COW

As soon as she's had a calf, the heifer becomes a cow. Cows are the most common source of meat. The quality of the meat depends enormously on the breed and age.

NUTRITION AND MEAT QUALITY

A tasty cow lives in the fields and eats grass. The flavor of this grass or of the winter fodder doesn't change the flavor of the meat, but of the fat that surrounds the muscles. The fat absorbs flavors and makes a big difference in the taste of the beef.

Before slaughter, cows go through a phase we call the "finishing phase," which lasts for three months, more or less. It's a very important period during which the cow is fattened. A good finishing has an effect on the quality of the meat and is done differently according to what the cow has been fed during the seasons.

Dry forage in autumn and winter
Straw, soybeans, linseed, sunflower seeds, rapeseed, wheat, barley, hay, soybeans . . .

Fresh forage in spring and summer
Grass, alfalfa . . .

WINTER

In the winter, there isn't enough grass to feed these animals, so they're given hay and dietary supplements. The hay makes the animal's fat taste of hay, but also gives it a stronger, more "gamy" flavor.

ON-THE-PLATE RESULTS

Fresh beef: deep flavors in December, January, February

60-day aged beef: deep flavors in February, March, April

SPRING

Winter was full of rain or snow, but now the sun slowly returns. The grass becomes lusciously thick and rich and full of wildflowers. The animals delight in this feast and provide us with a light, floral, and slightly grassy-tasting meat.

ON-THE-PLATE RESULTS

Fresh beef: light flavors in March, April, May

60-day aged beef: light flavors in May, June, July

SUMMER

Summer arrives and the sun burns. The thick grass begins to dry out a little, but the flowers remain. The meat has notes of dry grass and hay, but lighter than in the winter. It is still slightly floral with a "gamy" aftertaste.

ON-THE-PLATE RESULTS

Fresh beef: slightly gamy and floral flavors in June, July, August

60-day aged beef: flavors are slightly gamy and a little floral in August, September, October

AUTUMN

The grills have been put away and autumn and the rain are here. The soil is rich and heavy, the grass soaks up the goodness one last time, and the animals take advantage of this final feast before winter.

ON-THE-PLATE RESULTS

Fresh beef: summer flavors still very slightly perceptible in September, October, November

60-day aged beef: summer flavors still very slightly perceptible in November, December, January

BEEF CUTS

*Butchering is a true work of art.
The cow has large muscles that allow for different types of cuts,
depending on how they'll be cooked.*

FRENCH BEEF CUTS

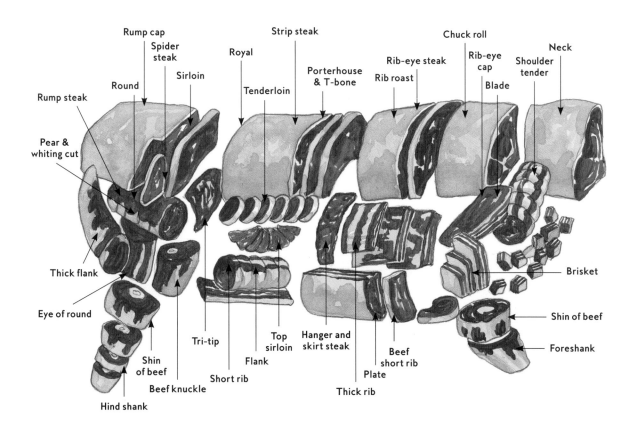

Rump cap
Spider steak
Royal
Strip steak
Chuck roll
Neck
Rib-eye steak
Rib-eye cap
Shoulder tender
Round
Sirloin
Porterhouse & T-bone
Rib roast
Blade
Rump steak
Tenderloin
Pear & whiting cut
Thick flank
Eye of round
Brisket
Shin of beef
Foreshank
Hind shank
Shin of beef
Beef knuckle
Tri-tip
Short rib
Flank
Top sirloin
Hanger and skirt steak
Beef short rib
Plate
Thick rib

ENGLISH CUTS

This cutting method is quite simple because beef is often boiled or braised: it's therefore unnecessary to separate all the muscles.

AMERICAN CUTS

Most American butchers adopt the French cutting method for finer cuts.

CHOICE BEEF CUTS

Don't order "steak" or "stewing meat" from your butcher. Ask him for precise cuts that will live up to your tastes and appetite.

 TRI-TIP STEAK
It can be cooked as a roast or a steak, but braising brings out its true colors and flavors. In French, its name *aiguillette baronne* comes from the word for "needle"—*aiguille*—because of its long, needle-like shape.

 SPIDER STEAK
This is a delicious piece of meat with deep flavors, tenderness, and length on the palate. Cook it rare or medium rare to avoid it becoming tough.

CHUCK ROLL
Situated in front of the ribs, it must be grilled or braised in thin slices to enjoy all its flavors. It has marbling, fat, flavor, and a consistency that requires chewing.

SHORT RIB
This fatty muscle sits against the skirt steak. Long and flat, this cut is used in stews.

TOP SIRLOIN
With its long, loose fibers and light marbling, this is the tastiest and more tender of steaks. Let it age to strengthen the flavors.

FLANK STEAK
Like the top sirloin, the flank steak is also formed of long, loose fibers. It's a little tougher and not as flavorful.

BEEF NECK
This cut isn't very well known; it's delicious but quite fatty, to be slow-cooked for a long period of time. Very tasty in stew.

 RIB ROAST
The rib roast surrounds the muscle that covers the dorsal vertebrae. Very marbled, very tender, it tastes incredible when aged well. Choose a thickness of at least 1½ inches (4 cm).

RIB-EYE STEAK
A boneless steak from the rib section. It has the same qualities as prime rib and can also be roasted. Avoid cuts that are too thin. At least ¾ inch (2 cm) is preferable.

OYSTER STEAK
Although twin sister to the spider steak, this does not mean that it shares its qualities. It's therefore used for delicious meat fondue such as the French fondue bourguignonne.

YUM! **STRIP STEAK**
Situated alongside the tenderloin, it's one of the best cuts: lean, very tender, and tasty with short fibers. Grill in thick slices.

TENDERLOIN
This muscle plays the role of shock absorber between the lumbar vertebrae and the digestive system. With its short fibers, it's extremely tender but not very flavorful.

TENDER FILLET
Incomparable to the tenderloin! Situated along the first dorsal vertebrae, it's a cut used in stews and casseroles, and sometimes as steak.

FLANK
A tough cut that consists of the abdominal muscles. Best boiled, it will enrich a stew with its many flavors.

SHIN OF BEEF (FORE AND HIND LEGS)
This tough, gelatinous cut should be boiled or braised to give a lot of flavor to a stock or broth.

EYE OF ROUND
This is the long, tender muscle from the middle of the thigh, often braised or stewed and sometimes roasted.

SKIRT STEAK
This is quite a delicate cut with long, distinct fibers that are located next to the hanger steak. Very tasty. Eat it rare!

SHANK (FORE AND HIND LEGS)
Quite tough and gelatinous, this is perfect for braising or boiling; the jelly will give the dish flavor and shine.

CHEEK
Largely unknown but delicious, it's lean, tender, and tasty. Braise it for the best results.

BRISKET
This can be divided into two cuts. The flat cut, which is used to make steaks, and the point cut, which is tougher, is boiled or braised.

SHOULDER TENDER STEAK
Situated just next to the blade, the shoulder tender steak is cooked as a steak. Once the central nerve is removed, the result is a lean, good-tasting meat.

WHITING CUT
This French cut gets its name from its long, flat shape, like a *merlan* or whiting fish. With its short fibers, it's very tender but not overly flavorful. Perfect as a steak.

HANGER STEAK
Wow! This is an absolutely delicious piece of meat, quite difficult to find due to its small size, which means it requires extra work from the butcher. It's tender and has strong flavors. Serve medium rare or rare!

MARROWBONE
Taken from the shank, in both the forelegs and hind legs, it's often used when boiling another cut of meat to give the broth more flavor. It can also be served lightly poached or grilled.

BLADE STEAK
Moist and tender, the blade can be braised or stewed. The top part can be made into a delicious steak, with distinctive flavors.

THICK RIB
Situated on the lower ribs, this tough cut needs to be cooked for a long time (boiled or braised) to become a tender and delicious piece of meat.

PEAR CUT
This small muscle, round and plump, gets its name from its pear shape. Very tender, with short fibers, it has a moderate flavor. Delicious as a steak.

PLATE
Although relatively unknown, this cut is delicious when boiled and also when marinated to make pastrami (p 194).

PORTERHOUSE AND T-BONE
These are cut in a T-shape from along the spine, just below the ribs. Both are composed of a piece of tenderloin and strip loin.

OXTAIL
Although quite fatty, oxtail is absolutely delicious in stew. Soft with gelatinous parts, it can also be used in terrines.

THICK FLANK
This is a long, round cut from the buttocks. It's tender, lean, and flavorful. The perfect shape for roasts or carpaccio of beef.

BEEF KNUCKLE
The top front part of the back leg. The bone gives good flavors when braised.

SIRLOIN
This can be divided into three tasty and short-fibered cuts: fillet, ball tip, and tenderloin. Sirloin never disappoints.

BEEF SHORT RIB
This is the muscle from the abdominal wall, streaked with fatty tissue and cartilage from the ribs. Slow cook to make it tender.

THE ROUND
With short fibers, this lean, tender cut is often cooked as a roast.

UNDER-THE-RADAR BEEF CUTS

RUMP CAP (TIP OF THE RUMP)
A nice layer of fat on the outside with a relatively lean meat underneath, a little like duck breast. The Argentinians' favorite cut. Delicious.

SURPRISE STEAK
Situated in the shoulder, this thin, short-fibered cut is very tasty, melt-in-the-mouth, and just as tender as tenderloin.

RIB ROAST: EXTRAORDINARY OR AVERAGE?

Be warned. What I'm about to show you is not the ordinary rib roast you may be used to: bought packaged in plastic from the supermarket. This is a new level of quality with wonderful flavors, aromas, texture, and incredible fat!

A proper rib roast is a sight to behold. It's beautiful to look at and will make your mouth water. It has wonderful color, marbling, and thickness, with just the right amount of fat around the muscle and the bone when clean and prepared. A good butcher will put a great deal of work into these cuts, aging the ribs for weeks. Once cooked, the meat will literally melt in your mouth and you'll be able to taste the land on which these animals were raised. The animals that these ribs come from are incomparable to typical lower-quality milk cows slaughtered because they were too old to make milk.

THE CHAROLAIS

This breed develops only a small amount of fat on and around the muscle, but this doesn't mean it isn't flavorful. The rib is large and thick. It has a gamy taste and its coarse grain gives it a firm consistency.

THE ABERDEEN ANGUS

The Angus tends to develop fat on the surface and the inside of the muscle. This breed, which isn't very big, yields quite a small rib that's less thick than that of other breeds. The meat is moist and well-balanced with a fine grain and floral notes.

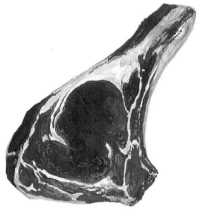

THE AUBRAC

This is a dark-colored meat. Its strong flavors are complex, deep, and have an aromatic, venison-like aftertaste. It has an intense aroma and a silky, velvety grain. It's a good choice for those unfamiliar with strong-tasting meat.

The 7th rib is always the best, the tastiest, the most tender, the one that lingers on the palate. This is because between the beginning and the end of the rack of ribs, certain muscles work harder in certain areas. Not only do ribs differ depending on the breed, but their position can make a difference, too!

THE RUBIA GALLEGA

Without a doubt one of the best ribs in the world. The meat is completely streaked with fat, and the fat along the edge of the muscle is absolutely divine. Spiced and salty notes can be detected and its length on the palate is phenomenal!

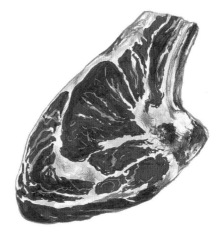

THE LONGHORN

The oldest English breed. This moniker says it all. It has a beautiful-quality marbling and a good fat quantity. Its flavors are intense, long on the palate, and it's the perfect mix of meat and fat. Cooking should be finished at a low temperature.

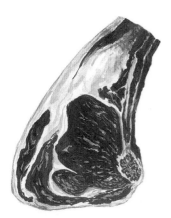

THE SIMMENTAL

Again, a lot of marbling and a very good fat quantity on the perimeter of the muscles and in between each rib. Pronounced, rich flavors that have length on the palate as well as succulence and a firm consistency. In short, a classic, tasty piece of meat.

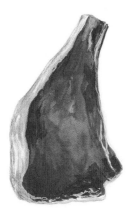

AND THE AVERAGE SUPERMARKET CHOICES?

Not an ounce of fat in there. Sad to the point of death. Sure to be dry, tough, tasteless—enough to put you off red meat forever. Any butcher who dares present this to you must have never tasted his own meat.

T-BONE AND PORTERHOUSE, TWO STEAKS IN ONE

The T-bone and the porterhouse unite two of the best pieces of beef.

T FOR TWO!

The T-bone gets its name from the T shape that the cut gives to the bone. It's exactly the same cut for the porterhouse. On one side of the bone you have the tenderloin and on the other, the strip loin.

Essentially, T-bones and porterhouses combine two steaks in one single piece of meat. The tenderloin, which makes the cut tender, and the strip loin, which makes it delicious. The bone gives both parts even more flavor. What more could you ask for?

NOT ENTIRELY THE SAME

The difference between the T-bone and the porterhouse lies in the width of the tenderloin. It's larger on the porterhouse because the porterhouse is cut from farther back on the animal than the T-bone is, where the tenderloin is wider. Because only four porterhouses can be cut from one animal, this cut is rarer and more expensive than the T-bone.

THE ORIGIN OF "PORTERHOUSE"

The name "porterhouse" supposedly comes from the big pieces of meat that were served in porterhouses, or bars, that were found in ports where people drank porter beer. Americans and the English disagree over the origin of the cut.

Position of the porterhouse on the animal

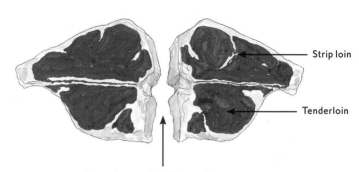

Strip loin

Tenderloin

Porterhouses (like T-bones) are cut from either side of the spine.

Porterhouse versus T-bone: the porterhouse tenderloin is wider than that of the T-bone because it is cut from the back of the animal.

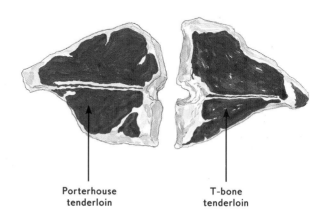

Porterhouse tenderloin

T-bone tenderloin

RIB ROAST VS RIB-EYE STEAK

The difference between a rib roast and a rib-eye steak is the presence or absence of the bone. They are essentially the same size. Does the bone really change anything?

To cook such a thick piece of meat, it must first be browned in a heavy-bottomed oven-safe pot or frying pan and then finished in the oven. As the meat cooks it contracts and releases its juices, whose flavors stick to the bottom of the pan.

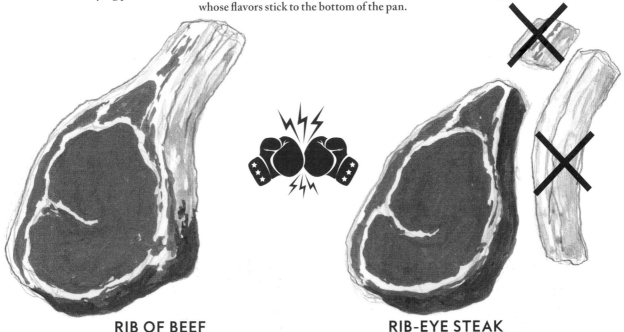

RIB OF BEEF

RIB-EYE STEAK

Because it's firmly attached, the part of the meat that sits against the bone cannot contract. And because the meat cannot contract, it can only release a very small amount of juice and so it remains juicy.

+ The bone contains marrow. As it heats the marrow melts, comes out of the bone, and creates juices that creep toward the meat and fill it with flavor.
+ Additional juices, created on the bone, naturally slide down toward the meat and give it more flavor.

The rib-eye steak browns all over, but there's no bone to give it additional flavor as it cooks. Additionally, the meat, which isn't held by the bone, contracts during cooking and so releases juice, which causes the meat to dry out.

RIB ROAST FOR THE WIN!

The same thing happens to all bone-in beef cuts: extra flavors are extracted from the bone and the meat attached doesn't contract, so it's more tender and juicier.

GROUND OR DICED?

Take a piece of meat, grind half of it and dice the rest into cubes.
Season both in exactly the same way and you'll get two different results.

GROUND MEAT

Most herbs and spices become stuck inside the ground meat.

To taste them, you'd have to chew the meat, but because the meat is ground you'll tend to swallow it almost immediately, without needing to chew. The flavors and aromas, buried in the meat, never reach your taste buds or your olfactory mucosa. Instead they go directly into your stomach.

PFFF...

Once in your mouth, the flavors stuck inside the meat don't stimulate the taste buds or the salivary glands.

RESULT:
Grinding makes most of your ingredients bland.

DICED MEAT

The herbs and spices coat the little cubes of meat and stay on the surface.

You can't swallow the pieces without chewing so you masticate and grind the meat, causing the herbs and spices to release all their flavors and aromas. Your salivary glands are working, producing saliva, which adds to the mix and intensifies the experience.

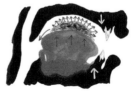

YEAAAHHH!!!

Once in your mouth, the flavors of the herbs and spices vigorously stimulate the taste buds and salivary glands.

RESULT:
Dicing accentuates the flavors and aromas of your meat and your seasoning.

DICING FOR THE WIN!

Diced meat has a firmer consistency than ground meat and a lot more flavor and length on the palate. For a light flavor, choose tenderloin; for a stronger taste, go for a hanger steak.

THE MARROWBONE, IN SLICES OR LENGTHWISE?

*Marrowbones can be cut in two different ways:
into slices for a classic cut or lengthwise for something slightly more classy.
The shape of the cut doesn't make much difference to the flavor
of the meat. It's how you cook it that matters.*

Marrow is found inside the long bones of a calf or a cow. The femur bone is traditionally used. Marrow can also be found inside thick ribs, but not as much of it. The marrow of a calf is slightly more delicate than a cow's.

The traditional cut, in thick slices.

The classy cut, in a baguette shape.

THE CUTS

Most butchers cut the bones into slices, but you can ask them to cut them lengthwise instead. This type of cut has numerous advantages: the cooking is a lot more even, the marrow more accessible, and if you brown it in the oven, a larger amount of the surface will turn crisp.

PREPPING LIKE A PRO

Nothing is more off-putting than bones with little bits of tendon and off-brown meat stuck to them, or a marrow full of filaments of clotted blood. To prep them like a pro, soak the bones for twelve to twenty-four hours in a big bowl of water with two tablespoons of coarse salt and a teaspoon of white vinegar. Then, take a paring knife and scrape off what's left. Using a small, hard brush works very well, too.

HOW TO COOK IT?

In a broth: the marrow melts slightly and releases its flavors into the liquid. It also makes it a little oily, which gives it a full-bodied flavor and good length on the palate. If you're a bit of a perfectionist, wrap the bones beforehand in gauze to stop the herbs from sticking to them.

Directly in the cooking dish: once removed from the bone and cut into thin slices, the marrow also releases a tasty fat that you can use to baste your meat and give it flavors that are to die for.

In the oven: the bone is cut lengthwise and is delicious when lightly broiled.

In a marinade: sprinkle the marrow with black pepper or spices and let it steep in them for twenty-four hours, after having soaked it in water.

Before soaking and scraping

After soaking and scraping

BEEF HAM AND DRIED BEEF

Bresaola, Grisons beef, wagyu ham, Cecina de León, pastirma, bresi, or biltong? Here's a tour of the world of dried beef...

Traditionally in northern climates dried meats were prepared in the autumn and made for a good source of protein throughout the winter. Killing the animal in the autumn also meant saving money on the fodder that would have had to been fed to it in winter. Small savings make a big fortune...

Wagyu or
Rubia Gallega ham

Biltong

Cecina de León

Bresaola

Grisons beef

BILTONG

In South Africa, biltong is made with strips of beef marinated for several hours in cider vinegar and then rubbed with a mix of salt, brown sugar, coriander, and black pepper.

The strips are then left to dry in the open air. Biltong has two different textures—hard on the outside and tender in the middle— and is something to nibble on while watching a Springbok match.

BRESAOLA

Let's move toward the north of Italy, all the way to the Swiss border for the most renowned dried meat, Bresaola della Valtellina. Like Cecina de León, it's made from the hindquarters of a cow, salted, spiced, and left to dry for two to four months. Serve with a drizzle of olive oil, a little lemon juice, and some Parmesan shavings.

BRESI

This is the Grisons beef's French cousin. Made in Franche-Comté, in the Jura Mountains, its name apparently comes from its rough-as-wood texture and its dark red color, reminiscent of brazilwood. The meat is salted and rubbed with seasoning before being dried and smoked. Serve with an old Comté cheese.

CECINA DE LEÓN

Originally from Castile and León in northwest Spain, the recipe has been around for more than 2,000 years. The square-shaped muscle from a relatively old cow's thigh is salted, smoked using oak wood, dried for two months, then aged for seven months. Bright red and lightly marbled with fat, the meat has very distinct flavors. Serve with a drizzle of olive oil.

CHARQUI (OR JERKY)

Originally, this was dried llama intended for South American travelers under the Inca Empire. Little by little it was replaced by brined or salt-cured beef, which was dried in the sun or smoked before being cut into thin slices. Today's jerky generally has a more sweet flavor.

DENDENG

A specialty from Padang in Indonesia, it's made using a specific method: the final drying stage is carried out by deep-frying the meat. The beef, cut into very thin slices, marinates in a mix of spices and coconut caramel. It's then left to dry for several hours before being deep-fried to complete the process.

WAGYU OR RUBIA GALLEGA HAM

Wagyu and the Rubia Gallega breed tend to produce a lot of intramuscular fat, like the Iberian pig breed. The production method is actually quite similar to that of the pig and drying takes up to thirty-six months to ensure an exceptional product quality. Get your hands on this if you're lucky enough to find any because it's even rarer, and tastier, than pure gold.

PASTIRMA

Originally made by the Balkan Turks, this meat is salted, pressed, lightly dried, and covered in a paste of crushed herbs and spices such as garlic, cumin, paprika, fenugreek, and chiles. It's left to dry again in the open air for another month. Serve raw, grilled, or add to vegetable dishes to give them more flavor.

SALATÉ

Its origins are unclear, but it's from somewhere near Spain. Salaté is made with tri-tip or shoulder tender, which is steeped in a mix of rosemary, thyme, garlic, and a few lemon slices and then covered in coarse salt. It's kept in a cool place for ten days and then the meat is rinsed, dried, and left to age for another ten days. Serve with a drizzle of olive oil and lemon juice.

GRISONS BEEF

Made in Switzerland in the canton of Grisons, the shoulder—depending on the method used—is or is not drenched in white wine, then washed and salted. Spices are then added before leaving it to dry for three to four months in the open mountain air. Don't hesitate to coat it in a thin layer of olive oil and lemon juice before serving.

THE BEST CALVES

Calves are no longer raised in wooden stalls, as they often have been in the past. Today, they're reared in a more natural manner and are free to roam for several months, despite the fact that Anglo-Saxon countries aren't big veal eaters.

NO MILK WITHOUT CALVES

Cows need to calve to produce milk. Without a calf to feed, there's no milk. The females born are kept to replace the dairy cow stock, but what to do with the males? Milk breeds being only very rarely good for meat, only the best males are kept to be used as breeding bulls. For a long time, only the purposeless males were slaughtered (it's mainly in France and in Italy that veal is eaten). There was a small market for veal in the United States and Great Britain, but the outbreak of mad cow disease practically stopped the consumption of veal in Anglo-Saxon countries.

A REVIVAL

Very recently, interest in veal meat has been revived. Quality breeding farms that ensure the well-being of the animals have developed and offer high-quality veal meat. In the United States, the majority of veal calves are raised in rural states in the Northeast (Pennsylvania, New York, Vermont) and in the Midwest (Ohio, Wisconsin, Michigan, Indiana), whereas in Great Britain, farms are more widespread. Demand for veal is increasing from year to year and production quality is improving, but France remains the biggest exporter of veal, principally to Italy.

The French are the champions in every category of veal offal consumption: brains, liver, kidneys, tongue, tail, sweetbreads, and even the head are used in dishes that are eaten on a regular basis in France. Blanquette of veal is part of French culinary heritage. However, Italy is not far behind with veal parmigiana, saltimbocca, piccata, and even vitello tonnato.

THE BEST

THE ROSÉE DES PYRÉNEÉS

A solely female calf descended from hardy breeds, raised exclusively on its mother's milk and on the grass of the Catalan pastures. It's slaughtered between five and eight months of age. Traditionally, suckling cows (mothers with calves) were sent high into the mountains to graze on the pastures that were difficult to access. In the autumn, the herds came back down and the calves were then eaten. This calf's unique characteristic to this day is that it is accompanies its mother to the summer pastures. During the summer grazing period, from June to November, the calves graze on a rich grass filled with flowers such as wild thyme, sainfoin, and licorice flower, which gives their meat intense flavors and a beautiful pink color.
Breeds: Gascon, Aubrac sometimes crossed with a Charolais bull
Live weight: 440 to 661 lb **Carcass:** 242 to 352 lb

THE SAÏNATA CALF

Pronounced [za-EEN-ata]. This striped breed is found mainly in Corsica and Sardinia. Raised practically free, feeding first on their mothers' milk and then on the leaves of wild olive trees, scrubs, grass, fodder, and even acorns. The calves are born beige, and the brindle pattern appears around three months old. Slaughter takes place at six months. The meat is dark pink with nutty flavors that are long on the palate. The tiger cow is another name for this breed, given to it by Jacques Abbatucci, a breeder in Corsica.
Breed: Saïnata
Live weight: 330 lb **Carcass:** 176 lb

THE AVEYRON AND SÉGALA CALF

Ségala is a French territory that extends to Aveyron and the common boundaries of the Lot, Cantal, Tarn, and Tarn-et-Garonne. Also called "the country of one hundred valleys," it gets its name from the rye (*seigle*) that used to be grown there. Farming is done the traditional way: the calves' mothers go to the pastures during the day and come to feed them in the morning and evening. After two and a half months, the calves are given additional, cereal-based food until they're slaughtered between six and ten months old. Their meat is quite hard to find because a large majority of the production is exported to Italy. It's tender, pink, and melts in the mouth. A must-try!
Breeds: Limousin, Gascon, Bazadaise, Aubrac
Live weight: 683 to 992 lb **Carcass:** 374 to 551 lb

THE FERMIER DU LIMOUSIN CALF

These calves come from the Limousin breed, a recognized meat breed. Located in the French departments of Limousin, Dordogne, and Charente, farming is still carried out in the traditional manner on small farms. The calves, male or female, are raised on their mothers' milk until they are between three and five and a half months old. They suckle directly from their mothers' udders when the mothers return from the pastures. A draconian selection is made at the moment of slaughter so as to keep only the best. A Prestige coat of arms is given to the best-ranking calves. The meat is pale pink, marbled, moist, and succulent with a fine grain.
Breed: Limousin
Live weight: 330 to 617 lb Carcass: 187 to 374 lb

A BRIEF HISTORY OF VEAL

At the beginning of their domestication, calves were raised only to grow and work because their meat wasn't something that people ate. Our taste for veal has since evolved.

THE NEW CALF

The low-quality battery-farmed calves don't drink their mother's milk, but instead are fed on powdered milk mixed with water and grain supplements to fatten them as quickly as possible. Of course, veal produced in this way is tasteless and loses all its succulence when cooked.

FROM SACRED CALF TO BATTERY FARM CALF

Long venerated, this animal fed on the milk of its mother and has been known as Golden Calf, Fatted Calf, Sacred Calf, or Calf of Grace.

In ancient times, veal was a delicacy intended for banquets, symbolizing prosperity and refinement. Only the wealthiest could afford to kill animals before they had been fattened.

During the Renaissance, Italy exported its culinary specialties all over Europe and new ways of cooking veal fed on their mothers' milk were discovered, as were eggs and biscuits.

In the seventeenth and eighteenth centuries, veal consumption developed all over Europe; it was often cooked in ragout, as blanquette, or fricassee.

In England, however, Scotch collops (slices of meat) of braised veal was preferred.

It was in the mid-twentieth century that things changed radically with the arrival of industrial farming. The objective became to obtain veal as cheaply and as fast as possible. Battery farming was born.

However, a few stubborn Welsh rebelled, to continue producing a quality meat from calves fed solely on their mothers' milk. They established labels such as "farm-reared veal" and "veal from suckled calves," which defend feeding calves almost exclusively on their mother's milk. The result of this is delicious meat.

WHICH VEAL TO CHOOSE?

*Calves aren't sold according to their breed,
but rather their age and unique characteristics.
Free-raised veal, milk-fed veal or grain-fed veal ... the names
are all a bit confusing. This will help you find your way.*

DIFFERENT TYPES OF CALVES

FREE-RAISED VEAL CALF

This is a rare and exceptional calf, reared solely on its mother's milk. Although the mother's diet changes with the seasons, this doesn't have much of an influence on the quality of her milk. The calf, slaughtered before weaning has begun (before three months of age) is often male and weighs between 242 and 330 lb. Its meat is very pale, soft, slightly sweet, and so tender that it melts in the mouth.

MILK-FED OR FARM-REARED VEAL CALF

This one also suckles its mother, but after two to two and a half months it's given whole cream milk from an automatic dispenser because its mother often doesn't have enough to feed it, especially if she's of a meat breed. When the calf begins to graze, its food varies. It's allowed to grow up to five months old, weighing more than 440 lb at slaughter. Its meat is a little pinker if it was born between February and March, because the grass it eats darkens its flesh and gives it slightly more intense flavors. The result is a beautiful, delicate veal with a lovely grain and fat that is well spread out between the muscles.

GRAIN-FED VEAL CALF

This is a type of veal you can find everywhere. It's a calf separated from its mother twenty-four hours after birth, fed a powder-based milk replacement, grain, and mostly grass to prevent its meat becoming too pink. At the most, its meat will have a slightly more pronounced flavor in winter and spring because this is when it's permitted to eat a little hay. The calf weighs around 661 lb at slaughter. The meat has a lot of fat, dries out very rapidly during cooking, and has lost much of its tenderness. It has barely any flavor. Basically, you should forget it exists.

THE "LABEL ROUGE"

There are numerous "Label Rouge" (Red Label) calves (Bretanin, Terre Océane, Veal Calves of Aveyron and Ségala, Limousin Veal, farm-reared calves raised on whole milk, veal from suckled calves, Vedelou). These are high-quality calves, usually from suckling cows and some meat breeds. The quality of the meat can vary greatly according to the breed. If possible, choose veal from the Limousin, Gascon, or Bazadaise breeds; they tend to fatten quite quickly, usually from 396 lb upward and make for a delicious meat with a well-spread-out fat.

VEAL SEASON?

There isn't really a season for veal. It's available year-round and the quality is consistent. That said, there's less veal in the butcher shop in September because summer calving is avoided.

THE COLOR OF VEAL

*Don't be fooled into buying pale veal.
It's not always a good sign.*

The difference in color in veal meat is mainly due to the calf's diet. The younger the calf, the more milk it's fed and the paler its meat is. As it grows, the calf's food varies. Its meat begins to darken a little. But its age, breed, and how it's been raised all play an important role. So, should veal be white, pink, or red?

White

GOOD SIGN

The meat of a free-raised veal calf is very pale because it's only been fed on its mother's milk. The meat isn't white because the milk is white, but because there's very little iron in milk. Free-raised calves are anemic—it's as simple as that. And their meat is absolutely delicious!

BAD SIGN

For a long time, you could only get very white veal. This is because it came from calves raised on battery farms, which were given food specially intended to make their meat white. This was done to the detriment of the animal's well-being and to the quality of its meat.

Pale pink

Dark pink

GOOD SIGN

As soon as a calf begins to grow, it skips about and feeds on grass as well as its mother's milk. The color of the meat changes from white to pale pink to dark pink. This is especially the case of milk-fed calves, whose meat is delicate with slightly deeper flavors.

BAD SIGN

Check the source of your veal: it could come from a calf raised on a battery farm.

Red

GOOD SIGN

The meat of certain calves is quite red because they're raised in a certain way, like the Aveyron and Ségala calf, the Corsicana calf, and the Rosée des Pyrénées. And that's good stuff!

BAD SIGN

Careful, it could be a slightly spoiled piece of veal!

"The key to choosing veal meat is being aware of its source, or even better, knowing a good butcher!"

VEAL CUTS

*These are still quite similar to beef cuts.
The muscles are already big enough to be able to separate
them from each other, depending on whether
you want to broil, boil or braise them.*

FRENCH VEAL CUTS

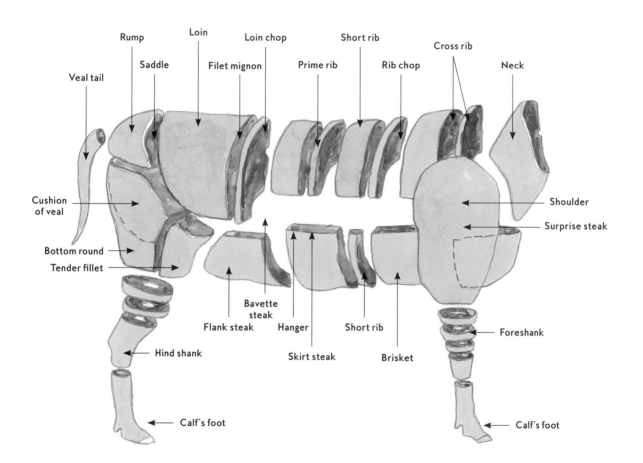

- Veal tail
- Rump
- Saddle
- Loin
- Filet mignon
- Loin chop
- Prime rib
- Short rib
- Rib chop
- Cross rib
- Neck
- Cushion of veal
- Shoulder
- Surprise steak
- Bottom round
- Tender fillet
- Bavette steak
- Flank steak
- Hanger
- Short rib
- Foreshank
- Hind shank
- Skirt steak
- Brisket
- Calf's foot
- Calf's foot

ENGLISH CUTS

As with beef, English veal meat cuts are best boiled or braised.

AMERICAN CUTS

The meat is cut in this way because in the U.S., meat is more often broiled than boiled.

CHOICE VEAL CUTS

Veal chops and cuts intended for ragout aren't the only choices you have! It's helpful to know the difference between a cross rib, rib chop, prime rib and loin chop, a surprise steak or tender fillet.

NECK
Not very well known but perfect braised or cooked in a ragout or stew, the neck is a moist and flavorful cut, although a little fatty.

CROSS RIB
The cross rib is only visible once the shoulder has been lifted. It's the smallest and toughest of the ribs. A calf has five of them.

LOIN CHOP
Taken from the loin, this large rib is covered in a beautiful, thin layer of fat. It's delicious when lightly seared and finished in the oven.

PRIME RIB
The prime rib has a smooth, thick, and tender eye and a straight bone. Ask for a thickness of at least 1½ inches (4 cm). There are five of these.

RIB CHOP
Almost certainly the best and the moistest of veal ribs, containing a good fat but a small amount of meat. A calf has three of them.

SHOULDER
Often sold boned as a roast because its cutlets aren't as fine as those taken from the cushion of veal. Buy it with its bone in for holiday meals.

TENDERLOIN
The tenderloin is found by removing the psoas muscle, which is attached to the loin chop. It's often cut into medallions or grenadines.

FILET MIGNON
The most tender part of the calf, it's so moist that it mustn't be overcooked. Brown in a frying pan and very gently slow-cook to finish.

FLANK
This is the thinnest and longest cut, gristly and moist with beautiful flavors. Braise or boil.

SHANK (FORE AND HIND LEGS)
The shank is fleshier in the hind legs than in the forelegs. It's more tender in the forelegs because the latter aren't under any strain during the hanging of the carcass.

CHEEK
Rare to find, this cut is delicious, tender, and lean. Gently braise on a very low heat.

SHORT RIB
The equivalent of beef thick rib and pork spare ribs. This cut is often used in blanquette or ragout.

LOIN
The loin is the lumbar region of the carcass. It's often sold deboned to be cooked as a roast. Gentle slow-cooking is a must.

CUSHION OF VEAL
This is the interior thigh muscle. Very tender with a very fine grain, it's often cut into delicious cutlets.

TENDER FILLET
Situated toward the front of the thigh, this cut allows for cutlets that are smaller, but just as tasty as those that come from the cushion. It owes its French name *noix pâtissière* (pastry nut) to the fact that it used to be reserved for pastry chefs who used it in puff pastry recipes and other dishes.

 MARROWBONE
Taken from the shank, it's more delicate than a cow's marrowbone, but the flavor has good length on the palate. Ask for a lengthwise cut so you can fit it in the oven.

YUM! **BRISKET**
The brisket cut also contains the short rib and the flank. It's a choice meat cut, tender and delicious when stuffed.

YUM! **RUMP**
This is an amazing piece of meat, the equivalent of beef sirloin. Composed of the top of the rump, it's very tender with a fine, fragile grain. Divine!

VEAL TAIL
More delicate and a little less fatty than oxtail, it's used in the same dishes, including stew, terrines, and pâté.

YUM! **HIND SADDLE**
Taken from the loin, this rare cut encompasses the ribs on either side of the spine. A cut for holiday festivities!

THE BOTTOM ROUND
This cut is situated at the back of the thigh and has a slightly coarser grain than the tender fillet. Order it in cutlets or as a roast, to be slowly braised.

SHORT RIB
The smallest area of the brisket with a nice amount of fat and cartilage. This is a delicate cut, to be broiled or braised.

UNDER-THE-RADAR VEAL CUTS

SURPRISE STEAK
As with beef, the surprise steak is situated in the shoulder, just above the blade. A very delicate cut and very, very difficult to find.

YUM! **HANGER STEAK**
More tender but less strong in flavor than beef hanger steak, veal hanger steak is a very tasty cut with long fibers.

SKIRT STEAK
This is truly rare. The cut is small and flat with long fibers. One of the tastiest. A must-try!

BAVETTE STEAK
Also very, very rare, but not any less delicious.

"**The abomasum,** or the calf's fourth stomach compartment, secretes rennet (a milk coagulant) which can be used to curdle milk and make cheese."

THE BEST PIG BREEDS

The best pig breeds are award-winning: marvels raised by people who take incredibly good care of them, lavishing on them love, space to roam, and the best food possible.

THE BEST OF THE BEST

THE TAMWORTH

Originally from the town of Tamworth in the center of the United Kingdom, this breed likely descends from the wild pigs of Northern Europe. Sir Robert Peel, Prime Minister of the United Kingdom (1834-1835 and 1841-1846) allegedly crossbred these with Irish pigs at his farm in Tamworth. These pigs were raised semiwild and fed on acorns that fell from the big oak forests. The breed was standardized in the middle of the nineteenth century and resulted in a pig that is red in color and of medium build with an elongated head and neck, erect ears, and long, strong limbs for traveling long distances. The Tamworth, which has likely recently been crossed with the Berkshire and the Yorkshire, grows slowly and develops a delicious intramuscular fat, which gives a lot of flavor to the meat. Traditionally considered to be a bacon breed, today its meat is highly renowned.
Boar: 661 lb **Sow:** 551 lb **Carcass:** 440 to 529 lb

THE BERKSHIRE

Legend has it that Oliver Cromwell's army discovered the Berkshire pig during the siege of the county of Berkshire, west of London, England, in the seventeenth century. Large, with colors varying from black to red, this pig was renowned for the quality of its bacon and ham. The breed was later improved by introducing Chinese and Siamese blood. This breed has remained pure for the last 200 years and was the first to have benefited from the status of breed in the eighteenth century. Very popular and even loved by Queen Victoria in the nineteenth century, the breed practically disappeared because it was unsuited to industrial farming. Dark in color with big ears, white feet and tail, and large hams, the Berkshire is a robust animal that takes a long time to fatten. Its meat is light red and well-marbled, succulent, tender, and tasty with short, fine fibers.
Boar: 617 lb **Sow:** 440 lb **Carcass:** 308 to 440 lb

"**You'll notice that** there aren't any little pink pigs here. Instead these pigs have big ears and long tails. There's no comparison to pigs from factory farms."

THE GLOUCESTERSHIRE OLD SPOTS

We can no longer be sure of the origins of the breed, but it's likely a descendant of the native pigs of the Vale of Berkeley in Gloucestershire, southwest England and the breed portrayed in eighteenth century paintings. It's also known as the Orchard Pig and the Cottager's Pig because it was partly raised in orchards where it ate the apples that fell to the ground. The Gloucestershire Old Spots was the first breed of all the species in the world to be awarded the designation of Traditional Specialty Guaranteed by the European Commission. Virtually extinct after the Second World War when pig production developed by moving away from pasture-raised pork, it's a large, sturdy animal with a thick round body and very large hams. It has a nice layer of fat across its back and a flavorful, truly succulent meat.
Boar: 661 lb **Sow:** 551 lb **Carcass:** 374 to 485 lb

THE BLACK IBERIAN PIG

The Iberian pig is one of the three original pig breeds—along with the Celtic and the Asian—from which all other pig breeds descend. Bred mainly in southwest and western Spain, this pig has quite a small head, a large snout, ears that fall over its eyes, slender limbs, and flat hams. This breed, weighing less than many others, is well suited to traveling long distances in search of food. It easily endures the humid winters and dry summers of this part of the Mediterranean rim. The Iberian pig's distinctive feature is its capacity to retain the oleic acid contained in the acorns that make up a big part of its diet during winter. Most well known for its pata negra ham and cured meats, it's a breed that makes for a divine meat: tender, succulent, with a melt-in-the-mouth intramuscular fat that is particularly delicious.
Boar: 617 lb **Sow:** 396 lb **Carcass:** 330 to 440 lb

THE BEST PIG BREEDS

THE BEST

THE CUL NOIR LIMOUSIN (BLACK-BOTTOMED)

The Cul Noir is an Iberian pig, originating from the Massif Central in France, which was practically extinct by the 1950s. Slow-growing, it has a large, stocky body. During the winter it feeds on chestnuts and acorns, which lend their flavor to its dark red meat. The Cul Noir is the only pig capable of producing a fat of an exceptional quantity—more than 4 inches (10 cm) in thickness along its back.
Boar: 551 lb **Sow:** 440 lb **Carcass:** 352 to 418 lb

THE LARGE BLACK PIG

Originally from southwest England, more precisely from the Devon and Cornwall regions, the Large Black is a large animal whose drooping ears cover most of its face and obscure its vision. Robust and tender, this breed has been classified as vulnerable since the arrival of industrial farming. The Large Black offers a delicious meat and world-renowned bacon.
Boar: 771 lb **Sow:** 661 lb **Carcass:** 374 to 485 lb

THE CINTA SENESE

Originally from the mountains around Sienna, the Cinta Senese, known to us since the Middle Ages, is also a pig that grows slowly. This breed has a light pink strip on the thorax and forefeet. Quite robust, it's raised wild or semiwild and feeds on chestnuts and acorns in winter and grass and roots in summer. Used to make Tuscan cured meats, its meat is tender and tasty with a delicious fat.
Boar: 661 lb **Sow:** 551 lb **Carcass:** 374 to 485 lb

THE DUROC

This breed was created in the eastern region of the United States at the beginning of the nineteenth century and takes its name from a famous ancestor, a boar of no particular breed. Since then the breed has been refined, is of medium length, and has drooping ears. Its color varies from deep orange to mahogany and its meat presents a lovely intramuscular fat which makes it very tender and deep in flavor.
Boar: 661 lb **Sow:** 551 lb **Carcass:** 330 to 485 lb

"Don't forget that the pig is a very intelligent animal, and also a bit of a joker."

THE BRITISH SADDLEBACK

Originally, it was a cross between Neapolitan boars and English Essex sows to improve the breed. This cross was then crossed with the Wessex to get the Saddleback. Very popular in the previous century, it's now quite rare. Its body is black with a large, pale pink strip that starts on the back and encompasses the forelegs. Its large ears point forward. It's almost certainly the breed that produces the best bacon.
Boar: 705 lb **Sow:** 595 lb **Carcass:** 418 to 507 lb

THE CORSICA NUSTRALE BLACK PIG

Nustrale means "ours" in Corsican. An inhabitant of the island of Corsica for thousands of years, this breed was recently saved from extinction. An Iberian pig, it's most commonly black in color with slender limbs and round, flat hams. It's raised semiwild and feasts on chestnuts and acorns found in the forests. Often used to make real Corsican cured meats, its meat is just as delicious and strong in taste when prepared simply.
Boar: 485 lb **Sow:** 352 lb **Carcass:** 242 to 330 lb

THE APULO-CALABRESE

This is one of the oldest Italian pig breeds, raised wild or semiwild in Calabria, in the far south of Italy. It's very likely of Iberian origin and fattens slowly. The Apulo-Calabrese is of medium build with slender limbs and an unfailing sexual vigor. Its diet, primarily composed of acorns and chestnuts in winter, makes for delicious cured meats and a tender, marbled pork with long-lasting flavor.
Boar: 551 lb **Sow:** 440 lb **Carcass:** 308 to 396 lb

THE RED WATTLE

The Red Wattle is thought to be from New Caledonia and was imported into New Orleans by French colonialists at the end of the eighteenth century. The breed was slowly abandoned in favor of others that developed with more fat. Practically extinct and then reintroduced in Texas in the 1970s, the Red Wattle makes for a lean, very succulent meat which is similar in taste and texture to beef. A breed full of surprises!
Boar: 661 lb **Sow:** 551 lb **Carcass:** 418 to 507 lb

THE MANGALITSA

The Mangalitsa is a special breed that deserves attention. In the winter it has a coat that looks like sheep's wool, but it's definitely a pig.

WHY IS IT BETTER THAN GOOD?

The first of the Mangalitsa's unique characteristics is its fat, an extremely large amount of intra- and extramuscular fat (up to 4 inches [10 cm] on its back!) This creamy, slightly sweet fat literally melts in your mouth (it starts to liquefy from 89.6°F) and contains barely any cholesterol. It's often called the pig version of wagyu or Kobe because the amount of fat it contains is almost equal to the amount of meat. The meat, a red color reminiscent of beef, has quite a strong flavor similar to that of the Corsica Nustrale Black Pig. Of course, the animal's food contains no soybeans, no antibiotics or other GMOs, and it lives outside year-round.

THE ORIGIN OF THE MANGALITSA

Considered the domestic pig breed closest to the wild boar (the piglets have the same stripes as wild boar piglets) the first traces of the breed appeared in Hungary in 1830. It's an Iberian breed, born of crossbreeding between several North-European breeds that produced large quantities of lard. Initially, there were three colors: blond, red, and black. The black is now extinct, but a cross between a Blond Mangalitsa and a Croatian pig created the Swallowbellied Mangalitsa, black with a light belly.

These pigs were raised in the open in forests, swamps, and wasteland. The breed developed quickly and became one of the most common in Europe because it produced a large quantity of fat at a time when the fat and oil industries didn't exist. The expansion of intensive agriculture and pig farming in pigsties almost resulted in the end of this magnificent breed. Numbers went from 18,000 animals in 1955 to 240 in 1965, and to 40 in 1970! Ultimate extinction was near when the National

Association of Mangalica Breeders was created in Hungary and began to take control, creating a breed register in which every birth has since been recorded. Today, there are farms everywhere—in France, the United States, and even in Japan.

THE BREED STANDARD

The Mangalitsa is of medium build, measuring 27 to 35 inches (70 to 90 cm) to the withers with a slender but very strong frame. It grows slowly, 154 lb to 176 lb at one year old, 308 lb to 330 lb at two years old, and up to 396 lb at three years old. Its ears are a medium size and point forward, and its eyes are brown.

THE COAT

The Mangalitsa's coat changes with the seasons, just like sheep's wool. It's short, fine, and smooth in the summer and thickens and curls in the winter. The color depends on the type.

THE CURED MEATS

Because they contain so much fat, the hams can be left to dry for longer, up to 40 months without issue. This intensifies the flavor while keeping the hams moist and deep red in color. Mangalitsa hams are regularly placed at the same level of quality as 100 percent Ibérico pata negra. That says it all.

The flavor and tenderness of its fat, as well as its immediate melt-in-the-mouth quality, make it one of the most popular charcuterie meats.

"Its nickname is the 'wagyu of pork.'"

THE MEAT

It's similar to the Cul Noir Limousin with a thick layer of fat and a lot of marbling. All of that results in a lot of flavors during the cooking process. The meat is very creamy, tender, and juicy with intense flavors and good length on the palate. To top it off, it's rich in Omega-3 and Omega-6 and contains antioxidants that effectively lower cholesterol levels. An exceptional meat!

A BRIEF HISTORY OF PORK

Pigs have not always been pink. They come from long ago and far away. Pork was already popular in Ancient Roman times.

DOMESTICATION IN THE WILD

The first signs of pig domestication can be traced back to 9,000 years ago in Turkey and in Cyprus, and then soon after in Asia, Africa, and Oceania with the successive migrations and in Europe from 1500 BC. Back then, pigs were dark in color—black, gray, or brown.

During the period of the Roman Empire, pork was by far preferred to other types of meat, but it was during the Middle Ages that pig farming began to develop. The pigs were left to wander through the cities and eat the trash, with little bells tied around their necks. This domestication ended in 1331 when King Louis IV the Fat issued a royal decree forbidding the free-roaming of pigs after one caused his son to fall off a horse.

THE FIRST PORK BUTCHERS

Meanwhile, in the countryside, pigs were already being slaughtered at the beginning of winter so as to have cured meats during the coldest months.

In the fifteenth century, pork butchers weren't allowed to sell fresh meat, so they cooked the pork before selling it.

MODERN FARMING

It wasn't until the seventeenth century that pigs changed in color and shape. By crossbreeding them with faster-growing Asian breeds, the dark-colored pigs became pink and grew in size.

Farming truly became industrial in the nineteenth century thanks to the distribution of potatoes, which were used to feed the animals.

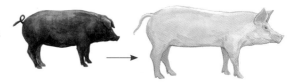

In the twentieth century, over time, all the beautiful, slow-growing breeds began to disappear in favor of pigs that fattened two to three times faster. Today, it's thanks to passionate breeders that we can still enjoy breeds such as the Gascon Black and the Cul Noir Limousin.

IS THE WILD BOAR ITS ANCESTOR?

Theoretically, no, but we can't be 100 percent sure. We don't know if pigs descend from a domesticated wild boar or from a domesticated wild pig. Opinions vary because the European pig shares some of the European wild boar's genetic characteristics, but none of the Asian wild boar's. The Asian pig, however, is similar to the Asian wild boar.

THE PIG FAMILY

*Several types of pigs make up the extended family.
Sow, gilt, and shoat—you've got to admit they have
interesting names!*

PIGLET

Up to 4 weeks old, the sow's young is called a piglet. It weighs
less than 13 lb and feeds exclusively on its mother's milk. Its meat
is very white, tender, and slightly sweet.

SHOAT

From 4 weeks to 6 months old, a shoat weights between 13 and 88 lb.
It isn't yet weaned but already eats grains. Its meat is very pale pink
and still tender.

If it's a factory farm breed   If it's a quality breed

BUTCHER HOG

At 6 months old, a factory-farm pig is an adult and is called
a butcher hog. So young and already at its maximum weight,
ready to be eaten.

HOG

A quality, purebred pig needs time to grow. It will be ready
and delicious at two years of age.

If it's male   If it's female

BOAR

The adult male becomes a sire.

GILT

This is a female that is not yet sexually mature but is intended
for breeding.

SOW

A female ready for breeding. Swollen teats indicate that a
sow is pregnant.

NUTRITION AND MEAT QUALITY

A tasty pig is raised semiwild and roams around to find food. Of course, nature provides it with forage that varies with the seasons. This food is what will contribute to the quality of its meat.

Pigs are omnivores and eat everything: roots, acorns, chestnuts, and also grass, vegetables, and even tree bark. A real glutton! And it's exactly that gluttony we're interested in..

It takes time for the food to flavor its meat. I'm obviously talking about purebred pigs that have been growing for two years and have roamed and lived semiwild, not the low-quality animals raised on factory farms.

Vegetables: carrot peels, potato peels … **Legumes:** peas, soybeans … **Grains:** barley, corn, wheat, oats … **And also:** chestnuts, acorns, roots …

WINTER

This is the pig's favorite season. He finds acorns, chestnuts, and damp roots. He roots around furiously in the earth to eat everything he can. In short, he exerts himself like crazy and builds up fat and muscle.

ON-THE-PLATE RESULTS

Absolutely divine in February, March, and April.

SPRING

The earth begins to dry, the grass grows back, underground life resumes, and the pig continues to roam, eating grass and everything else he can find. Life is good, even though his favorite food, burrowed underground, isn't as easy to find.

ON-THE-PLATE RESULTS

Very, very tasty in May. Very tasty in June and July.

SUMMER

A sad season for our pig. The earth dries out so there's nothing much to be found in the dirt and the grass isn't as rich. He's given vegetables and grain so he doesn't waste away.

ON-THE-PLATE RESULTS

Very tasty in August, September, and October.

AUTUMN

Finally, autumn is here. The earth is reborn and a lot is happening beneath the falling leaves. The season of acorns and chestnuts is on its way. The pig's tail shivers with delight as he digs up everything in his path.

ON-THE-PLATE RESULTS

Good in November. Very good in December. Very, very good in January.

PORK CUTS

Because French gastronomy encompasses a multitude of dishes, pork butchery yields more than you might imagine. Be it slow-cooking or fast-cooking, each cut has its own unique cooking method.

FRENCH PORK CUTS

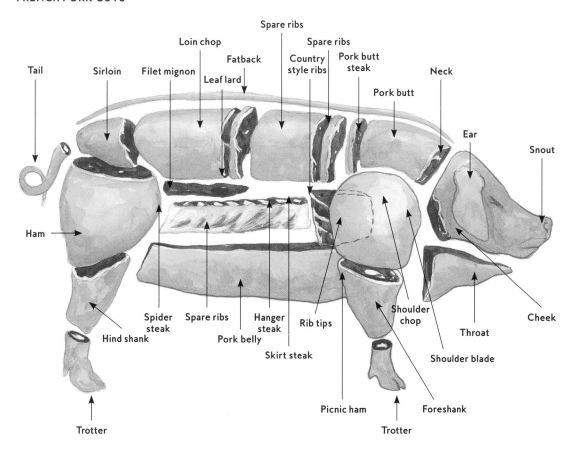

Tail · Sirloin · Filet mignon · Loin chop · Leaf lard · Fatback · Spare ribs · Country style ribs · Spare ribs · Pork butt steak · Pork butt · Neck · Ear · Snout

Ham · Spider steak · Hind shank · Spare ribs · Pork belly · Hanger steak · Skirt steak · Rib tips · Picnic ham · Shoulder chop · Shoulder blade · Throat · Foreshank · Cheek

Trotter · Trotter

ENGLISH CUTS

In England, pork is cut in a similar way to the French method.

AMERICAN CUTS

This cutting method favors big cuts for lots of dinner guests.

CHOICE PORK CUTS

There's more to pork than ribs. Consider the shoulder chop, skirt steak, spider steak, pork neck, or even leaf lard. Here's a lesson on each cut.

PORK BUTT STEAK
This part of the pork butt provides the best steaks. They're the most tender and have a delicious fat. This cut is difficult to dry out and requires a slightly longer cooking time than other steaks.

LOIN CHOP
Situated toward the back of the animal, these chops are generally cut in a T shape with the bone in, like a T-bone steak. Deboned, this cut becomes the tenderloin, which is served as roast and dries out very fast.

SPARE RIBS
The second section of the ribs is situated to the front and touches the pork butt. The first section sits between the second section and the loin chops. Be sure to order these with the fat and rind for extra flavor.

PORK BUTT
Comprising part of the neck and the first five ribs (equivalent of the beef chuck roll) this is one of the best pork cuts. Cooked as a roast or as individual steaks, it's tender, moist, and very tasty.

FILET MIGNON
Be careful not to confuse this with the tenderloin! The filet mignon is a long, narrow muscle, a very tender and succulent choice cut. Brown on a low heat in a pot while being extremely careful to avoid overcooking, which would make it dry and pointless to eat.

THROAT
This is fatty—very fatty. It's a cut generally used in terrines, pâtés, and other recipes to make them more flavorful. Part of the fat is drained after cooking.

COUNTRY-STYLE RIBS
Taken from between the shoulder and the ribs, it's a flat cut with elongated fibers; quite fatty, tender, and moist when not overcooked. It's often used in curries. Grill and serve pink, always.

SNOUT
Often used in salads, the snout is also delicious cooked simply in a pot on a low heat.

HAM
The top part of the hindquarter is the famous ham that can be cooked to make boiled ham, or salted and dried to make cured ham. It can also be cooked whole or in slices (pork round).

SHANK (FORE- AND HIND LEGS)
Also called hocks, the fore- and hind shanks are very different from each other. The foreshank is leaner and more tender while the hind shank is plumper but tougher, because the animal is hung by its hind legs after exsanguination.

CHEEK
Contrary to what you might think, the cheek is a lean cut. Rare, but absolutely delicious, it requires gentle braising. Don't hesitate to order in advance from your butcher.

FATBACK
This is from the top of the back. It has a rind attached and is a cut used in cassoulet or to give flavor to certain soups. With the rind removed, it can be diced and used to cook lean meats.

PICNIC HAM
This cut is usually ground to make sausage meat.

EARS
At one time, pigs had big ears that were poached before being grilled. They contain a lot of delicious cartilage.

SHOULDER CHOP
This cut is divine. The top part can be grilled like the beef blade steak. And if you cook it whole, the central nerve will give a lot of flavor and shine to your braising liquid.

BLADE

YUM! Located in the top area of the shoulder near the pork butt, the blade with its bone is a choice cut and should be braised or roasted in the oven. When the bone is removed, the blade becomes a tender and tasty roast with beautiful fat marbling.

LEAF LARD

This is the white, silky, shiny fat that surrounds the kidneys. It's removed and melted before being filtered to make lard. Its salty taste limits its use in cooking, but it's often used in bakeries.

TROTTERS

Usually poached and then grilled, they're also often added to terrines, patés, and broths for their tasty gelatin.

RIB TIPS

The rib tips are situated to the front of the rib cage. The crowning cut of the *petit salé*, a French salted pork dish, it can also be bought fresh and slow-cooked in a ragout or braised for a moist, tender meat.

SIRLOIN

Situated above the ham, this is the equivalent cut to beef sirloin. It's a leaner cut than the pork butt, but not as dry as the middle part of the tenderloin. It's generally boned to make premium roasts.

PORK BELLY

A choice cut, to be broiled in the oven. It's often called "lean bacon" and is used to make *ventrèche*, the French version of bacon. It's different to fatback because the latter has no meat.

TAIL

Again, a cut that is rarely used. Cooked in a broth, it's then broiled, sometimes covered in bread crumbs.

BABY BACK RIBS

The top section of the rib bones in the rib cage.

UNDER-THE-RADAR PORK CUTS

NECK

YUM! This cut was discovered by Eric Ospital, a butcher in Bayonne in southwest France. With old and heavy pigs, he removes the two small muscles situated between the head and the top of the back. Pork neck can be roasted until very tender and juicy, and should always be served pink.

SPIDER STEAK

YUM! Taken from the leg, the butcher often keeps this choice cut for himself. Pigs have two of them, whereas cows only have one. Its texture is similar to poultry breast but with a much more distinctive taste.

HANGER STEAK

YUM! Ah, pork hanger steak! Situated in the same area as the cow's, it's smaller but also requires aging and has the same qualities: lots of flavor and tenderness.

SKIRT STEAK

YUM! This is the holy grail of pork. Very difficult to find, this delicate, slender piece of meat has long fibers and is lean and very tender. It should be grilled for a short time to serve pink. It can also be marinated overnight.

PORK CHOPS OR PUREBRED PORK CHOPS?

I'm not talking about those dry, tasteless chops
that come in trays and are covered in plastic wrap.
I'm talking about pork chops from pigs raised slowly
and fed good food with lots of love.

Rib steaks are miles apart from the pale, tasteless pork rib chops you get in the supermarket. They're darker in color with fat streaked through the inside and around the outside. After cooking, they melt in your mouth like candy, full of flavors and aromas that linger—chestnut, acorn, hazelnut. And you eat them pink. Please don't overcook these beauties!

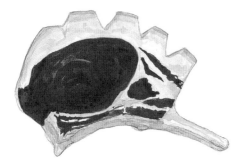

THE GASCON BLACK

Notice the fat streaked inside and around the muscles, and the other very white layer of fat that surrounds the meat. The deep red color and the thick, tender cut has the flavor of acorn, hazelnut, and almond.

THE CUL NOIR LIMOUSIN

The pork equivalent of wagyu, this is essentially fat with meat inside. Chestnut and acorn flavors and a fat that literally melts in your mouth.

THE CORSICA NUSTRALE BLACK PIG

With fat marbling between and on the side of the muscles, this rib smells of mountain grass, of Corsican scrubs, and of chestnuts and acorns and hazelnuts,

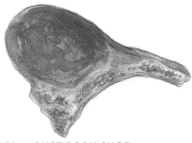

SUPERMARKET PORK CHOP

It's difficult to find words to describe this inferior cut. This pig was not raised with love and was fed so much to make it grow fast that the poor pig didn't have time to build up any fat. The meat is so pale that it's almost transparent.

CURED HAM AND COOKED HAM

*Take two of the same cuts of pork, some salt, and two ancient procedures; you'll get two very different hams.
The first, dried, will keep for many months,
whereas the second remains moist and only lasts a few days.*

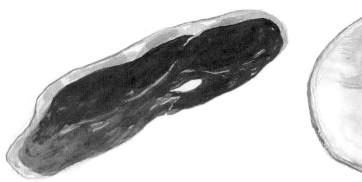

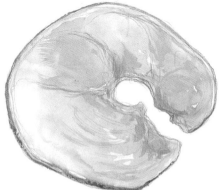

CURED HAM

Apart from a couple of regional differences, the method is always the same. The bottom section, called the knuckle or the hock, is removed, rubbed with coarse salt, and left in the cold, in the salt, for about fifteen days. Then it's washed, rinsed and left to dry. The drying process, during which the salt disperses itself evenly through the meat, can take up to a year. Finally, we move on to the aging process, during which the yeast and bacteria will work to develop some very distinct flavors. The longer the aging process, the richer and more complex those flavors will become. For a good-quality ham, there must be a minimum of twenty-four months of aging between curing and sale. And for an exceptional quality ham, we're talking around thirty-six to forty months.

DRIED HAM VERSUS CURED HAM

A cured ham is a dried ham, but a dried ham isn't a cured ham.

A cured ham must dry for at least four months, whereas a dried ham doesn't have a minimum drying duration. But both are raw. Both are served at room temperature, at about 68°F to 77–78°F so that their flavors and aromas can develop.

COOKED HAM

The hock is also removed for cooked ham, as are the femur bone and the fatty vein. Once the bone is removed, the ham divides into two pieces, which are soaked in a brine containing salt, sugar, and a mixture of various herbs and spices. To accelerate the process, some of this brine is injected directly into the meat. The brining process can last from several days to just over two weeks, depending on the desired result. Before cooking, both pieces are placed together and tightly squeezed into a kind of large sock. The ham is either steamed or boiled in a broth, but is always cooked slowly until the temperature of the center reaches 159–161°F. It's left to cool and then kept in a cold place.

INDUSTRIAL COOKED HAM

These hams practically double in volume due to the water injected into them. The hams are churned (meaning they're mixed at 400 to 500 watts in immense vats), then reconstructed, molded, cooked, and cut into slices. A bit of fat or rind is even added around the edges to make them look like real ham slices.

THE BEST CURED HAMS

Hamstring, ham, it's the same etymology. Hams come from hamstrings. Except that certain hams don't come from pigs' hamstrings but from other areas of their bodies. Honestly, we're not going to be picky, as long as it's good.

Cured ham is part of the heritage of many regions, each of which has developed its own characteristics depending on the breed, the salt quality for curing, and the climate for drying. Here's a little tour of the best cured hams.

San Daniele hams are recognizable by their guitar shape.

🇫🇷 FRANCE

CUL NOIR (Limousin)

In the northern Périgord, Jean Denaux has developed an incredible ham, the Cul Noir du Limousin. These animals are raised in semi-freedom, feeding on acorns and chestnuts all winter. The drying and ripening last for nearly 36 months to yield a very mild, low-salt ham, with flavors, not surprisingly, of hazelnut and chestnuts. It's one of the best hams in the world!

EXCEPTIONAL 👍

IBAÏMA (Bayonne)

A pure French Basque country ham made with the Basque breed, Basque salt, and Basque wind (there's a lot of that!). Curing is carried out with a particular salt from Salies-de-Béarn, which is extracted from salty spring water. Aged for almost twenty months, it's dark red, finely marbled with fat, and develops nut and grilled spice flavors.

LUXEUIL HAM (Luxeuil-les-Bains, Vosges)

Following a process that's over 2,000 years old, the meat is marinated in a mix of Jura red wine and spices for one month and is removed, sponged, and dry-salted on a regular basis during this time. Then it's put to dry on a wicker rack and smoked with conifer and wild cherry wood. Aging takes seven to eight months.

PRISUTTU HAM (Corsica)

Corsica Nustrale Black pigs are raised semiwild. They eat chestnuts and acorns during winter and shrubs, bark, and leaves the rest of the year. Lightly salted and aged for two to three years, this ham develops strong flavors of thyme, marjoram, shrub, and hazelnut.

GERMANY

MAINZ HAM (Mainz)

Showcased by Rabelais in the novels *Gargantua* and *Pantagruel*, renowned in the eighteenth century but nonexistent at the beginning of the twentieth century, Mainz ham came back with a bang. Quite similar to Bayonne ham, the flesh is quite tough with a beautiful fat around the edge and delicate flavors.

ITALY

CULATELLO HAM (Zibello, near Modena)

Taken from pigs fattened on wheat bran, barley, and whey, Culatello is made solely from the best part of the leg, the center. This ham is brined in a mix of salt, pepper, garlic, and white wine and then sewn into a pig's bladder to be aged for over 400 days. Foggy winters and hot, humid summers create a pinkish-red ham with deep, almost sweet flavors and a melt-in-your-mouth texture. An incredible ham!

NEBRODI HAM (Sicily)

Raised wild or semiwild in the north of Sicily, in the oak and beech forests of the Nebrodi mountains, the Nebrodi black pigs are very similar to wild boar. Very difficult to find because the breed is in danger of extinction, the ham develops a delicate taste, with flavors that are both intense and mild at the same time.

PROSCUITTO DE PARMA HAM (Parma)

Large White and Duroc pigs feed on pastures and bushes and their diet is supplemented with Parmesan whey. The meat is then lightly salted in a mixture of garlic and sugar, which, after two years of drying, results in a pink, partially tough ham with slightly sweet flavors.

SAN DANIELE HAM (Friuli-Venezia Giulia)

Made from pigs that cheerfully reach 440 lb, from which each ham weighs up to 26 lb, this ham is aged for eighteen months in the air that descends from the Alps and in the Adriatic breeze. It's then pressed (to remove as much water as possible), which gives it its characteristic guitar shape. The flavors are mildly sweet and salty.

SPECK (South Tyrol)

From the Trentino–South Tyrol region in the north of Italy, on the Austrian border, speck is seasoned with a mixture of salt, sugar, garlic, juniper berries, and various spices before being lightly cold-smoked, dried and aged for two years. The ham is dark red and the fat, very white, develops fruity flavors that are very long on the palate.

SPAIN

MANGALITSA HAM

From the Hungarian Mangalitsa breed, this ham, made principally in Spain, has more intra- and extramuscular fat than the Iberian breed and, most importantly, a fat that melts at a low temperature. Very rare (the breed has just been saved from extinction), it has a strong taste with hazelnut notes and an extraordinary length on the palate.

100 PERCENT IBÉRICO HAM

This is made from the Black Iberian pigs, whose unique characteristic is that they can absorb oleic acid. They feed mostly on acorns during the winter and build up a large amount of intramuscular fat. The ham is dried for about three years in the very particular southwestern Spanish air. The result is one of the best hams in the word, a product of exceptional quality!

SERRANO HAM (Teruel, between Valencia and Zaragoza and Trevélez, between Málaga, Almería and Granada)

The Sierras, mountainous regions of Spain, gave their name to this ham. Bigger and less fatty than Ibérico, Serrano is dry-salted, washed in hot water, and left to dry and age for fifteen months in the dry, fresh mountain air. The color varies from dark pink to purple with a white, slightly yellowish, and very tasty fat.

Teruel ham is AOC-certified. This Serrano is produced in the Teruel province using pigs fed on milk and then barley. It's aged for up to twenty-eight months.

Trevélez Serrano is also a Serrano and is IGP designated (a guarantee of origin for foods produced in specific areas). It's produced in the highest village in Andalusia and is also aged for up to twenty-eight months.

Both of these hams are of very, very high quality and can be sold at the same price as a 100 percent Ibérico ham.

PATA NEGRA OR BELLOTA 100 PERCENT IBÉRICO?

Pata negra is a renowned ham that is the pride and joy of Spanish gastronomy.

THE LIFE OF THE IBERIAN PIG

The Iberian breed is an ancient one that takes a long time to reach adulthood. Its unique feature is the ability to absorb the oleic acid contained inside acorns and to develop fat inside its muscles. It's this fat that gives it such a distinctive taste.

THE ORIGIN OF THE IBERIAN PIG

A huge reforestation project was begun after the civil war in part of the southwest region of Spain. A system that dated back to the Middle Ages, called *dehesa*, was used. This was the planting of trees with evergreen foliage (evergreen oaks, cork oaks, beeches, pine trees) while favoring pastures and crops.

THE RHYTHM OF THE SEASONS

During the summer months, the Iberian pig doesn't have much to eat. It's almost a period of famine. Then autumn comes and October brings the start of the *montañera*, the period during which the acorns fall from the oak trees. Our animal stuffs himself and stores the fat in preparation for the next summer's fast.

During its second summer the pig is still growing and weighs almost 220 lb, but again, the poor creature is starving. Once again, autumn arrives with its astronomical quantity of acorns. Unable to resist after having gone without for so many long months, he becomes a beast, eating up to 22 lb of acorns per day.

Once the *montañera* is over and the pig's muscles are swollen with oleic acid, before it can begin to draw energy from its fat reserves, the animal is slaughtered.

A MASTERPIECE

After slaughtering, the hindquarters are cut off and placed in a very humid cold-storage room for six or seven hours so that their temperature quickly drops to 42°F.

SALTING

They are then covered in salt for six to ten days, during which time the meat loses a bit of humidity. Then they're rinsed in tepid water to remove any salt remaining on the surface.

POST-SALTING

Once washed, the hams are put into a cold-storage room for the third time for one to two months. This gives the salt time to disperse itself evenly across the meat, helping to preserve it.

NATURAL DRYING

The hams are placed in a dryer—usually in the natural, open air— for six to nine months. As the ham slightly dehydrates, Maillard reactions slowly begin to take place (see p 174). Then the sugars condense, the fats oxidize, begin to melt, and little by little penetrate the meat. Bacterial and mycological flora aren't without purpose and also begin to develop. There's a lot of hard work going on in there.

AGING

The hams are moved (again!) to a humid cellar so that the natural yeasts can develop. This is when the ham produces both its most delicate and intense flavors and takes on notes of dried fruit, hazelnut, etc. The best hams are left another thirty to fifty months.

PATA NEGRA AND THE OTHERS

Spanish legislation, which was vague at the very least, has recently changed. It differentiates the pata negra from other hams of the Iberian breed, which don't exactly meet the same criteria.

PATA NEGRA BELLOTA 100 PERCENT IBÉRICO HAM

Since the legislation changed, this pata negra must be of pure Iberian breed, free range, fed on grass and fruit in the summer and on acorns in the winter. But remember, this ham is very rare and represents less than 0.5 percent of Spanish hams. It is considered a "black label" ham, distinguished from other hams.

BELOTTA IBÉRICO HAM

This comes from a 75 percent purebred pig that is free-range, fed on acorns in winter, and grass and fruit in summer. It has a red sticker.

CEBO DE CAMPO IBÉRICO HAM

This is from a 75 percent purebred pig, free-range, fed on grains, grass, fruits, etc., but not acorns. It has a green sticker.

CEBO IBÉRICO HAM

This comes from a 50 percent purebred pig that was raised in converted barns, fed on grains and grass provided to them by man. It has a white sticker.

DON'T BE GULLIBLE...

When you're told that pata negra is from pigs fed exclusively on acorns, remember that there isn't an unlimited amount of acorns to eat in autumn, spring, or summer. That's a legend that some of the people who sell the ham would have you believe.

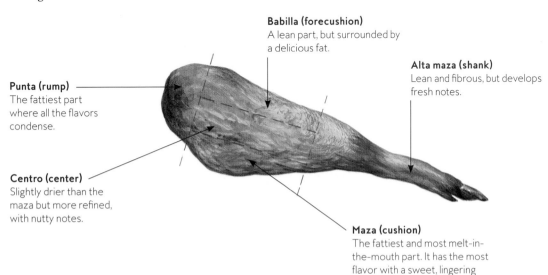

Babilla (forecushion)
A lean part, but surrounded by a delicious fat.

Alta maza (shank)
Lean and fibrous, but develops fresh notes.

Punta (rump)
The fattiest part where all the flavors condense.

Centro (center)
Slightly drier than the maza but more refined, with nutty notes.

Maza (cushion)
The fattiest and most melt-in-the-mouth part. It has the most flavor with a sweet, lingering aftertaste and hazelnut notes.

THE PATA NEGRA CUT

BRING HOME THE BACON!

*Although French bacon is nothing to boast about,
the word "bacon" is French and refers to a flitch of salted bacon,
which meant the side of pig cut lengthwise. But, in fact, bacon
originated in Denmark.*

BACON, WHERE DO YOU COME FROM?

The Danish, who have been eating it for ages as a side to their potatoes, imported bacon to England in the 1850s. The English appropriated the cut to themselves and used it to make the bacon we know today. Today still, most of the bacon consumed in Great Britain comes from Denmark.

WHICH PART OF THE PIG?

English and Danish bacon are taken from the animal's back. The cut takes part of the meat that's found in the ribs as well as a part of the fat that surrounds it. But other parts can be used, too. American bacon is taken from the side of the pork belly; Canadian bacon, like French bacon, is taken from the sirloin, and others use the cheek or the bottom of the shoulder.

THERE'S BACON AND THERE'S "BACON"

FRENCH BACON

The French don't understand a thing about bacon. Theirs is dry, without fat, tasteless, and barely even browns. Basically, it's the same bacon you get on hamburgers from fast-food chains. Out, and into the trash!

ENGLISH SIRS, SHOOT FIRST

Ah, English bacon! Incomparable. There are pig breeds raised specially to produce prize-winning bacon, like the Tamworth or British Saddleback, or even the Berkshire or the Gloucestershire Old Spots that also make for delicious bacon. These animals are raised with love for our greatest satisfaction.

HOW DO MAKE IT?

As with all salting processes, there are two possibilities:

DRY-SALTING

This is the artisanal method, the tastiest but also the one that takes the most time. The meat is rubbed with a mixture of salt, sugar, and spices and left to rest for several days, during which the process is repeated numerous times. Next, it's hung to dry for two weeks and then aged for several months to a year. Some are smoked with apple, beech, and cherry wood.

IN A BRINE

This is the most commonly used method and the fastest, but it develops fewer flavors. The meat is soaked in water that has been salted and sweetened with sugar or maple syrup for between two days and a week. Then, it's hung for two weeks to allow it to dry a little.

For bacon intended for mass distribution, lots of stuff is injected into it to accelerate the process and chemically improve the flavor. Yuck!

Once the salting process is complete, the bacon is ready to be eaten. It's called "green bacon," and if it's smoked, it becomes smoked bacon.

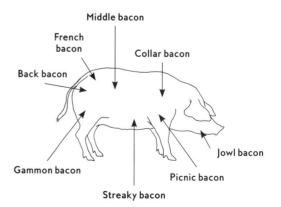

BACK BACON

Located on the back part of the animal, the back bacon is a cut particular to the United Kingdom. Its meat is lean and surrounded by a delicious fat. It's the most commonly eaten bacon in England and Ireland.

MIDDLE BACON

Cut from the side of the pig, the middle bacon sits between the back bacon and the streaky bacon in terms of flavor and fat quantity. Cook it very slowly and finish by deep-frying.

COLLAR BACON

Cut from the shoulder, the collar bacon has an interesting marbling that stops it from drying out too much during cooking. It requires the same type of cooking as the middle bacon to accompany dishes that may be a little dry.

EXCEPTIONAL 👍

JOWL BACON

When it's unsmoked, it's the same as the Italian *guanciale* used in carbonara. Basically, it's an absolutely divine piece of fat with a little bit of meat inside. Fry as a side for vegetables.

PICNIC OR COTTAGE BACON

Taken from the pig's shoulder, the picnic bacon doesn't have a lot of fat and it's the toughest of all the different types of bacon. Its flavors are very mild.

STREAKY BACON

This comes from the belly and has thick streaks of tasty fat. It's the most common bacon in the United States and is sold smoked and unsmoked in France as *poitrine*, It's the same as pancetta.

EXCEPTIONAL 👍

GAMMON OR WILTSHIRE BACON

Gammon or Wiltshire bacon is made following a process that dates back to the mid-nineteenth century. It's a flavorful, mild bacon that can be cut into slices of varying thicknesses depending on the desired texture. It's without a doubt the most interesting bacon.

FRENCH AND CANADIAN BACON

It's made in an industrial manner, is full of water, has a poor-quality smoked flavor, and doesn't brown.

BRING HOME THE BACON

~~~~~~~

In fairgrounds, the most coveted prize was given to the champion able to catch by hand a pig coated in grease. The women encouraged their husbands by shouting, *"Bring home the bacon!"*

EXTRAORDINARY LARD!

I'm talking about something extraordinary here: lard that's been dried, aged, and nurtured with love for months to create an exceptional-quality product.

Forget the thick slice of lard that's added to flavorless dishes or soups to give them some taste. Just as an extraordinary ham, like pata negra, is worked on for more than three years to produce an array of incredible flavors, so too can lard be worked to create something you can't find anywhere else.

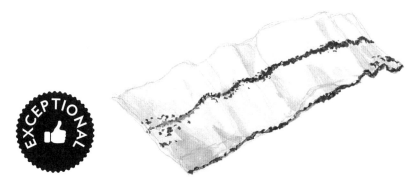

EXCEPTIONAL 👍

COLONNATA LARD

This is of a very, very high quality, without a doubt the best lard in the world, whose recipe dates back to antiquity. Taken from the backs of pigs of ancient breeds, this lard is created in Colonnata, a suburb of the town of Carrara in Tuscany. It's no coincidence that Carrara is also the town that produces the timeless marble.

Seventy-two hours after slaughter, the lard, at least 1 inch (3 cm) in thickness, is put into marble vats rubbed with garlic. Garlic, rosemary, sage, oregano, salt, and pepper and also star anise, cinnamon, clove, and nutmeg are added one after the other. It's aged for almost two years. During the aging process, the salt absorbs the water contained in the fat, which becomes white and creamy and absorbs the flavors of the herbs and spices in which it soaks. The impermeable marble acts as insulation and ensures that the temperature remains consistent during the entire process.

Once removed, the result is a lard of unimaginable delicacy—deep, pearly white and almost transparent in color, with fresh, peppery, herby, and spiced aromas and soft, very elegant, almost evanescent flavors.

Colonnata lard should be cut into very thin slices, as thin as cigarette papers, and served at room temperature or a tiny bit warmer if possible. Once it reaches 77-78°F, it's the best it can be.

It's eaten raw on toasted slices of rye bread so that its melts slightly, with cheese or honey or simply on its own, letting it melt in the mouth. This lard is also delicious wrapped around pan-fried asparagus, gently dripping off its burning-hot surface. I could write pages about it.

"**When my wife's still asleep,** I cut myself a couple of slices for breakfast. It's my own guilty little pleasure. But don't tell her . . . "

LARD D'ARNAD

Another absolutely exceptional lard. It's lesser known than Colonnata lard, yet just as sublime. Arnad is a little village in the Aosta Valley in the north of Italy (not very far from Chamonix, for those of you who know your mountains). Lard d'Arnad is made with fat from the pork butt, at the top of the shoulder.

It's aged in brine (water and salt) and herbs found in the valley, including rosemary. This whole mixture is put into traditional wooden molds made of oak, chestnut, or larch. The aging process takes around three months and creates a lard with deep, herbal flavors. It's eaten in the same way as Colonnata lard.

BELLOTA 100 PERCENT IBÉRICO LARD

Iberian pigs, used to produce true pata negra, develop a fat of infinite flavors, especially along the top of their backs. Salted, rinsed, and finally left to dry with the hams, the lard absorbs part of their aromas and flavors. Fruitier and slightly more intense than Colonnata lard, this pearly white lard develops notes of dried fruit, such as hazelnut and walnut. Condensed into this lard is everything that makes Bellota 100 percent Ibérico ham so magical.

GUANCIALE

Originally from Rome, guanciale is the fat from the pig's cheek and jowl, inside of which is a small amount of lean meat. There are various ways this can be prepared, but the best is the one used in the Lepini mountains in the Latium region. The lard is rinsed in wine, and rubbed with salt, red pepper, and spices before being left to dry for two months. This extremely white lard is of quite a firm texture with distinct grassy and musky flavors. Lightly cooked, it's the must-have ingredient in carbonara or amatriciana pasta.

IBERIAN PIG VENTRÈCHE

Taken from the same breed of pigs as Bellota lard, this ventrèche is also made in the southwest of Spain. Once salted and dried, the aging process takes place in the open air for several months. The lard develops a pearly color with nutty, fresh, and slightly sweet flavors.

GASCON FLAT VENTRÈCHE

Flat ventrèche is made of fat taken solely from the pork belly. This lard, which is first covered in salt and cracked black pepper, is dried and aged for over six months. It's light pink in color and its flavors have peppery, slightly sweet notes. The Gascon Black pig has the ability to produce a high-quality fat.

THE WORLD OF BLOOD SAUSAGE

Blood sausage is made of blood and pork fat. It's one of the oldest known cured meats. It was supposedly invented during ancient times and was usually eaten at the time of year when pigs were slaughtered, in the autumn.

Black, white, red, green; small or large; eaten cold, hot, deep-fried, pan-fried in thick or thin slices, crushed onto bread: blood sausage can be appreciated in many different ways. Each country has its specialty and its secret ingredients. Here's a little world tour of the blood sausages you should try at least once in your life.

🇫🇷 FRANCE

GALABART (Greater South-West)
This is pig's intestine filled with a stuffing made of blood, pig's head and rind, and sometimes tongue, lungs, and heart. It can also contain bread and hard fat.

SANGUI (Corsica)
Made with blood from Corsica Nustrale Black pigs and wild herbs from the scrublands, it can also sometimes contain wild onions, mint, and juniper berries.

CREOLE BLOOD SAUSAGE (Antilles)
It can contain sheep's or goat's blood instead of pig's. Composed of bread crumbs, spices, and chile pepper-infused water, it's very creamy.

🇧🇪 BELGIUM

VÈTE TRËPE (Centre, province of Walloon Brabant)
Made of white pork meat and spices, a third is then filled with a mix of cabbage and green kale. This blood sausage is green.

🏴󠁧󠁢󠁳󠁣󠁴󠁿 SCOTLAND

STORNOWAY BLACK PUDDING (Western Isles)
Very famous in the United Kingdom, this blood sausage of Scottish origin contains rolled oats and fat from beef kidneys. It has a crumbly texture and peppery flavors.

🇩🇪 GERMANY

THÜRINGER ROTWURST
(Centre-East, near the border)

This oldest-known recipe dates back to 1613. It's made with pieces of pork shoulder and cheek brined for twelve hours. Liver and rind are then added to the mix.

🇮🇹 ITALY

BIROLDO (Tuscany)

Very dark, with a very fine texture, this blood sausage is made with the pig's heart, tongue, and lungs, which are mixed with spices (clove, fennel seeds, etc.)

BURISTO (Siena)

This very large blood sausage contains pig's head and fat, lemon, orange zest, sage, and sometimes pine nuts. Serve on crusty bread.

🇪🇸 SPAIN

MORCILLA DE BURGOS
(Burgos in Castile, Northern Spain)

This is made with pig's blood and fat, onion, rice, lard, and chile peppers. In certain parts of Castile, squash and raisins are also added.

MORCILLA DULCE (Canary Islands)

This very sweet, black blood sausage contains almonds, honey, cinnamon, and even pine nuts and raisins. It can also be found in Galicia.

🇫🇮 FINLAND

MUSTAMAKKARA (Tampere, Southwest of Finland)

This very old recipe is made with ground rye, flour, and onions. It's eaten with cranberry jelly, hot milk, or red wine.

🇮🇸 ICELAND

SLÁTUR

Another ancestral recipe, made of blood, offal, sheep's kidney fat, and oats. This blood sausage is often sold as a kit: people can choose the amount of each ingredient and put them into the intestine themselves.

🇸🇪 SWEDEN

BLODPUDDING

Slightly sweet, blood pudding is made of pig's blood, diced lard, milk, rye, beer, molasses, and spices. It's eaten with ice-cold milk.

🇺🇸 THE UNITED STATES

BIROLDO (San Francisco)

Of Italian origin, American biroldo can contain cow's blood instead of pig's blood, pig's snout, pine nuts, grapes, and spices.

BOUDIN ROUGE (Louisiana)

With a slightly grainy texture, this blood sausage contains pork liver, rice, spring onions, and red pepper. Don't confuse it with Cajun boudin, which doesn't contain blood.

🇧🇧 BARBADOS

BLOOD SAUSAGE (Caribbean)

Made of pig's blood, sweet potato, onion, and herbs and spices from Barbados, it's traditionally served with the pig's trotters and ears.

🇬🇾 GUYANA

BLOOD SAUSAGE (South America)

The blood used in this is generally cow's blood mixed with rice, spices, and herbs like thyme and basil. It's usually served with a spicy pepper sauce.

🇧🇷 BRAZIL

COURIÇO OR MORCILLA OR MORCELA

The entire range of Portuguese blood sausages. Very popular, they're served as starters at *churrascos*, Brazilian barbecues.

THE BEST LAMB AND SHEEP BREEDS

Here are some amazing breeds. Some are well-known and delicious, but others are rare and exceptional. It's essential that you don't just ask for lamb or mutton, but for a specific breed.

THE BEST OF THE BEST

THE NORTH RONALDSAY (UK)

North Ronaldsay is the northernmost island of Orkney, off the north coast of Scotland. This ancient breed feeds almost exclusively on fresh seaweed. It has modified its digestive system so that it ruminates several times a day instead of once during the night. Its meat is dark in color, slightly tough with little outer fat, and an intense, gamy flavor. Many consider the North Ronaldsay to be the best type of lamb and mutton.
Lamb: 22 to 33 lb **Carcass:** 17 to 24 lb

THE TUNIS (U.S.)

A few specimens of the Tunisian Barbarin breed were gifted to George Washington in 1799. A federal judge who owned a farm in Pennsylvania developed the lineage and named it Tunis. The breed gained a foothold just about everywhere after the Chicago World's Fair in 1893, despite having become virtually extinct during the civil war. Similar to the Suffolk but smaller, the Tunis is renowned for its delicious meat, smooth and silky with a mineral aftertaste.
Lamb: 33 to 44 lb **Carcass:** 22 to 33 lb

THE SOAY (UK)

Probably introduced to Scotland by the Celts 3,000 years ago, the Soay takes its name from the Isle of Soay in northwest Scotland. This breed is small, stocky, and looks a little like the Mediterranean mouflon. It's quite robust, surviving in a hostile environment with violent winds, extreme temperatures, and numerous cliffs. Because the lambs are quite small, the Soay is eaten when fully grown, producing a lean, tender meat with deep, gamy flavors.
Sheep: 55 to 88 lb **Carcass:** 39 to 61 lb

THE WELSH MOUNTAIN (UK)

Originally from Wales, the Welsh Mountain is white with no wool on its face. Numerous varieties of the breed exist, such as the Badger Face (with a black belly and limbs) and the Black Welsh Mountain (completely black). This breed dates back to the Middle Ages, during which time it was raised mainly for its wool and its milk. Today, however, it's bred for its meat. Small and robust, its meat is lean with a fine texture and deep but soft flavors.
Lamb: 26 to 37 lb **Carcass:** 19 to 26 lb

"These animals are magnificent. You won't find lambs like these on industrial farms."

THE BEST

THE SUFFOLK

Formerly known as the Northside Norfolks or "black face," the Suffolk was created at the end of the eighteenth century by crossing Norfolk Horn ewes with Southdown rams. Easily recognizable with its black face and large ears, drooping in males and horizontal in females, the breed has developed all over the world and is often used to crossbreed and improve local breeds. The Suffolk ewe provides plenty of milk and produces heavy, stocky lambs with a beautiful outer layer of fat.
Lamb: 39 to 50 lb **Carcass:** 26 to 33 lb

THE HAMPSHIRE

Born of a cross between the Wiltshire Horn, the Berkshire Knot, and the Southdown at the beginning of the nineteenth century, the Hampshire or Hampshire Down is a robust, low-maintenance breed that adapts to all climates, and which has wool on most of its head and the tops of its feet. Its breeding season is earlier than that of other breeds and so provides lambs for the beginning of the year. These lambs grow rapidly and make for a tender meat with a delicious fat.
Lamb: 44 to 55 lb **Carcass:** 33 to 39 lb

THE DORSET

Very likely born from a cross between a Spanish wool breed and an English breed, two varieties exist: the original, horned variety called the Dorset Horn and the hornless variety called the Polled Dorset, which was developed in Australia. Known for its prolific lambing, year-round and up to twice a year, the Dorset ewe provides plenty of milk and suckles her lambs for a long time. The Dorset produces stocky lambs with good legs and a long loin. The meat is quite lean with a beautiful color, tender and flavorful.
Lamb: 44 to 55 lb **Carcass:** 30 to 44 lb

THE WILTSHIRE HORN

Originally from the south of England, it was eaten back in the eighteenth century but was mainly raised to provide manure and urine to fertilize cultivated cropland. The Wiltshire Horn naturally loses its wool in the spring and almost went extinct in the nineteenth century when sheep were predominantly raised for their wool. Saved from extinction by several breeders, its meat is tasty, tender, and lean, with a fine grain.
Lamb: 39 to 55 lb **Carcass:** 26 to 35 lb

THE BEST LAMB AND SHEEP BREEDS

OTHER BREEDS NOT TO BE MISSED

THE TEXEL

Originally from the island of Texel in Holland, this breed was recently imported to England and to the United States. Texels are very muscular and their meat is quite tender.

THE SCOTTISH BLACKFACE

This is a very ancient breed whose origins we can't be sure about, but it has been traced as far back as the sixteenth century. Its meat responds to current demand for mild flavors and very little fat.

THE SHROPSHIRE

Robust and of medium build, the Shropshire offers quite a fatty meat, which gives it a lot of flavor. Unfortunately, the breed is being modified to obtain a leaner meat.

THE RYELAND

The Ryeland is one of the oldest breeds in the United Kingdom and was in danger of extinction until recently. Although quite rare, the lambs offer a meat that is highly sought after by the best chefs.

THE DORPER

The Dorper was born in South Africa in the 1930s of a cross between the Dorset Horn and the Blackhead Persian sheep. Its beautiful cover layer of fat reveals a good-quality meat, tender and juicy.

THE SOUTHDOWN

Originally from Sussex in England, the Southdown belongs to the "Downs" group, along with the Hampshires, Suffolks, Shropshires, and Oxfords. Its meat is very tender and very flavorful.

THE OXFORD

Created by crossing Cotswolds and Hampshires (and probably some Southdowns) in the county of Oxford in England, the Oxford is among the biggest and heaviest breeds of sheep.

THE BORERAY SHEEP

From the island of Boreray in the St. Kilda archipelago in northwest Scotland, the Boreray, in contrast to the Soay, was domesticated quickly. Very small and very rare, its meat is delicious.

THE PORTLAND

Portlands produce carcasses that mature for longer than other breeds. The delicate, lean meat has rich, complex flavors that are long on the palate. One of the best breeds.

THE KARAKUL

The Karakul, originally from Central Asia, is undoubtedly the oldest domesticated breed. The fat in its tail is used in many dishes in the Middle East. The meat has soft, elegant flavors.

WHICH LAMB TO CHOOSE?

*In France, lamb meat isn't sold according to its breed
but to where it was raised, be that a Label Rouge,
Protected Geographical Indication or Protected Designation
of Origin area. But it's not that complicated . . .*

The quality of lamb meat depends on various factors: the parents' breeds, where and how it was raised, the lamb's diet, and the age at which it was slaughtered.

THE PARENTS' BREEDS

Ewes from breeds that produce good-quality meat generally have very little milk to feed to their lambs and have no maternal instinct. The young lambs have to very quickly learn to look after themselves by eating grass and grains. This is unfortunate because lamb tastes so much better when it's been fed on its mother's milk for a long time.

THE SOLUTION

Ewes from breeds that produce good, nurturing mothers are bred with rams that produce very good-quality meat. This ensures that, on the one hand, that the mother will feed good milk to her lamb, and on the other, that the lamb will inherit its father's qualities and produce good meat.

LAMB-REARING METHODS

MILK-FED LAMB

A milk-fed lamb is fed solely on its mother's milk. Its meat is eaten from winter to June–July, depending on the region. The quality of its mother's diet, which is fresh grass or hay, has very little influence on the quality of her milk.

SHEEPFOLD LAMB

As made clear by its name, this type of lamb is raised in a sheepfold. Lambs are born year-round. Kept inside, it's fed the same food no matter the season. The quality of its meat and its availability are therefore consistent throughout the year.

GRASS-FED LAMB

Born in the winter in a sheepfold, it eventually begins to eat grass. If it's raised in salt meadows, its meat is available from the beginning of June until January, because it needs time to graze on the grass along the bay, which is rich in iodine.

DESIGNATIONS

The Label Rouge (Red Label) is an official stamp that guarantees a quality superior to that of other, more common products of the same type. When awarding this label, the breed, diet, and rearing method, among other things, are taken into account.

The IGP (Protected Geographical Indication) is a European label that guarantees the product's quality, geographical origin, and any other characteristics that can be linked to the geographical region.

The AOC (Protected Designation of Origin) is a French label that designates a high-quality, values expertise, and allows producers to protect themselves against poor imitations of their products.

These labels signify high quality and some lambs of outstanding quality hold both a Label Rouge and an IGP. These designations indicate which animals are first-rate.

A BRIEF HISTORY OF LAMB AND MUTTON

While the sheep's ancestor, the Ovis aries, is well known, we know very little about the evolution of its wild ancestors. The most common hypothesis is that it descends from European and Asian mouflons.

SYMBOL OF PURITY AND SACRIFICE

The first traces of sheep domestication go back to about 10,000 years ago in Mesopotamia. Later, India, China, North Africa, and Europe also began to domesticate sheep. Greek and Roman civilizations regularly sacrificed sheep to appease divine wrath or celebrate the renewal of nature. From the very beginning of Christianity, the lamb symbolized Christ: "Behold, the lamb of God who takes away the sins of the world." Passover, Easter, and the Muslim Ramadan continue this tradition.

A DELICACY

In the Middle Ages, rams and ewes were eaten, but mainly raised for their wool and milk. Lamb was one of the delicacies eaten by the wealthy and the aristocrats. The people made do with mutton, which had a stronger flavor.

At the end of the nineteenth century, breeders began once again to show an interest in lamb meat, carefully selecting stock to improve the qualities of certain sheep according to their needs: either wool, milk, or meat.

The different sheep breeds often carry the name of the region in which they were raised, exactly as with chickens and cows.

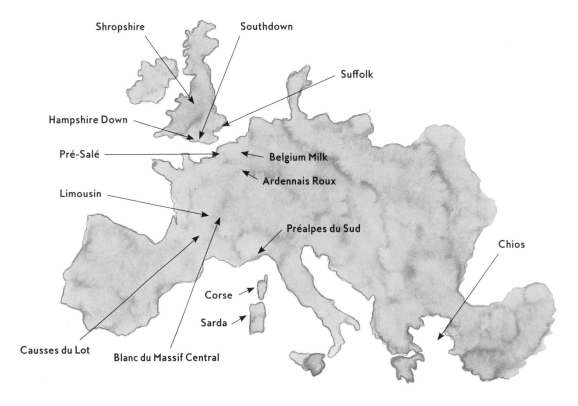

Shropshire
Southdown
Suffolk
Hampshire Down
Pré-Salé
Belgium Milk
Ardennais Roux
Limousin
Préalpes du Sud
Chios
Corse
Sarda
Causses du Lot
Blanc du Massif Central

THE SHEEP FAMILY

With its frolicking and playful temperament, the lamb has bundles of charm. But things change as the lamb grows up.

MILK-FED LAMB

Up to five or six weeks, this is what the ewe's baby is called. It weighs between 13 and 17 lb and is fed solely on its mother's milk. Its meat is very pale, almost white, very tender, mild, and slightly sweet.

SPRING LAMB

Up to three or four months, the spring lamb weighs between 30 lb and 39 lb and is fed mostly on cow's milk. When slaughtered at this age, its meat is pale pink and is beginning to develop a stronger taste.

A spring lamb left to grow **up to five months** weighs over 44 lb. It begins to eat grass and sometimes grain. Its meat is a darker pink and its flavor is beginning to mature.

LATE SEASON LAMB

Over 5 months old, it weighs between 66 and 77 lb and eats grass and grains every day. Its meat is now a light red color and its flavor has reached maturation. For the late-season lambs raised in salt meadows, it's at this age that they're slaughtered.

EWE

The female is a ewe. She is used for breeding and she'll give birth to up to four lambs per year. She bleats.

WETHER

A wether is castrated male sheep. Its meat has a very strong taste.

RAM

This male is also used for breeding. It's a force of nature and grunts like a camel.

NUTRITION AND MEAT QUALITY

Even though you can get it all year round, lamb tastes better at certain times of the year. The quality and the particularities of what the lambs have been eating, as well as their age, result in very different meats.

As we've seen, there are three types of lamb: the milk-fed lamb, the sheepfold lamb, and the grass-fed lamb.

For the sheepfold lamb, the seasons have no influence because lambs are born on a regular basis and their food is the same all year. However, for the milk-fed lamb fed on its mother's milk, and for the grass-fed lamb that feeds on grass, hay, and sometimes salt meadows, the seasons are highly influential on the quality of their flavors. And because these lambs are principally born in the winter until the beginning of spring, we can talk about the seasonality of lamb meat.

Hay and short grass

Rich grass and a few small flowers

A finer, sparse, more scraggly grass, a few small white flowers, a lighter-colored soil

Thick, short grass without flowers

WINTER

The animals go into the sheepfold to keep warm. They have access to outside but mostly eat hay. The milk-fed lambs have just been born and suckle their mothers.

ON-THE-PLATE RESULTS

Milk-fed lamb: very, very good
Grass-fed lamb: very good at the beginning of the winter, with aftertastes of hay after that.
Prés-salés (salt meadow) lamb: the last of them are still for sale at Christmas and are still very tasty.

SPRING

The lambs born at the beginning of winter start to graze. Little flowers appear in the fields where the animals are happy and frolic in delight.

ON-THE-PLATE RESULTS

Milk-fed lamb: very, very good
Grass-fed lamb: some aftertastes of hay at the beginning before more floral notes begin to surface.
Prés-salés (salt meadow) lamb: not the season for these (the lambs are only just starting to graze).

SUMMER

The animals wander in fields that offer a grass that is less green than before, except in the mountains. The grass on limestone plateaus dries out a little in the sun. And in the salt meadows, the plants are thriving.

ON-THE-PLATE RESULTS

Milk-fed lamb: it's no longer the season; there are usually none left.
Grass-fed lamb: the lambs raised in the mountains take on delicate grassy and floral flavors. Those raised on the dry limestone plateaus develop stronger flavors.
Prés-salés (salt meadow) lamb: the season is beginning. Floral and salty notes develop.

AUTUMN

The first cold weather arrives, and the lambs slowly begin to take shelter in the sheepfolds. In the mountains, they come down from the summer pastures; in the salt meadows, our friends still have access to the unusual plants that grow there.

ON-THE-PLATE RESULTS

Milk-fed lamb: the season begins again, hurrah!
Grass-fed lamb: the lambs raised in the mountains still have beautiful floral flavors.
Prés-salés (salt meadow) lamb: they're at their very best with more intense flavors than in the summer.

LAMB CUTS

Because lambs are small, the cutting is simplified as much as possible to get large cuts that can be shared between several people. But there are a still a few secret, smaller pieces.

FRENCH LAMB CUTS

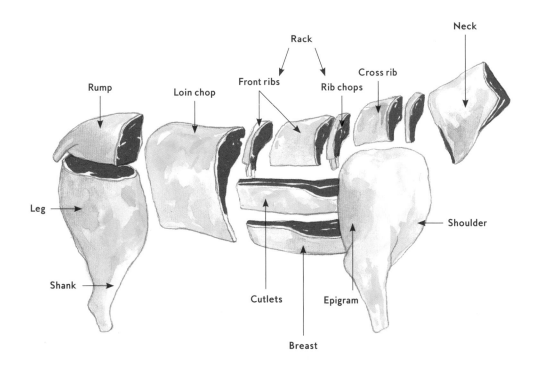

ENGLISH CUTS

Here, too, the cutting is done depending on the desired size of the meat pieces.

AMERICAN CUTS

This cutting method allows for even bigger cuts.

CHOICE LAMB CUTS

If you've never heard of the royal rib, the baron of lamb, or the butterfly or the lamb roast, don't worry, I'll guide you through them.

 CANNON OF LAMB
This is the eye of the loin rolled into a roast. Beautiful!

RACK
Both the prime rib and rib chops together. A good butcher will cut it from the fourth to the eleventh rib so as to ensure the filet meat is proportional across each rib, therefore allowing for an even cooking of the whole rack.

NECK
Boned or not, the neck is gently slow-cooked, usually to give depth to the flavor of a stock or to lamb-based sauces.

CROSS RIB
Located just behind the neck, it's composed of the first five ribs with a beautiful fat that gives it a lot of flavor and tenderness. It's the equivalent of the beef chuck roll. Not as presentable as the other ribs, it nevertheless has the strongest flavor.

LOIN CHOP
After the cross rib are the loin chops, which aren't real ribs, they're lumbar vertebrae with flesh attached. There is no bone. Loin chops can be cut in various different ways: into filets, double lamb chops, as part of the saddle, or into eye of loin.

 FRONT RIBS
Composed of the four ribs that come after the rib chops. The first of the ribs is called the "royal rib" and has a perfectly equal meat/fat ratio. The rib eye is large, the bone long with very little fat.

RIB CHOPS
The four ribs after the cross rib. The eye, which is the circle of meat in the center of the rib, is a good size and its flavors are intensified by the strip of fat that sits alongside the bone. A very good balance between meat and fat, and tasty flavors.

LAMB CHOPS OR MUTTON CHOPS
This is one of the loin chop cuts. It's cut with the entire vertebra at a thickness of ½ inch (1.5 cm) for the lamb chop and 1 inch (3 cm) for the mutton chop. It's the equivalent of two T-bones stuck together.

 SHOULDER
Fattier and more tender than the leg, the shoulder can be prepared whole or in pieces for sautéing. Roast it with the shoulder blade in or boned and rolled into a roast, stuffed or unstuffed. Choose a round shoulder cut rather than one that is long and thin.

EPIGRAM
Delicious and full of flavor with a beautiful fat! It's a cut taken from beneath the shoulder and contains part of the breast. It's best with the bone in. Broil it, braise it, or boil it. Delicious!

TENDERLOIN
Another variation of the loin chop. It's the same cut but boned and without the chops. There are two tenderloins, one on each side of the loin.

LEG OF LAMB
The classic lamb cut for a family meal encompassing the back leg cut with the rump. It can be sold in different forms: whole, boned and rolled, cut into small roasts or into steaks. It's divine gently slow-cooked in a pot.

LEG OF LAMB, RUMP OFF
The same cut as the leg, but without the rump.

CUTLETS
This cut is from the rib bones. The meat is tougher because many of the bones contain marrow. This flavorful piece is delicious when slow cooked on a low heat in a braising liquid or a broth.

EYE OF LOIN

Another loin chop variation, this is the central part of the prime rib or the loin chops without the bone or the surrounding fat.

FEET

These are part of the offal. They are often used to make a delicious and very delicate gelatin that is used to enrich terrines and patés, or as a side dish to certain cold meats.

BREAST

This is the lower part of the animal and contains several cuts such as the cutlets and the epigram. It's rich in bones and cartilage and is made up of different abdominal muscles. If cooked whole, it should be boiled or braised.

RUMP

This is the top part of the lamb's rear, which is equivalent to rump of veal and the back part of beef sirloin. Its meat is succulent and it's usually boned and sold whole as a roast or in slices. It's the best!

SADDLE

This loin chop variation is formed of five of the loin chops. A cut fit for a king. Try it as soon as you get the chance!

SHANK

The bottom part of the back leg. Soft and gelatinous, the shank can be sold separate from the leg. If you have time to slowly confit it, it will be delicious.

UNDER-THE-RADAR LAMB CUTS

CULOTTE

This is made up of the hindquarters of the lamb—both legs and the entire rump.

YUM!

BARON OF LAMB

This is the culotte and the saddle—both legs, the rump, and the saddle.

ROSBIF

This French cut is composed of the baron and the rib rack. Basically, this is all of the lamb except for the breast, the shoulders, and the neck.

BUTTERFLY

Another French cut, this includes the shoulder and the neck, unlike the rosbif cut.

THE BEST CHICKEN BREEDS

Just as with other animals, the breed has an enormous influence on the quality of the chicken that you find on your plate. Here are the tastiest breeds.

THERE'S CHICKEN AND THEN THERE'S "CHICKEN"

Certain breeds produce very good laying hens but bland meat. Others produce good laying hens and tasty meat. Then there are what we call "broiler chickens," renowned for the quality of their meat. Some are tough in texture, others more tender, some have a lot of fat, others less, some have dark meat, others white, etc.

FREE-RANGE CHICKEN

If you want a very good-quality bird, choosing a free-range chicken is a minimum requirement, but it's not enough. The "free range" designation is concerned with the farming method, not the place where the chicken was raised or its breed. Ask your butcher which breeds his free-range chickens are from, and if he can't answer, find another butcher!

THE NAMES OF THE ANCIENT BREEDS

Ancient breeds often take the name of the town in which they were bred. So don't be surprised by the names of chickens—they're not mistakes. When we talk of the Barbezieux breed we call it "the Barbezieux" and when referring to the Le Mans breed, we call it "the Le Mans." Now that that's cleared up, let's move on!

THE BEST OF THE BEST

THE BRAHMA

It owes its name to the Brahmaputra River, which stretched from the north side of the Himalayas to northeast India. The Brahma, born from crossbreeding the Malay with the Cochin, is an American creation that was then introduced to Europe in the mid-nineteenth century. This animal is big, massive even, with a deep, full breast, a pea comb, orange-red eyes, and feathered feet. Slow-growing, this breed makes for a succulent meat.
Rooster: 9.9 to 11 lb **Hen:** 8.8 to 9.9 lb

THE DORKING

Created in England, the Dorking is one of the most ancient breeds. It carries the name of a locality in a county called Surrey, near London. Its origins possibly go back to the first century. Columella, a Roman writer, described a poultry bird like today's Dorking, with five toes and with the same coloring. Another origin, the Picardie region of France, has also been suggested. It's a slow-growing bird whose meat is very pale, almost white, delicate, tender, and juicy.
Rooster: 9.9 to 13 lb **Hen:** 7.7 to 11 lb

> **"Don't hesitate to ask** your butcher for the exact breed you would like. He'll know he's dealing with someone who knows what they're talking about."

THE JERSEY GIANT

This breed was created in New Jersey in the 1870s from crosses between black Langshans, Brahmas, black Javas, and Cornishes, to respond to the demand for heavy breeds. The largest breed of chicken in the United States, it's robust but its slow growth (the development of the skeleton and of the meat require up to at least a year) means that it's only raised on small-scale farms. Its meat is extremely tender, juicy, flavorful, and perfect for large meals.
Rooster: 12 to 13 lb **Hen:** 8.8 to 9.9 lb

THE BARBEZIEUX

Because it grows very slowly, this breed completely disappeared at the beginning of the twentieth century. A true show-off, this strong and noble animal has long legs and a magnificent comb. It looks a little more like a large Bresse capon than a traditional chicken. Its white meat is both firm and tender at the same time. Its flavor is very different from the flavor we usually associate with chicken and therefore a little difficult to discern, but the female tastes much better than the male. This breed is fabulous gently roasted at a low temperature.
Rooster: 9.9 lb **Hen:** 7.7 lb

THE BEST CHICKEN BREEDS

THE BEST

THE RHODE ISLAND RED

Red birds with yellow tarsi already existed in Rhode Island and Massachusetts at the beginning of the nineteenth century, and red-colored poultry was in fashion. These roosters were therefore crossbred with other birds to obtain red chickens. Boats brought large, Asian birds to the area as these were also used to crossbreed. The Rhode Island Red has a long, horizontal back and makes for what we would call good, free-range meat.
Rooster: 6.6 to 8.8 lb **Hen:** 5.5 to 6.6 lb

THE CORNISH

Created in England at the beginning of the nineteenth century by Sir Walter Raleigh Gilbert, the Cornish was formerly called the Indian Game or Chicken Indian Game. The stated goal was to produce a breed of gamecocks by crossing several indigenous breeds with Asian breeds. The result was inadequate for cock fighting, but its wide breast and muscular limbs made for delicious meat. The pullet tastes very good, which is rare for an ancient breed.
Rooster: 9.9 to 11 lb **Hen:** 7.7 to 8.8 lb

THE LANGSHAN

Also called the Croad Langshan in honor of Major Croad, who established the breed in England. Originally from the Langshan monastery near the mouth of the Yang-Tsé-Kiang River in China, it was brought to England in the second half of the nineteenth century. It was often mistaken for the Cochin, as crossbreeding between the two breeds was common. This bird has a large, full breast and long, black feet that are white underneath. The skin and the meat are almost white and flavorful.
Rooster: 8.8 to 9.9 lb **Hen:** 6.6 to 7.7 lb

THE CHANTECLER

Created in Quebec in the 1920s, its origins go back to crosses between several breeds: Cornish, Leghorn, Rhode Island, Wyandotte, Plymouth Rock. This breed is perfectly adapted to temperatures below 32°F and when the water freezes, it hydrates itself by eating snow. Its meat is slightly dark in color, similar to duck. The breast is small and the thighs thick. A slow-cooking method is recommended so that the breast meat remains tender and flavorful.
Rooster: 7.7 to 8.8 lb **Hen:** 5.5 to 6.6 lb

THE WYANDOTTE

This breed has been traced back to the mid-nineteenth century, found in the eastern region of the United States under different names such as the American Sebright and the Sebright Cochin. It was recognized as a breed in 1883 and quickly spread across the world, arriving in England in 1884 and in France in 1888. The breed standards recognize a multitude of colorings, but the most remarkable is the Silver-Laced, whose white feathers are bordered by a black edging. It's a good layer and shouldn't be roasted, as its meat is quite lean.
Rooster: 7.7 to 8.8 lb **Hen:** 4.4 to 6.6 lb

THE IXWORTH

This breed was created near Ixworth in Suffolk, England, in the 1930s by crossing the White Orpington, White Sussex, White Minorca, and the Cornish. Its creator, Reginald Appleyard, was a renowned breeder and we have him to thank for the famous Silver Appleyard duck breed. The Ixworth is a dual-purpose breed, raised for its eggs and very white, very succulent meat. Unfortunately, it was almost extinct with the arrival of new American intensive breeds.
Rooster: 7.7 to 8.8 lb **Hen:** 6.6 to 7.7 lb

THE PLYMOUTH ROCK

The doctor J.C. Bennett created this breed in the mid-nineteenth century by crossing, among other breeds, the Malay, Cornish, Dorking, Java, and Cochin. The first birds were brown, but Dr. Bennett succeeded in obtaining the cuckoo color by crossbreeding them with the Dominique breed. This Plymouth Rock was then crossbred by other breeders and new colors such as black, white, and fawn were established before the breed was imported to England in 1872. This bird is at its best when simply roasted.
Rooster: 8.8 to 9.9 lb **Hen:** 6.6 to 7.7 lb

THE LA FLÈCHE

Originally from Sarthe, the breed goes back to the fifteenth century. Traditionally black in color, it can also be blue, white, pearl gray, and speckled. It's at its highest quality at around eight to ten months of age. This is a proud creature and its comb, which is separated in two and points forward, can make it look vicious. Its dark meat is tough and flavorful. It's best cooked in a pot and is also delicious roasted, but at a low temperature.
Rooster: 8.8 to 9.9 lb **Hen:** 7.7 to 8.8 lb

THE BEST CHICKEN BREEDS

THE LE MANS

This breed disappeared completely in the mid-twentieth century, but a few passionate breeders worked to reintroduce it by crossbreeding other ancient breeds. This animal has quite a heavy body, black plumage with green tints, and a very red comb. The meat from both male and female are equally as good, and from a quality point of view, it could be said that it's similar to the meat of a male Barbezieux chicken. Its meat is very, very tender with a beautiful fat.
Rooster: 6.6 to 7.7 lb **Hen:** 5.5 to 6.6 lb

THE FAVEROLLES

Created around 1860 with the aim of feeding the people of Paris, the Faverolles chicken was the most common breed in France before 1940. It was born of a cross between the Houdan and other breeds and has five toes, a beard, and muffs (very nineteenth-century!). Imposing and majestic, its face looks a bit like that of an owl. Its meat is delicate and of great quality. Delicious either as capon or poularde.
Rooster: 7.7 to 8.8 lb **Hen:** 6.1 to 7.7 lb

THE HOUDAN

Born from different crosses in the nineteenth century, the Houdan has a beard, muffs, and a tuft of hair (really!), feathers on its feet, a comb in the shape of an oak leaf, and five toes. This breed doesn't have a specific color. Once considered a laying chicken, the Houdan evolved and is now raised for its tender, dark meat whose flavor is similar to that of the partridge. As it fattens well, it's often sold as capon or poularde.
Rooster: 6.1 to 6.6 lb **Hen:** 5 to 5.5 lb

THE GÉLINE DE TOURAINE

This is another breed that almost disappeared during the Second World War with the arrival of industrial breeds. Fully grown at four months of age, which is slower than most free-range chickens but faster than those mentioned above, it's nicknamed "The Dark Lady." Its meat is very white, finely textured, delicious, and very juicy, and is devoured by discerning eaters and children alike.
Rooster: 6.6 to 7.7 lb **Hen:** 5.5 to 6.6 lb

A BRIEF HISTORY OF CHICKEN

Don't be fooled, chicken isn't just a farmyard animal. It's come a long way and provides us with the very best of what it has. A large number of chickens were almost extinct not very long ago.

AN UNSUSPECTED GLOBETROTTER

In Asia, hens and roosters were wild and lived in the trees. They were arboreal animals.

Chickens were among the first animals domesticated by man over 8,000 years ago. First in Persia and Greece, then in Europe about 3,000 years ago.

THE MODERN CHICKEN

In the mid-nineteenth century, the criteria for certain breeds were well defined, until suddenly giant Asian breeds were introduced to Europe to increase the size of poultry.

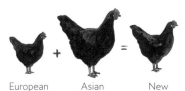

European chicken + Asian chicken = New European chicken

At the end of the nineteenth century, precise standards were agreed on. Chickens became "pedigree chickens" and no longer lived only on old manure stacks.

In France, the interwar period brought on the golden age of high-quality chicken farming.

But after the Second World War, the industrialization of farming allowed for the arrival of more prolific, intensive farming breeds, with the aim of optimizing the growth of the animals.

Many breeds were almost completely extinct, including the Barbezieux, Coucou de Rennes, Géline de Touraine, Janzé, Le Mans, and Le Merlerault.

In the 1980s, people once again became interested in these ancient breeds and they were all eventually reintroduced, thanks to passionate breeders supported by consumers who were inclined to buy good-quality poultry. Today, all is well for these breeds, but they (and we) only narrowly avoided disaster!

THE COUNTRY OF THE ROOSTER

The name "Gaule" comes from the Latin *galls gallus*, which means "rooster." The Romans allegedly called the French "Gaulois" (Gallic) because they raised many roosters. And now the rooster is the emblem of France.

OTHER POULTRY BIRDS

There are other common poultry birds to be found besides our cherished chickens, and not only during the hunting or festive seasons.

GUINEA FOWL

Quite timid, the guinea fowl is originally from Africa, where is still lives in the wild. Its meat tastes slightly gamy and dries out very easily. The common guinea fowl is the most well-known, but other delicious breeds also exist. Choose a young guinea fowl, which is more tender and flavorful. Slow-cooking in a pot is recommended and roasting should be avoided.

Guinea fowl: 2.6 to 3 lb **Young guinea fowl:** 1.7 lb

DUCK

The Muscovy duck (the best), the Nantes duck, and the Rouen duck have a milder flavor than wild ducks do. The Mulard (also spelled Moulard), a cross between a female Rouen and a male Muscovy, is intended for gavage. Only the male's liver can be sold as foie gras and the rest of its meat is used for duck breast and confits. The female duck has a more delicate meat than the male. Serve it pink to preserve the flavors.

Duck: 3.5 to 7.7 lb **Mulard:** Up to 15.4 lb

QUAIL

The common quail is among the most common wild breed. The farm quail, known as the Japanese quail, is a strong-tasting alternative. It's eaten roasted and is often encased to protect the white meat. Spatchcock cooking should be avoided, as it dries out the breast meat.

Weight: 5.2 to 8.8 oz

DOMESTIC PIGEON

The domestic pigeon, whose plumage is generally white, can be of an American breed, like the Texan, the Hubbel, and the King, or of a French breed like the Carneau. Young pigeons are much more tender and delicious than adults.

Weight: 14.1 to 17.6 oz

PHEASANT

Originally from Asia, the pheasant acclimatized to our part of the world a long time ago. Usually raised and then released just before the hunt begins, the common pheasant is the most well-known. Choose a wild bird. It will have more distinct flavors and a meat that is almost red. The female tastes more delicate than the male, but is also smaller.
Female: 1.9 lb **Male:** 3 lb

GOOSE/GANDER

Don't confuse the goose, the female, whose meat is a lot more tender and smooth, with the gander, the male. The Normandy goose is probably the most delicate, and the Bourbon goose, the Toulouse goose, and the Landes goose are chosen for their fatty meat and potential to make a good foie gras! Careful, this animal loses a lot of its weight during cooking.
Weight: 9.9 lb

TURKEY

Turkey comes from Mexico and is formerly from East India. The turkey hen tastes better than the turkey cock, the male, whose meat is reserved for carving. The Black Sologne and the Red Ardennes turkeys are without a doubt the tastiest breeds. Roast on a low heat.
Weight: 6.6 to 11 lb

RABBIT

What's a rabbit doing here? It's a leporid mammal, not poultry! Yes, yes, I know, but commercially, it's classed as poultry. So let's stick to that. The most popular are the Fauve de Bourgogne, with its tough, dense texture, and the Alaska, completely black (yes!) with a very delicate meat. There's also the Giant Papillon, a creature of over 6.6 lb with a fine-textured meat.
Weight: 4.4 to 6.6 lb

OSTRICH/EMU

Over the last few years, the ostrich and the emu have become easy to find. Of Australian origin, these animals are now also raised in France. The meats are similar to each other: dark red, very tender, and with a flavor that's similar to beef, but slightly milder. Of course, you can't buy these animals whole but as roasts, steaks, terrines, etc.
Ostrich: 220 lb **Emu:** 88.1 lb

THE CHICKEN FAMILY

He who steals an egg steals a prize-winning chicken in the making!

CHICK

When it's born, the chick is naked or covered in a light down.

JUVENILE

It doesn't matter whether it's a male or a female. It weighs around 1.3 lb and eats grains. Its meat is tender but can dry out fast.

It grows some more and becomes an adult ...
CHICKEN

If it's a chicken of an ancient breed, it needs a lot of time to grow into an adult—about 300 days. It weighs between 4.4 and 6.6 lb and the flavor of its meat depends on the breed, but I can tell you that it tastes absolutely fantastic!

If it's a battery farm chicken, it will be ready to eat at eighty-two days old. Its meat is tasteless and water is sometimes injected into it to make it heavier. Yuck.

As it grows older, its gender becomes critical.

If it's female

If it's male

HEN

She has chicks and weighs over 4.4 lb. The older she gets, the tougher her meat will become, but it can still be used in many dishes!

POULARDE

She's at least 120 days old and a spinster. She tastes even better when a little older. She weighs between 3.9 and 5.5 lb. Without a doubt, an exceptional product!

ROOSTER

He's very active, sexually speaking. He's the one who rules the farmyard. He weighs between 5.5 and 8.8 lb. His meat is very tough and requires a long cooking time to become tender.

NON-BREEDING ROOSTER

He's banned from any close relations with young and pretty hens. He weighs between 5.5 and 8.8 lb. Rare to find and absolutely delicious.

CAPON

We take it upon ourselves to gently castrate him. He loses his comb and weighs between 5.5 and 8.8 lb. He's a bit fat but he's the most handsome, most tender, and the juiciest. Basically, he's exceptional!

NUTRITION AND MEAT QUALITY

We don't ever think about it, but chicken tastes better in some seasons than it does in others. That depends on what it can find to eat.

Chickens are omnivorous, meaning they eat everything. The quality of a chicken's food is important to obtaining a good-quality meat. Its meat varies in flavor depending on what nature has to offer throughout the seasons. So, a chicken slaughtered in July won't taste the same as one slaughtered at Christmas.

Chickens roam the fields from about one month old. The age at slaughter and the maturation period varies depending on the breed. Free-range chickens are slaughtered at a minimum of eighty-one days old, whereas ancient breed chickens are left to grow for more than 300 days.

| Wheat | Corn | Triticale | Vetch | Field bean | Woodlouse | Larva | Centipede | Earthworm |

WINTER

The earth is hard, the grass almost doesn't grow at all, and underground life is reduced to a minimum, as is the food that winter-born chickens find in the fields.

ON-THE-PLATE RESULTS

Free-range chickens: very, very good in August, September, October
Ancient breed chickens: exceptional in November, December, January

SPRING

The worms are out and fertilize the soil, the larvae and the insects are having the time of their lives in the growing grass. This makes for very good food for the spring chickens who roam happily and peck at the ground. Their muscles fill out and provide a meat of a very high quality.

ON-THE-PLATE RESULTS

Free-range chickens: normal in November, December, January
Ancient breed chickens: very good in February, March, April.

SUMMER

The earth begins to dry out a little, there are few larvae, and the worms sleep deep in the earth to protect themselves from drought and heat. The chickens born in this season therefore have food of a lesser quality and make very little physical effort.

ON-THE-PLATE RESULTS

Free-range chickens: good in February, March, April
Ancient breed chickens: very, very good in May, June, July

AUTUMN

It's no longer as hot, the earth humidifies with the rain, the worms come out and fertilize the soil, some larvae are back, and the insects are content in this humid environment. Our autumn-born chickens roam around like crazy and find fresh food.

ON-THE-PLATE RESULTS

Free-range chickens: normal in May, June, July
Ancient breed chickens: very good in August, September, October

THE ANATOMY OF THE CHICKEN

*Chickens are majestic animals,
not just a pile of breast meat and legs!*

THE MORPHOLOGY OF CHICKENS

Be honest, did you know that chickens have primary and secondary feathers or that their feet are covered in scales, like dinosaurs?

Here are a few tips to better understand their anatomy.

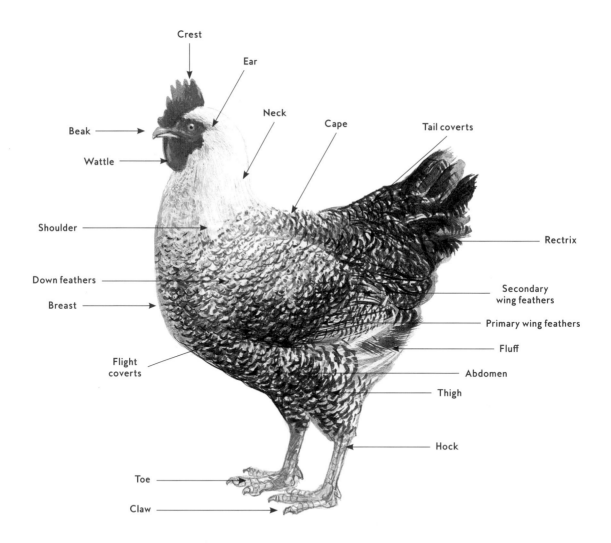

Crest

Ear

Neck

Cape

Tail coverts

Beak

Wattle

Shoulder

Rectrix

Down feathers

Breast

Secondary wing feathers

Primary wing feathers

Fluff

Flight coverts

Abdomen

Thigh

Hock

Toe

Claw

DO CHICKENS HAVE LIPS?

It's an age-old question. What we know is that chickens don't have teeth! They swallow straight away. But because nature knows best, it found a solution for good digestion—and the digestive system of the chicken is an impressive machine.

The swallowed food accumulates in the crop, where it mixes with saliva and goes down into the proventriculus, where it mixes with digestive juices. This combination lands in the gizzard, and that's where everything happens. Chickens swallow small stones with their food, which are stored in the gizzard. These little stones grind up the grains, insects, and larvae it eats so that its organism can digest them. Next, everything goes into the intestines; the nutrients are absorbed into the body and the rest is feces, evacuated through the cloaca.

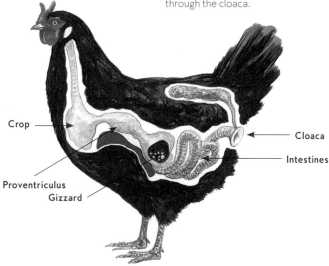

Crop

Cloaca

Intestines

Proventriculus

Gizzard

CHICKEN CUTS

Carving a chicken isn't as complicated as it looks. You simply need to be able to identify the different parts.

Parson's nose

Wing tip

Tenderloin

Fillet

Drumstick

Thigh

Drumette

Wingette

PREPARING A CHICKEN

*Depending on whether it's prepared by a butcher or a poulterer,
chicken can be sold in different ways.*

Whole, gutted, or eviscerated—chicken isn't only sold already cut or already roasted. In the past, chicken was sold whole and with its feathers. Up until recently, poulterers would remove the digestive systems just before sale and would leave the heart, the gizzard, and the liver. However, there are almost no poulterers left today and butchers buy their chickens preprepared.

Whole chicken: plucked, bled but not gutted.

Gutted chicken: plucked and bled, the intestines removed but not the other viscera (heart, liver, lungs, and gizzard).

Eviscerated or ready-to eat chicken: plucked and bled, the intestines, heart, liver, lungs, and gizzard removed.

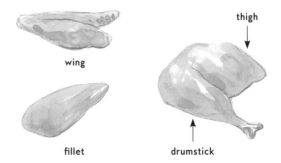

wing

fillet

thigh

drumstick

Cut-up chicken: raw or cooked pieces.

> **"When you see a chicken at the butcher shop,**
> the breast meat is on top and the animal is presented on its back. But
> when the animal is alive, the white meat (breast meat) is underneath."

GOOSE FOIE GRAS OR DUCK FOIE GRAS?

Foie gras is like politics: there are unwavering advocates for both goose and duck, people who'll never change their minds, often out of spite!

AN ANCESTRAL PRACTICE

About 4500 BC, the Egyptians had already begun trapping migratory geese just before they migrated, because they realized that they were tastier at that time of year. The geese were stuffing themselves with food to gather enough strength for their long journey home. Once the Egyptians had understood the reason for the geese's succulence, they began stuffing them with food themselves.

AN ALTERNATIVE GAVAGE METHOD

The quality of foie gras depends most of all on the animal's breed and the quality of the sanitary conditions in which it's raised. Gavage is generally done by feeding the animal corn over a period of about twelve days.

Farmers have developed a goose- and duck-fattening process that is more respectful of the animals. The food is offered to them in small quantities, but often. These super-greedy animals pounce on the food and they fatten naturally. The livers produced are less fatty, but each person must weigh for himself the importance of a humanely raised animal over a fattier product.

FOIE GRAS BREEDS

Geese that are force-fed or fattened for foie gras are usually from the Landes and Toulouse breeds. For ducks, the star is the Mulard, born from a cross between a Muscovy male and a Rouen or Pekin female.

SO, WHAT'S THE DIFFERENCE?

Goose foie gras is bigger than duck foie gras. Its texture is a tiny bit firmer and it has a lovely pink color when raw, but turns a grayish color once cooked. Its flavors are dainty and long on the palate.

Duck foie gras, on the other hand, is more tender, with a magnificent orangey-beige color; strong, deep flavors; and a bigger loss of volume during cooking.

FOIE GRAS IN ITS MANY FORMS

In shops, you can find foie gras in various different forms:
• "whole foie gras" is a foie gras composed of several whole lobes
• "foie gras" is made of compacted pieces of foie gras
• a "block of foie gras" is a reconstituted liver containing pieces of foie gras.

"**Contrary to what you may often hear,** you can't denervate foie gras. There are no nerves in a liver! Not a single one! But there are veins, so you can devein it."

CHOICE POULTRY CUTS

The names of the different cuts are quite easy.
They're also mostly quite obvious: the wing, the thigh, the breast meat.
However, there are other cuts you may not be familiar with
like the chicken oyster, the coat, or the parson's nose.

TENDERLOIN
The tenderloin is a small, thin piece of meat that's hidden between the fillet and the wishbone, the bone that separates the two breasts. Delicious!

WING
The wing is separated into three parts: the drumette, the wingette, and the wing tip. Stuffing can be added beneath the skin when served alone.

NECK
Duck and goose neck can be boned and stuffed. Chicken necks (which are often removed) still have delicious strands of meat attached.

THE PARSON'S NOSE
Fat, fat and more fat! The parson's nose has its aficionados, like my mother-in-law, for example. The parson's nose is her favorite cut. She makes sure that nobody else has their eye on her cherished piece of meat. I usually hide it for her. Then I marinate it before serving it to her. Her eyes crinkle and a smile lights up her face. Pure happiness!

THIGH
As with the wing, the thigh is composed of several parts, whose flavors and textures are very distinct.

FILLET (OR BREAST MEAT)
This is the breast, the leanest cut. It cooks much faster than the other cuts and therefore requires attention.
   With a rabbit, it's what's left attached when you've boned the saddle and removed the belly flap (the parts not attached to the ribcage).

WING TIP
This is the last part of the wing. Honestly, it's useless. It's generally removed because it barely contains any meat.

LEG
This cut is composed of the thigh and the drumstick, boned. For rabbit, the meat from the ribcage is also boned. It's often served stuffed.

SCRATCHINGS (DUCK OR GOOSE)
These are the little bits of meat or skin that turn a golden brown when duck or goose fat is melted.

THIGH
This is a truly tasty piece of meat, the juiciest of poultry cuts, with a firm consistency. It's a morsel fit for a king.

OYSTER
Round, tender and juicy, it's located almost in the center of the back, in line with the thigh bones.

DRUMETTE
This part of the wing is the plumpest and the closest to the body. It can be frenched by scraping the bone to push the meat to one side.

WINGETTE
This is by far the most flavorful part of the wing, with its two long bones. Kids love to eat it with their fingers.

COAT
This is the entirety of the flesh pulled from the carcass in one whole piece. The fillets, thighs, and wings stuck together by the skin make you think of a coat.

FOOT
Composed of four or five toes depending on the breed, chicken's foot is mostly eaten in Asia. In Europe, this part is usually removed.

DRUMSTICK

This is the bottom part of the leg, containing muscles that have worked hard. It's tough and contains a big nerve.

SADDLE (RABBIT)

This is the whole middle part of the rabbit between the hind legs and forelegs. Roasted whole or boned and stuffed, it's the best part of the rabbit.

SUPREME

When the breast meat is lifted from the carcass with the tenderloin and the drumette, you get a supreme. The little bone from the drumette brings many flavors to this cut.

UNDER-THE-RADAR CUTS

~~~~~~~

INSIDE THE WING

In the central part of the wing—the wingette, to be exact—is a small, elongated muscle that is absolutely divine—tender, juicy, but unfortunately so small!

INSIDE THE THIGH

In the top part of the thigh that's attached to the body, there's a short, thick, and wide muscle that is incredibly tender and juicy.

INSIDE THE CARCASS

After having removed all the parts, two small pieces of flesh remain attached to the carcass. These are delicious and you can scrape them off with your fingers.

"Magrets come from ducks that have been fattened for their livers. The same cuts are called breasts when they come from nonfattened ducks."

OFFAL AND GIBLETS

Before we had mastered fire or knew how to cook meat, offal and giblets were our favorite food because they're more tender than raw meat. Today still, they're eaten all over the world. Let me take you on a little tour.

Offal and giblets are part of what we call the fifth quarter, as opposed to the other four quarters of traditional meat cuts. They're classed in two categories: white and red. The white are usually blanched (soaked in hot water) or even cooked, which is what gives them their beautiful, pearly white color. The red are sold raw and without any alteration except the removal of the fat. Veal generally produces the finest offal.

BEEF MARROW Beef, veal
This is the part of the spinal cord situated along the backbone toward the front of the animal. Absolutely delicious, it's prepared in a similar way to brains.

HONEYCOMB TRIPE (RETICULUM) Beef, veal
The reticulum ensures the regurgitation of food. Its lining looks like honeycomb. A small part of it is used to make the Lyonnais specialty *tablier de sapeur*.

INTESTINES Pork
Intended for sausages, dried sausage, blood sausage, etc.

RED TRIPE (ABOMASUM) Beef, veal
This is the final stomach compartment, with a smooth, dark lining. It secretes rennet, which curdles milk. This rennet is often extracted from the abomasa of young ruminants and used for cheese-making.

BRAIN Beef, veal, lamb, pork
Lamb brain is the daintiest, but honestly, they're all delicious and melt on the tongue. Poached and then fried in butter, or deep-fried in batter.

HEART Beef, veal, lamb, pork, poultry
Lamb's heart is often sold along with the liver and called "pluck." Cow and pig's hearts are firm and have a distinctive flavor. Veal, lamb, and chicken hearts have a very delicate taste.

STOMACH Pork
This is principally used to make andouille and andouillette sausages.

LEAF TRIPE (OMASUM) Beef, veal
It's composed of multiple "leaves" between which food is ground, hence its name.

LIVER Beef, veal, lamb, pork, poultry
Beef liver is sold as ox liver. Veal liver is the finest, but lamb, heifer, poultry, and rabbit livers are also delicious.

CALF'S CAUL Veal
This is the membrane that surrounds the intestines. Cooked, it can be eaten hot or cold, or even fried in batter.

GIZZARD Poultry
The gizzard is a muscular part of the stomach, whose purpose is to grind the swallowed food. It's delicious in a salad.

FAT Beef, poultry
Beef fat is commonly used in Belgium to cook fries and give them a delicious flavor. Goose and duck fat are perfect for frying potatoes or for browning asparagus in a pan.

PLAIN TRIPE Beef, veal
This is the thickest part of the stomach, but it's not at all fatty. Sold precooked, it can be sautéed, fried, broiled, or used as an ingredient for minestrone soup.

SKIRT STEAK Beef, veal, pork
Skirt steak is from the muscle that joins the diaphragm to the ribs. Beef skirt steak is delicious, veal skirt steak is a little finer, and pork skirt steak, which is also fine, is unfortunately very rare to find.

CHEEK Beef, veal, lamb, pork
Cheek is a lean meat that can be slow-cooked for use in stews and terrines.

TONGUE Beef, veal, lamb, pork
Out of all of these types of tongue, it's once again the calf's tongue, as the most delicate, that wins the prize. It can be served raw or cooked.

MARROW Beef, veal
A good, delicate fat. In French, the word for marrow—*moell*e—inspired the name "*moelleux*," a very soft cake which used to be made with marrow.

LUNGS Beef, veal, poultry
The lungs are inedible because they're too difficult to chew, but cats love them, so I've included them here.

SNOUT Veal, pork
This is generally sold with the chin. It can be served whole or in slices.

HANGER STEAK Beef, veal, pork, lamb
Located just above the skirt steak, the hanger steak is composed of two small muscles joined together by an elastic membrane. Beef hanger steak is delicious, but veal and pork hanger steak are even better.

 EARS Pork
Boiled and sometimes grilled, the ears are quite delicate. A good bet for those less familiar with cartilaginous cuts.

RUMEN Beef, veal
The rumen is the main part of a ruminant's stomach. Its external surface is ribbed, whereas its interior surface is smooth. Served whole, it contains the reticulum, the abomasum, and the omasum.

PLAIN TRIPE Veal
The calf's stomach is used to prepare dishes like the feet, stuffed sheep's tripe, and *tripoux*.

 FEET Veal, lamb, pork, poultry
Pig's feet are delicious boiled and sometimes grilled. Calf's feet are braised or boiled to add creaminess to a dish or to make gelatin. Lamb's feet make an absolutely delicious gelatin.

TAIL Beef, veal, pork
Beef and veal tails are both used in the same way, in slow-cooked dishes. Pig's tail is served as a side to the ears and feet.

 SWEETBREAD Veal, lamb
Sweetbread is the culinary term for the thymus, a gland situated at the back of the throat. There are two different sweetbreads: heart sweetbread, the most refined, and the throat sweetbread, reserved for side dishes. Both disappear when the animal becomes an adult. This is the king of offals, the finest. They can be blanched in milk before being sautéed.

KIDNEYS Beef, veal, lamb, pork
Heifer, veal, and lamb kidneys are tender and tasty. Beef and pork kidneys are firmer and have a more distinct flavor.

HEAD Beef, veal, lamb, pork
Cow's head is usually sold in pieces. For the calf's head, the inferior jaw and nasal bones are removed. Sold boned and rolled, you can buy it whole. Pig's head is perfect for making headcheese. Finally, lamb's head is generally sold without the brain, the tongue, and the cheeks. It's mostly bone that remains.

TRIPE Beef, veal, lamb
Tripe is made up of various ruminant stomachs.

"No, no, you haven't misunderstood: the skirt steak, hanger steak, and cheek that you saw on this list are actually offal. They're sold as much by meat butchers as they are by tripe butchers."

UNDER-THE-RADAR OFFAL AND GIBLETS

TESTICLES Beef, veal
Bull or ram testicles have a similar consistency to sweetbread. They're prepared in the same way as kidneys are, or cut into slices that are rolled in flour and sautéed.

COMB Poultry
Rarely used nowadays, royalty used to feast on them. But to be honest, they're nothing special.

UDDER Beef
Heifer or cow udder was once a sought-after specialty. It's not as fashionable today, despite being very tender.

THE GAME THAT ROAMS OUR LANDS

Game can be put into two categories:
ground game and winged game. Most of these animals are eaten
when they're quite young, during their first year of life.

GROUND GAME

Direct sale of game by the hunter to the consumer is illegal, but it can be given free of charge. Picking up injured game is strongly discouraged and banned in many countries. That's fine; game can be found in good butcher stores during the hunting season, from mid-September to the end of February.

Preparing game for cooking must be done in a particular way: the offal must be removed as fast as possible and kept cool until you're able to refrigerate them.

For all these animals, the best cuts are the rump, the haunch, and the chops. They should always be served pink.

ROE DEER

He lives in the woods or in on the edge of forests, and sometimes appears in the crop fields. Very elegant and very fast, the roe deer is, unbeknownst to himself, a drug addict. He's a great lover of alder buckthorn, a plant containing an alkaloid that has psychoactive effects. His meat is dark red and quite mild.
Size: 2 ft 1½ in (65 cm) to the withers/55 lb

DEER

The stag is a majestic animal that lives in big forests. At the end of September, the beginning of the rutting season, he grunts to alert the females to his arousal and to warn off other males. The doe, smaller and a lot more slender than the stag, is Bambi's mother. Their meat is a little stronger-tasting than roe deer meat.
Stag: 4 ft 7 in (140 cm) to the withers/330 lb
Doe: 3 ft 11 in (120 cm) to the withers/176 lb

FALLOW DEER

The fallow deer behaves in the same way as the deer and adapts easily to life in captivity. His tender meat is a lot leaner than deer meat and requires a rapid cooking process so as not to dry out.
Buck: 2 ft 11 in (90 cm) to the withers/132 lb
Doe: 2 ft 7 in (80 cm) to the withers/ 77 lb

WILD BOAR/YOUNG WILD BOAR

The wild boar is a very intelligent animal that seeks out a forest habitat with numerous watering places (he's an excellent swimmer). He doesn't hesitate to wander around the outskirts of villages. Dark in color, his meat is lean (the fat is around the muscles) and strong in flavor. The young wild boar is more tender and tastes more refined.
Wild boar: 2 ft 11 in (90 cm) to the withers/374 lb
Sow: 2 ft 3½ in (70 cm) to the withers/220 lb
Piglet: 8 in (20 cm) to the withers/44 lb

HARE

The hare is a lot bigger than the wild rabbit and doesn't dig warrens. The best-tasting hare is one that is between six and eight months old. His meat is such a dark red that it can look black.
Hare between 6 and 8 months: 12 in (30 cm) to the withers/5.5 lb

EUROPEAN RABBIT

The European rabbit lives in dry regions and seeks out undergrowth to build its warren. Its meat is pale like the meat of farm-raised rabbits, but a lot tougher and more flavorful.
Size: 8 in (20 cm) to the withers/3.3 lb

THE GAME THAT ROAMS OUR LANDS

WINGED GAME

Some of the winged game is raised before being released into the wild. This is the case for the pheasant, the partridge, and certain ducks. However, the great majority are born in the wild before being hunted.

It's always better to pluck and eviscerate birds before storing them in the refrigerator, because the feathers and the blood carry bacteria. Wrap your fowl in a cloth or an air-permeable bag to preserve them.

Don't hesitate to freeze your fowl so as to be able to enjoy them at any point during the year. In this case, plucking and eviscerating aren't necessary.

PHEASANT

Originally from Asia, the pheasant is considered the king of game. Saint Louis filled the Bois de Vincennes with them, and the kings that followed did the same in their own forests. Pheasants are polygamous and rule over their harems. The meat of the female is a lot more delicate than the male's, and the younger the animal is, the better it tastes.
Size: 2½ ft (75 cm)/2.2 lb

MALLARD DUCK

This is the most common and well known duck in the Northern Hemisphere. The male has an emerald green head and neck. Its red meat, with its subtle wild flavor that can even verge on tasting slightly bitter, is tougher and a lot less fatty than the meat of farm-raised ducks.
Size: 1 ft 11 in (60 cm)/3 lb

GREY PARTRIDGE

The grey partridge lives on the plains, in heather fields, and among the crops. A few big partridge farms have recently appeared and are producing good-quality birds. Be careful not to cook a partridge on too high a temperature because it's quite small and its meat will dry out! The young partridge has a delicate and delicious meat.
Size: 12 in (30 cm)/14 oz

"**Net hunting developed** in regions where certain migratory birds stopped off to rest."

WOODCOCK

This is one of the finest and most renowned game fowls. It's generally found in forests and marshy areas. Its dark meat is highly appreciated by gourmets. It's usually left to hang by the beak until its body softens and drops. This takes about 40 days. It's recommended to serve it rare.
Size: 13¾ in (35 cm)/10.5 oz

QUAIL

Quail can be found in the wheat fields, but not only there. Prairies and dry areas also suit them perfectly. Monogamous, bigamist, polygamous, sexually speaking, it's quite a free animal. Its meat is so much tastier than the meat of farm-raised quails, which are easy to obtain.
Size: 7 in (18 cm)/3.5 oz

SKYLARK

No bigger than a sparrow, the skylark lives on crop land, prairies, and marshland. The French culinary term for Skylark is *mauviette*, named so by famous chef Escoffier. Its meat is pale pink. It can be cooked in the same way as the ortolan, but it's most often used in patés and terrines.
Size: 8 in (20 cm)/1.5 oz

ORTOLAN

It's forbidden to hunt it, but this bird became legendary for the way it is consumed: caught in nets, it's fattened for three weeks on white millet, then drowned in Armagnac and finally roasted. You eat it by letting it melt in your mouth and then chewing the whole thing, bones included, without spitting any of it out.
Size: 6⅔ in (17 cm)/0.88 oz

THE GAME THAT ROAMS OUR LANDS

TURTLE DOVE

Very timid and difficult to see, the turtle dove returns from Africa in the spring and stays in Europe until it begins to get cold. The female is a good layer (up to eight broods per year). Its meat is similar to the meat of stock doves, but not as delicate as the ring dove's (wood pigeon).
Size: 11 in (28 cm)/5.2 oz

STOCK DOVE AND RING DOVE

They're also called wood pigeons. These are the most common wild pigeons. The wood pigeon is especially renowned in southwest France, where the hunt for it is an ancestral tradition. Its meat is red and its liver without bile. It's usually eaten in a ragout or on a spit. Choose a young one, with a beak that's still quite supple.
Size: 1 ft (33 cm)/10.5 oz

HAZEL GROUSE

The hazel grouse is from the same family as the western capercaillie and lives in the foothills. Like the western capercaillie, it buries itself in the snow when it's too cold and feeds itself in the same way. Its white meat makes it one of the most appreciated game birds in Northern Europe. Be aware that this one tastes slightly of pine resin!
Size: 1 ft 4 in (40 cm)/10.5 oz

GROUSE

The grouse is originally from Scotland, where it can find the young heather, wild blackberries, and sorrel seeds that are essential to its diet. It can be hung for a few days or even longer. It's highly sought-after by gastronomists for its very distinctive taste—these true experts can grasp the nuances of its flavors.
Size: 21 in (55 cm)/14.1 oz

WESTERN CAPERCAILLIE

Discreet and timid, the western capercaillie is a mountain bird that burrows into the snow as soon as the temperature drops below freezing. It hides in forests for the rest of the year, where it can find seeds and berries like the wild blueberry. Its meat can have a slight taste of resin because it eats pine needles during the winter.
Size: 1 ft 11 in (60 cm)/ 2.6 lb

GREYLAG GOOSE

This is the most common wild goose. It migrates from Northern Europe to the Mediterranean in search of warmer temperatures and adequate food, and lives for about twenty years. Due to the fact that its meat is quite fatty, roasting on a low temperature is the best cooking method.
Size: 2 ft 11 in (90 cm)/ 7.7 lb

SONG THRUSH

This is without a doubt the best type of thrush, but like the others, it's illegal to sell it. The only way to eat it is to hunt it or have a hunter friend. You don't eviscerate the thrush. Only the gizzard, crop, and eyes are removed. The intestines melt during cooking and give the meat a unique flavor.
Size: 9 in (23 cm)/2.6 oz

BLACKBIRD

There's a French proverb that goes "For lack of thrushes, one eats blackbirds." Forget this proverb; blackbird doesn't taste great.
Size: 9½ in (25 cm)/3.5 oz

Secrets of the Butcher

THE ANATOMY OF A KNIFE

A good knife is like a good pot—you keep it forever (in fact, they're guaranteed forever). With a good knife, you'll be able to make easy, clean cuts and get the best out of your meat.

THE PARTS OF A KNIFE

Tip

Knife back

Blade

Cutting edge

Branding

Bolster

Finger guard

Tang

Rivet

Pommel

FORGED BLADE OR STAMPED BLADE?

A forged blade is made by hand. A stamped blade is cut out of a sheet of metal, of lower quality but less expensive. There's no comparison—the forged blade is better! It's heavier, a lot more solid, and stays sharper for longer.

THE CUTTING EDGE AND THE TIP

The cutting edge is the part that cuts and the tip is just above it. For the cutting edge, there are two possibilities: the European edge, with an angle between 20° and 30°, and the Japanese edge, a lot sharper, with an angle between 10° and 15°.

European edge

Japanese edge

20/30°

10/15°

Tip

Edge

SHAPES AND USES

THE INDISPENSABLES

THE CHEF'S KNIFE

This is a kind of big, do-it-all knife. It can cut a roast into slices or a steak into strips, move pieces of meat by placing them on the blade, and crush garlic cloves. Basically, if you can only have one kitchen knife, this is the one you want.

THE JAPANESE HALF BROTHERS

Japanese knives are known for the quality of their blades— their tremendous sharpness inherited from ancestral sabers—but also for the neat design. The gyuto is specially used for meat, with its long, slightly curved blade, whereas the santoku is more universal.

FOR SLICING

THE TRANCHELARD

This is the ideal knife for cutting thin slices from a big piece of meat like a leg or a cured or cooked ham. The blade is narrower than a chef's knife's blade and its cut is more precise for big slices.

ITS JAPANESE YOUNGER BROTHER

Another Japanese knife that shares the same qualities as the gyuto and the santoku, but with a long, thin blade for cutting meat. The chutoh's blade, shorter than the tranchelard's, is also good for preparing and paring meat.

THE BUTCHER'S KNIFE

THE BONING KNIFE

Perfect for boning, of course, but also for removing tendons and fat. This is a small knife with a very rigid blade. It's a butcher's favorite for preparing meats that are complicated to cut.

THE GOOD-FOR-EVERYTHING

THE UNIVERSAL KNIFE

Like the chef's knife, this is indispensable for all work that doesn't involve meat, because there are a lot of other things you need to cook as sides for your main dish from the butcher shop.

THE UNEXPECTED

THE POULTRY SHEARS

This is super useful for when you need to cut poultry as well as other difficult meats, or to break thin bones.

The chef's knife
Blade length between 4¾ to 12 inches (12 and 30 cm).

The gyuto

The santoku
Blade length between 6 and 9½ inches (16 and 24 cm)

The tranchelard
Blade length between 7 and 12 inches (18 and 30 cm)

The chutoh
Blade length between 6 and 8 inches (16 and 20 cm).

The boning knife
Blade length between 4¾ and 7 inches (12 and 18 cm).

The universal knife
Blade length between 4 and 6 inches (10 and 16 cm).

The poultry shears
Blade length between 8½ and 10 inches (22 and 26 cm).

CHEF'S KNIFE VS. BREAD KNIFE

Of course, the purpose of a knife is to cut, but the way in which it is used to cut your meat will have a big influence on the taste, texture, and consistency. Let's compare.

THE CHEF'S KNIFE

This is the most commonly used knife in cookery. Very sharp, it cuts in a perfectly straight line. The sides of the piece of meat are smooth and even. The knife is so precise that its contact with the meat is minimal.

THE BREAD KNIFE

This is different. The teeth of the blade "rip" through the fibers of the meat, and the surface of the cut is very uneven. The sides of the meat are irregular and rough. The knife's contact with the meat is maximal.

"**The shape of the knife** has an enormous influence on how much of the meat's surface the knife will come into contact with. So, cutting with a bread knife results in the knife encountering a larger surface area and creating an uneven cut of meat."

CONCLUSION

For tender, grilled meats, there's no doubt about it, the chef's knife is a much better choice. But for tough pieces of meat that require a long cooking process (braising or boiling) or that are cooked in a sauce, a toothed knife (or bread knife) is more effective.

THE RESULTS PUT INTO PRACTICE

PAN-FRYING:
LONG LIVE THE BREAD KNIFE!

When pan-fried in fat, meat cut with a bread knife will brown across a larger surface and will therefore develop even more flavors, partly thanks to the Maillard reactions.

GRILLING:
LONG LIVE THE CHEF'S KNIFE!

For grill cooking, it's the opposite. The smooth cut obtained using the chef's knife increases the size of the surface contact area between the meat and the grill: it browns more and tastes better.

BOILING:
LONG LIVE THE BREAD KNIFE!

The large surface contact area allows the meat to not only release more of its flavors during the making of a broth, but also to absorb more flavors when cooked in a stew or a blanquette.

MEAT COOKED IN A SAUCE:
LONG LIVE THE BREAD KNIFE!

The irregular cut of the bread knife creates craters in the meat in which the sauce can sit. Each mouthful will contain more sauce than it would have had a chef's knife been used.

ROASTING:
LONG LIVE THE BREAD KNIFE!

Meat cut with a bread knife has a lot more holes for the juices to fill. The meat will be a lot more flavorful thanks to this uneven surface, compared to a smooth surface where the juices just slide off.

CUT AND CONSISTENCY:
IT DEPENDS ON THE LENGTH OF
THE COOKING TIME AND THE MEAT

For tender meats, a neat cut creates a good consistency because the cleanly cut fibers are easy to chew. However, a tough piece of meat, tenderized by several hours of cooking, is also easy to chew; there's no difference.

GOOD EQUIPMENT FOR A GOOD CUT

Now that we know everything there is to know about blade shapes, let's take a look at what knives are made of and how to choose a chopping board.

THE DIFFERENT POSSIBLE METALS

STAINLESS STEEL

Knives made of stainless steel don't rust and require little maintenance, but the quantity of chromium used makes the blades less sharp than those made of carbon steel.

CARBON STEEL

The higher the chromium content, the harder and sharper the blade is; but it's more fragile. Carbon steel is susceptible to corrosion and requires more upkeep than stainless steel.

DAMASCUS STEEL

It's possible to mix various different steels together in successive thin layers, to benefit from certain of their characteristics. This method results in blades that are infinitely customizable. With very high-end blades that cost thousands of dollars, the number of layers of steel can reach 300.

CERAMIC

More solid than knives made of steel, ceramic knives are strong for cutting. However, they're fragile when used to cut in anything but a straight direction and are unsuitable for boning.

TITANIUM

Just as sharp as ceramic but suppler, the main characteristic of titanium knives is that they're very light.

THE SOLIDITY OF THE STEEL

The more rigid the steel is, the stronger the blade and the finer, sharper, more precise—but also more fragile—its edge.

The less rigid the steel, the less clear-cut the tip is and the more you'll have to sharpen it.

"**The solidity of the steel** is measured in HRC numbers (symbol of Rockwell hardness). From 52 for quite a soft steel, it can go up to 66 for an extremely hard steel."

THE UPKEEP OF A GOOD KNIFE

A good-quality knife shouldn't be washed in a dishwasher; it needs to be rinsed soon after it's been used, before being dried with a soft cloth. If you can't avoid using the dishwasher, place your knife on the rack intended for glasses, the blade lying horizontal with nothing on top of it.

Even if they look strong, cutting knives are fragile. They don't appreciate collision with other metal objects that could damage their edges.

> **"Whatever type of material you choose** for your chopping board, there must be a groove around the edges to catch the juices that will leak out of the meat during the cutting."

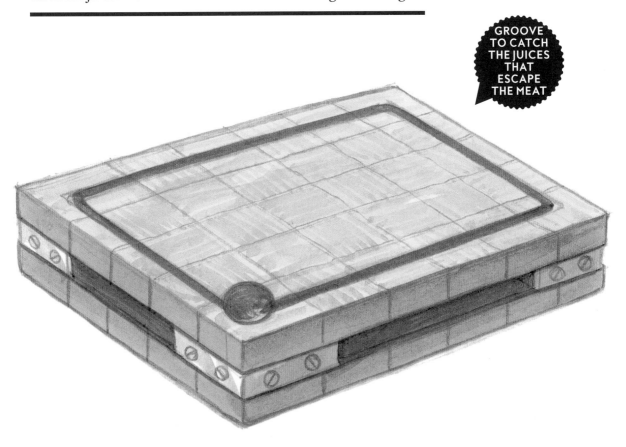

GROOVE TO CATCH THE JUICES THAT ESCAPE THE MEAT

WHICH CHOPPING BOARD?

Surely, with such good knives, you're not going to cut your meat on a glass or granite board and risk damaging the entire knife edge? You need a chopping board that's a little less hard.

A WOODEN BOARD!

I know, you've been taught that wooden chopping boards aren't very hygienic. That's what we all thought for a long time, and then they made a comeback.

Choose a cutting board made of bamboo. It's the most hygienic, robust, the hardest, and the best at resisting humidity and protecting your knives' blades.

But you can also choose beech, oak, or hornbeam which are very good, too.

WHICH COOKWARE FOR MY BEAUTIFUL PIECE OF MEAT?

You may be one of those people who cooks their meat in any old pot or pan. Let me explain why it's important to choose the right cookware for the right piece of meat.

A FRYING PAN FOR PAN-FRYING STEAK

THE STRENGTH OF THE FLAME

This is the most important thing when browning a steak. With a strong flame, the whole surface of the pan is burning hot and perfectly sears your steak.

THE MATERIAL THE PAN IS MADE OF

This is also important, not as much for the cooking as for the creation of juices, because juices are delicious. There are materials that create more juice than others, and it's these juices that make the meat tasty.

WEAK >>>THE MATERIAL'S CAPACITY TO CREATE JUICES >>> STRONG

NONSTICK

Forget pans with nonstick coatings because they barely brown the meat and create very little juice.

CAST IRON

This develops the flavors but needs time to accumulate heat. So be aware of the inertia of this material!

STAINLESS STEEL

Stainless steel creates a lot of juices and heats up quickly. It's a very good material to use.

IRON

Iron creates a lot of juices and both heats and cools rapidly. Honestly, it's the best of the best!

A POT FOR BOILING OR BRAISING

Here, the material is crucial. It can change the quality of what you're cooking. When you make stew, you cook the meat in water (or in a broth). The water heats and cooks the meat. How does the material influence this? Let's compare.

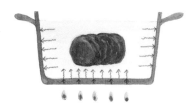
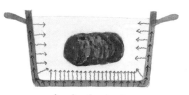

Iron distributes the heat through the pot very unevenly.
The sides of the pot aren't heated by the flame, but by the water, which in turn is heated by the bottom of the pot in contact with the flame. The meat nearest to the sides cooks at a lower temperature than the meat at the bottom of the pot.

Cast iron distributes the heat very well.
It accumulates the heat and distributes it throughout the pot. The heat of the flame spreads through the metal and up around the sides. The temperature is the same everywhere and the cooking is even.

COOKWARE FOR THE OVEN

Here too, the material is of great importance. It can accelerate the cooking and brown only the bottom of the meat, or it can ensure that the top and the bottom cook at the same speed. You should choose your cooking vessel based on the size of the piece of meat you're cooking and the necessary cooking time.

MATERIAL	COOKING	+ PROS +	- CONS -
CERAMIC 	Everything cooks slowly at the oven's temperature	Ceramic stores the heat well and releases it slowly. Perfect for slow cooking.	Be careful with black vessels because they store and release more heat. There will be fewer juices if you cook at below 320°F.
GLASS 	The meat cooks slowly and browns at the oven's temperature. The bottom of the meat cooks and browns simultaneously.	Because they're transparent, glass vessels allow the radiant heat to pass through, which means the bottom of the meat can brown easily.	Be careful not to cook at too high a temperature so as to avoid burning the juices.
CAST IRON 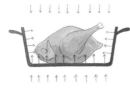	The meat must be of the same height as the vessel. The top cooks slowly and browns at the oven's temperature. The bottom cooks a little faster and browns at the same time.	Cast iron absorbs heat and diffuses it progressively. It creates a gentle heat inside. There's a large quantity of juice and the cooking is even.	 **ALSO BRILLIANT FOR BRAISING**
IRON AND STAINLESS STEEL 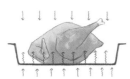	The top cooks slowly at the oven's temperature. The bottom cooks more than the top because iron and stainless steel store and then violently release the heat.	Perfect for quick cooking. The meat in contact with the metal browns and cooks a lot faster than the top. With iron and stainless steel there will be a lot of juices.	Avoid for slow cooking as the cooking of the top and bottom of the meat isn't even.
TERRACOTTA 	These vessels are usually soaked in water before going in the oven. The water evaporates in the heat and creates humidity.	The meat heats slowly in a very humid atmosphere. It remains very juicy and creates a beautiful jus.	One inconvenience: the meat doesn't brown.

THE SIZE OF THE COOKWARE

This is super important. Using cookware that's too big or too small causes you to lose a large amount of your meat's qualities and juice.

FRY IN A LARGE FRYING PAN

A frying pan that's a lot larger than your piece of meat will make it crispier and create more juices. Don't forget: put the oil on the meat, never directly in the pan!

LARGE FRYING PAN

The meat doesn't take up much of the surface area; the pan stays hot. There's space around the meat so the juices evaporate easily and create a lot of flavor. Because the juices evaporate so well, the meat cooks at the temperature of the pan, around 392°F, and browns perfectly.

SMALL FRYING PAN

The meat takes up the whole surface area, which cools the pan. There's no space around the meat, so the juices it releases don't have room to evaporate and create flavors. Since the juices don't evaporate well, they stay beneath the meat and boil it.

BOIL IN A SMALL POT

For a good balance of meat and broth, there shouldn't be too much space around the meat and the water should only just cover it. If the water evaporates during the cooking, you can add a bit more.

SMALL POT

The meat releases its flavors into the water, but because there isn't too much of it, the water boils down before the meat has lost too much of its taste. The broth is very flavorful because the meat's juices are released into a very small quantity of water. An equal balance between a meat that keeps its flavor and a broth that tastes good.

LARGE POT

The meat releases its flavors into the water and becomes bland before the water reduces. The broth is also tasteless because the meat's juices are diluted in too big a quantity of water.

BRAISE IN A SMALL POT

Using a pot that's just a little bigger than the meat will result
in a more even cooking and a tastier base for your sauce.

SMALL POT

With only a small volume of water to heat, a gentle heat
beneath the pot will be enough and will result in a very
tender and juicy meat. The amount of water is small so
the juices released by the meat aren't diluted and create a
flavorful sauce base. A tender, succulent piece of meat, along
with a very rich sauce base.

LARGE POT

There's a large volume of water to heat so the heat below
the casserole dish needs to be higher, which means risking
burning the juices and the vegetables (and making the
whole thing taste bad). There's a large quantity of water
so the juices released by the meat are diluted and create a
tasteless sauce base that will need to be reduced.

"**Don't forget this basic tip:** check the size of your
cooking vessel by placing your meat inside, still in its packaging.
You can't go wrong."

ROAST IN A SMALL DISH

There needs to be a bit of space around the meat (but not too much) to allow for
even cooking, good-quality flavors, and a very tasty jus.

SMALL DISH

There's enough space between the meat and the dish for
the juices to evaporate a little and create lots of flavor. The
herbs and spices cook slowly, create juice, and don't burn,
because the meat protects them from the oven's heat. The
top and bottom cook evenly. The result is a uniform cooking,
a lot of flavors, and a great-quality jus.

LARGE DISH

If there's too much room between the meat and the dish, the
juices evaporate too fast. The herbs and spices, which aren't
protected by the meat, cook too fast and burn because the
oven's heat is too intense. The bottom of the meat absorbs
the bitter taste of the burnt herbs and spices and the fat
spits everywhere inside the oven.

TEMPERATURES AND COOKING THERMOMETERS

It's rather infuriating to have a medium cooked piece of meat when you wanted a medium rare one. What you need to never get this wrong again is one—or several—thermometers.

TOUGH MEATS

The meats we class as tough are those that contain a lot of collagen, like the meat you would use in a stew or blanquette, for example. To make them tender, you need to melt the meats' collagen, which happens from about 154.4°F.

At this temperature, the meat heats up and releases water. The collagen melts and turns into gelatin. And bam, just like blotting paper, the gelatin reabsorbs the water.

Essentially, during the cooking of a stew, for example, the meat dries out, then sucks up all the water it released and becomes juicy again. Amazing, isn't it?

1 The meat heats, releases water, dries out, and the collagen melts.

2 As it melts, the collagen turns into gelatin.

3 The gelatin absorbs the water released by the meat. And you end up with a tender and juicy piece of meat.

TENDER MEATS . . . THAT SHOULD STAY THAT WAY

For tender meats, it would be simpler if they all became medium rare or medium well at the exact same temperature. But Mother Nature didn't make life simple.

For a piece of meat to stay tender and juicy, certain proteins must be modified, but others must not be; if they are, the meat will be as tough as rubber.

Simply put, the myosin must be distorted (except in beef), but the actin mustn't change much. And the temperatures that cause these modifications are different for each animal.

A GRAPH MAKES THINGS EASIER

HERE'S A RECAP OF THE IDEAL COOKING TEMPERATURES FOR EACH ANIMAL
These are "core temperatures," meaning they're taken in the center of the meat.

Temperature range in which the myosin is modified

Temperature range in which the actin is modified

Temperature range suitable for the type of animal

167 –
158 –
149
140 –
131 –
122 –
113 –
°F

Poultry   Veal   Beef   Pork   Lamb

COOKING TEMPERATURES CHEAT SHEET

	RARE	MEDIUM RARE	MEDIUM	MEDIUM WELL	WELL DONE
POULTRY	-	-	149°F	158°F	167–176°F
WINGED GAME	113°F	122°F	140°F	158°F	167–176°F
VEAL	-	131°F	143.6°F	158°F	167–176°F
BEEF	113°F	122°F	131°F	149°F	167–176°F
PORK	-	-	149°F	158°F	167–176°F
LAMB	131°F	140°F	149°F	158°F	-

NOTE: if your meat needs to rest before being served, reduce by 37°F because the temperature of the meat will continue to rise.

THE RIGHT THERMOMETER

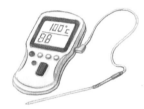

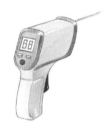

THE PROBE THERMOMETER

This is a thermometer that allows you to read the temperature of the inside of the meat without even opening the oven, and to be alerted as soon as the desired temperature is reached. This is also very useful for cooking in water. Prices start at about $23. For that price, it's silly to deprive yourself of such a tool. One overcooked roast, and you've lost more than $23!

THE OVEN THERMOMETER

The temperature indicated by the thermostat is rarely precise because its thermometer is on the inner wall and not in the center of the oven, where the meat is placed. The difference between the true temperature and the one indicated by the thermostat can be quite large. This little accessory will allow you to check the thermostat's precision and to correct it, if necessary.

THE INFRARED THERMOMETER WITH LASER TARGETING

This doesn't go into the meat but measures the outside temperature. Very useful for checking the temperature of a pan or grill before placing the meat onto them, or of oil as it heats.

"You don't measure the temperature just anywhere! It should be measured in the center of the meat— that means in the middle of its thickness AND of its length!"

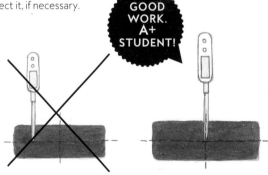

You're right in the middle of the thickness, but not of the length. Review your geometry lessons.

Certain bones transmit heat and others don't. Bones or no bones, place your thermometer in the center of the meat.

GOOD WORK. A+ STUDENT!

HOW TO SEASON YOUR MEAT WITH SALT

Salt and meat have a long history together. Everyone will tell you to "season before cooking" and "never add salt just before serving!" Just for fun, what if we looked into what actually happens, scientifically, when you season meat with salt?

NO NO NO

DOES THE SALT PENETRATE THE MEAT?

Here's the real question we need to answer first. It seems so obvious that we don't even wonder.

I know that when we put salt onto meat, we think it's going to penetrate it. However, the fact is that during cooking, the penetration of the salt is laughably minimal.

IF I ADD SALT BEFORE COOKING ANYWAY, WHAT HAPPENS?

 1

 2

 3

 4

UNIVERSAL GRAVITY

You're familiar with the law of gravity? This law also applies to the salt added to meat. It falls off during cooking. Exactly how much falls off is a mystery, but basically you'll never know how much salt stayed on your meat and how much of it ended up at the bottom of the cooking dish. That's the first problem.

FAT

You know that salt dissolves in water but not in oil. If you brown your meat in oil or butter, the fat will coat some of the grains of salt and will prevent any contact between the salt and the humidity of the meat. It won't be able to dissolve. That's the second problem.

EXPULSION

During cooking, the surface of the meat contracts, dries out, and expels some of the juices it contains. On a grill or in a frying pan, this is very violent: the steam exits with such force that it pushes some of the grains of salt away. In an oven, this isn't as brutal, but the same thing happens. Again, some of the salt sprinkled onto the meat serves no purpose. But how much of it? It still isn't measurable. We haven't got the foggiest idea. Problem number three.

AND IN A STOCK?

This is different. If the stock was salted before you added the meat, the salt will stop the meat juices from being released into the stock. The meat will be more flavorful. It's the same for braised meat if you sprinkle the exterior with salt—but the salt won't actually penetrate.

 **CONCLUSION**

Adding salt just before cooking is essentially pointless. Sorry!

THE SPEED OF SALT PENETRATION

FOR THE SALT TO PENETRATE BY ⅓ INCH (1 CM), JUST ONE TINY CENTIMETER, IT NEEDS ABOUT:

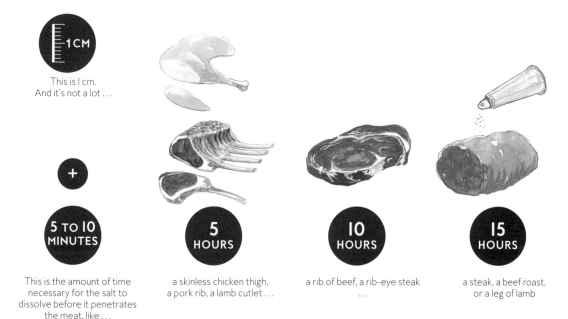

1 CM

This is 1 cm.
And it's not a lot . . .

+

5 TO 10 MINUTES

This is the amount of time necessary for the salt to dissolve before it penetrates the meat, like . . .

5 HOURS

a skinless chicken thigh, a pork rib, a lamb cutlet . . .

10 HOURS

a rib of beef, a rib-eye steak . . .

15 HOURS

a steak, a beef roast, or a leg of lamb

"**Before penetrating the meat,** the salt needs to dissolve. And to dissolve, it needs more time than it takes to cook a steak!"

THE TRUTH AND LIES ABOUT SALT

SALT CAUSES THE MEAT TO RELEASE JUICES.
Yes! That's true, it's been proven. But it depends on which meat and which part of the meat: it's faster for poultry and pork, and a lot slower for veal or beef. But in both cases, it takes quite a long time.

TRUE!

SALT IS A FLAVOR ENHANCER.
We're often told this, but it's completely false. Salt doesn't enhance flavors, but modifies them. In many cases, salt reduces the acidity or bitterness of a dish even better than sugar does, like for a tomato sauce, a grapefruit, or chicory, for example.

FALSE!

THE MEAT BOILS IN ITS JUICES.
This is another thing we often hear: "I don't add salt to my meat because it'll boil in its own juices." It's just that the pan isn't hot enough or isn't big enough for the juices to turn into steam. These juices remain beneath the meat, and boil it. It has nothing to do with salt.

FALSE!

HOW TO SEASON YOUR MEAT WITH SALT

SO, WHAT'S THE POINT OF ADDING SALT?

During the cooking process, the proteins inside the meat twist and release juices.

So, for a juicy piece of meat, these proteins need to twist as little as possible. And for this to happen, there's one infallible thing: our beloved salt!

When the salt seeps deep into the meat, it modifies the structure of these proteins. Once it has caused them to deteriorate, they'll twist a lot less and so will release far fewer juices.

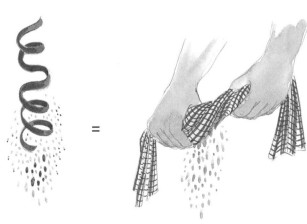

Protein that twists during cooking = Laundry that you wring out by twisting it

When you wring a wet cloth, you expel the water it contains. It's the same for proteins; the effect of the heat causes them to twist and expel the water inside the meat.

"**Attention, newsflash:** never again will you season your meat with salt like you used to . . . That's great!"

DO YOU ADD SALT BEFORE, DURING, OR AFTER COOKING?

Take a good piece of meat. Here are the different solutions and explanations to help you season it with salt.

3 WEEKS BEFORE	2 DAYS BEFORE	4 TO 5 HOURS BEFORE
BENEFICIAL	**DIVINE!**	**VERY GOOD**
A protective crust forms: the meat can then age slowly, without the risk of putrefaction.	The salt penetrates the meat and lightly dries out the exterior. The meat will better retain its juices during the cooking process and will crisp up on the outside.	The salt slowly penetrates the meat: the exterior turns slightly dry. The meat will be juicier and the outside will crisp up faster.

"Seasoning meat with salt long before you start cooking it is a secret of star chefs and something they definitely don't want revealed."

HOW DO I EFFECTIVELY SEASON MY MEAT WITH SALT?

SEASON BEFORE COOKING

The trick is to add salt well in advance, a long time before cooking—up to two days.

I know, it sounds crazy. You'll say, but won't the salt make the meat release some of the juices? Yes, that's true. But then the meat will reabsorb them, and it will be more tender and a lot juicer once it's been cooked.

SEASON AFTER COOKING

This is better, because you know exactly how much salt is on your meat. There are two solutions: either you season before the meat has rested, or you season it afterwards.

Before resting: a large quantity of the salt will dissolve and the outside of the meat will be evenly salted.

After resting: the salt won't dissolve and when you chew, the little grains of salt will crack beneath your teeth and stimulate the taste buds.

THE CLASSIC ERROR TO AVOID

If you coat your meat in oil before you season it, the oil will form a light film that will prevent the grains of salt from coming into contact with the humidity of the meat.

The result: the salt will have great difficulty dissolving and most of it will remain in the cooking dish.

I HOUR BEFORE	JUST BEFORE	DURING	AFTER
GOOD	**POINTLESS**	**POINTLESS**	**ALSO GOOD**
The salt slowly dissolves and begins to slightly penetrate the inside of the meat. In the areas where the salt has soaked through, the meat will be juicier—but only in those areas.	The salt won't have had time to dissolve or to penetrate the piece of meat. Most of it will fall or be pushed off. The worst-case scenario.	The salt won't have had the time to humidify or dissolve, so it won't stick to the meat and most of it will fall into the cooking dish.	This way, you know exactly how much salt there is on the meat. The salt stays crunchy and this stimulates the taste buds. Not a bad solution.

THE DIFFERENT SALTS TO USE

Forget fine salt, that's the one you can get everywhere. It's a salt that doesn't have a particular taste and hasn't got any personality. There are many salts with different textures and surprising flavors. Don't hesitate to switch between them depending on their qualities and on your recipe.

All cooking salts are composed mostly of sodium chloride. It's what they contain besides the sodium chloride that makes the difference, as well as the shape of the salt crystals. Here's a short list of salts to try.

FINE SEA SALT

Collected from salt marshes, this is the most common salt after fine salt. Tastier, it's the most basic salt to have for seasoning cooking water. It's better unrefined (slightly gray) so as to benefit from all of its natural mineral salts.

COARSE SEA SALT

Like fine salt, but . . . coarse. It's usually a grayish color because its falls to the bottom of the salt marshes and takes on some of the color of the clay on which it sits. It's a little rough, but perfect for the English-style cooking (in boiling water) of certain vegetables.

FLEUR DE SEL

Formed of very fine crystals, this is the thin layer of salt that skims the surface of the salt marshes and sticks together in clumps around the marsh edges before it's collected. The flavors change according to production regions. Use after cooking to benefit from its crunchiness.

KOSHER SALT

This is a pure salt (so, unrefined), slightly grayish in color, made up of grains that are quite big. Not very well-known in Europe although very commonly used in the United States, it's a delicious salt that is unique in that it's difficult to dissolve and offers a light crunch, perfect for using at the end of the cooking process.

PINK HIMALAYAN SALT

This salt doesn't come from the Himalayas, but from the northeast region of Pakistan, in the geological zone of the Himalayas! Its pink color is due to its high iron levels. It's an unrefined, noniodized rock salt, fine with a crunchy texture and a hint of acidity. Use it just before serving to get the most out of its qualities.

PERSIAN BLUE SALT

From the most ancient salt mines in the world, situated in Iran (formerly Persia), this salt has been hand-collected for centuries. It gets its name from the fact that some of its crystals contain sylvinite, which gives it a blue hue. With its strong, spiced flavors, it's perfect on poultry or foie gras.

HAWAIIAN BLACK SALT

It gets its black color from the lava rocks that used to hurtle down the sides of the island's volcanos and onto the shores. Today, a few rocks are added to the saltworks to obtain this intense black color. Its flavors are bold and slightly smoky. Use sparingly just before serving, on foie gras or white meat.

HAWAIIAN RED ALAEA SALT

From the island of Molokai, part of the Hawaiian Islands, this salt takes on the red color of the volcanic clay called alaea, which is added to it during the drying process. In contrast to a lot of other rare salts, this one can be used in cooking due to its predictable nutty flavor.

CHARDONNAY OAK SMOKED SALT

This is a fleur de sel salt harvested from the Pacific Ocean off the coast of California. It's cold smoked and then placed in barrels used for producing Chardonnay wine. Definitely the finest of smoked salts, it develops flavors that are woody, tartly balsamic, citrusy, and of course, smoked. Use after cooking.

MALDON SALT

Originating from the town of Maldon in the east of England, this very white salt is obtained by heating seawater until salt forms due to precipitation. Its consistency, made up of very pure flakes that are light and crumbly, crunchy, highly iodized, and which dissolve with difficulty, have made it the favorite salt among star chefs.

HALEN MÔN ANGLESEY SALTS

These salts, from the island of Anglesey near Wales, are so light and airy that they look like snowflakes. They're obtained using a very particular method: water from the Atlantic Ocean is successively filtered through coal, a bed of mussels, and then sand. It's then heated sous vide and put into crystallization containers so that salt crystals form.

UNSMOKED HALEN MÔN

Very white, crunchy, slightly sparkling, and highly iodized, it looks like snowflakes.

SMOKED HALEN MÔN

Smoked on wood chips, it has the same characteristics, with a soft, smoked flavor.

> "Of course, salt should be stored away from light and the humidity of the air!"

CHEF'S TIP

Here's a secret from Hervé This (physiochemist, inventor of molecular gastronomy) that Pierre Gagnaire uses every day: he mixes a bit of salt with a few drops of olive oil. A microscopic layer of oil coats the grains of salt and stops them from dissolving when they come into contact with the meat. When you eat it, there's a slight crunchiness that stimulates the taste buds. Exceptional!

HOW TO SEASON YOUR MEAT WITH PEPPER

Many people add pepper before grilling or roasting meat. Is there any point in adding pepper to your meat?

NO NO NO NO

DOES PEPPER PENETRATE THE MEAT?

As with salt, this is the big question. The answer is no, pepper doesn't penetrate! You can pepper your meat like crazy, but it won't flavor the meat as it cooks. Nyet, nada, nothing, zero. Salt already requires several hours to penetrate by 2 to 3 mm. The same is true for pepper.

"Like Pierre Gagnaire, elected best chef in the world by his peers, said: **'You must always, always, always add pepper at the end to preserve its flavors.'"**

IF I ADD PEPPER ANYWAY, WHAT HAPPENS?

 1

UNIVERSAL GRAVITY

As with salt, the law of gravity must be taken into account. Some of the pepper that you put onto the meat will fall onto the grill, into the pan, or into the cooking dish. Again, you have no idea how much pepper has fallen off or how much is still on the meat. Also, if you prepare a sauce with the juices from the cooking dish, there's already pepper in it, but you don't know how much.

 2

IT BURNS!

When you cook meat, fish, or vegetables on too high a heat, they burn. And when you heat pepper too much, not only does it burn, but it also becomes bitter and acrid. Pepper is very fragile and it burns at quite a low temperature, from 284°F.

 3

AND IN A STOCK?

This will also go wrong. The pepper infuses when heated in a liquid. As it does so it becomes astringent. Season your stock with pepper after cooking. In the past, pepper was added to broths for its antiseptic properties, not to give the broth flavor.

CONCLUSION

Adding pepper before cooking is even more counterproductive than adding salt. It doesn't penetrate, burns if cooked at too high a heat, and becomes astringent in a stock. You should always, always, always add it after cooking, never before.

WHAT EXACTLY IS A PEPPER PLANT?

A pepper plant is a tropical vine from the southwest region of India. These vines are twisted around wooden posts (often around live wood in India) that are 6½ ft (2 m) high and act as stakes. To thrive, the pepper plant needs a constant temperature between 68°F and 86°F. The pepper grows in little clusters along the vines. Green, black, white, and red pepper are the same fruit, but at different degrees of maturation.

GREEN PEPPER

Peppercorns start off with a green color. This pepper is fragile when it's just been picked. It can often be found dehydrated, in brine, and sometimes freeze-dried. It has a fresh flavor, vegetal and not very spicy.

BLACK PEPPER

If you let it ripen, green pepper turns pale yellow. It's picked, dried, and its pericarp (skin) turns black. Its flavor is warmer— woody and spicy. It offers a complex aromatic palette.

WHITE PEPPER

If you let the pepper ripen some more, the peppercorns turn orange. They're soaked in rainwater for about ten days, then left to dry. The pericarp is removed to reveal the white peppercorn. It's a little more aromatic than the black and not as strong.

RED PEPPER

And if the pepper is left to ripen even more, the result is deep red peppercorns that are soaked in hot water to set the color before drying. This time, the pericarp is left on the peppercorn. Rare, red pepper is hot and full-bodied.

THE DIFFERENT PEPPERS TO USE

Get rid of that powdered pepper! When I say pepper, I mean pepper that has flavor, aroma that overwhelms your taste buds but doesn't sting, full-bodied with length on the palate— pepper that transports you.

Don't use powdered pepper anymore. They put everything in it: dust, detritus . . . powdered pepper is the equivalent of the battery-farmed chickens of poultry. So, away with it and into the trash can! Opt for two or three peppers that you grind just before serving. Here's a little tour of some exceptional peppers, a few of which cost no more than the powdered peppers commonly found at the store. These peppers have all been harvested and sorted by hand, just like the grapes of good wines.

WHITE BIRDY PEPPERCORNS "BIRD PEPPER"

In Cambodia, the birds peck the ripest peppercorns directly from the vines. When the pepper is in the bird's crop, an enzymatic reaction modifies its flavors. After having digested the pericarp, the bird spits out the peppercorn, which is then collected by hand from the ground, hence its expensive price. Use with white meats.

KAMPOT PEPPER

In 2009, Kampot peppers were the first peppers to benefit from the IGP (Protected Geographical Indication) status. Practically nonexistent since the Khmer Rouge began to prefer cultivating rice in 1975, Kampot pepper has gradually reappeared over the course of the last twenty years. It's a pepper that's grown near the sea, very fresh and very elegant.

BLACK KAMPOT PEPPER

A pepper with floral notes, slightly sweet, strong, warm, and with good length on the palate. Use with red meats and lamb.

WHITE KAMPOT PEPPER

This pepper has vegetal, undergrowth notes (menthol, eucalyptus) and also notes of grilled peanuts. Incredible on white meats and in sauces.

RED KAMPOT PEPPER

Picked when ripe, this is a very warm pepper, with sweet, spicy, elegant flavors. Use in terrines, meat salads, or with foie gras.

HOW TO PROPERLY GRIND PEPPER

The flavors and aromas of pepper are concentrated in the center of the peppercorn and the spiciness lies in the exterior layer, on the pericarp.

The finer you grind your pepper, the stronger the spiciness and the more it will mask other flavors. The coarser your pepper is, the stronger its flavors will be and the more you'll be able to enjoy its richness.

To get the most out of its characteristics, crush the peppercorns with a pestle and mortar or adjust your pepper grinder for the coarsest grind.

Very fine grind: the spiciness dominates

Medium grind: a mix of spiciness and flavors

Coarse grind: the flavors dominate

WILD VOATSIPERIFERY PEPPER

This pepper is found wild in the southern region of the island of Madagascar, on vines that grow at the tops of trees that are up to 66 ft (20 m) tall. Its shape is similar to the shape of *Piper cubeba* (tailed pepper). It appeared in Europe only a few years ago and is still very rare. Eat it whole or slightly crushed.

WILD BLACK VOATSIPERIFERY PEPPER

Intense flavors of fresh soil with woody, fruity, and citrus notes and a distinct, lasting spiciness that isn't too strong. Extraordinary on duck, pork, and lamb.

WILD RED VOATSIPERIFERY PEPPER

This has the same characteristics as the black variety but with warmer flavors. Perfect for pork and lamb.

LONG RED PEPPER

This can be found in various countries (Indonesia, Cambodia, etc.) but it's in Japan, on the island of Ishigaki-Jima, that the most surprising kind is found. Shaped like ears of grain, this pepper develops flavors of cacao, coffee, butter, and also dried tomato. Best grated, crushed, or ground, it's ideal for pork, lamb, and poultry. This long peppercorn is the ONLY one that is the best for making infusions (stocks)— the only one!

MADAGASCAR BLACK PEPPERCORN

Pepper was introduced to Madagascar at the beginning of the twentieth century by Frenchman Émile Prudhomme. The little Madagascan black peppercorns develop sweet flavors of brioche, pine nuts, and even of cacao and gingerbread, which are balanced out by notes of acid green fruits. Quite spicy, it's ideal for red meats and marinades.

MALABAR PEPPER

Originating from the Malabar coast, between Goa and Kanyakumari in southwest India, this pepper benefits from two monsoons each year to develop the finesse and long-lastingness of its musk and burnt wood flavors. It's also slightly sweet with a very light touch of acidity. Unbelievably good on white meat and poultry.

TASMANIAN MOUNTAIN PEPPER ("FALSE" PEPPER)

This "aboriginal pepper" is a "false" pepper (so-called because it is not a true peppercorn) that grows wild in Tasmania, in southeast Australia. At first pleasant on the palate and then hot, its peppercorns develop flavors of bay leaf, unripe nuts, and black fruits (blackberries, blueberries, and blackcurrants). Delicious with game, pork, lamb, and white meats.

TIMUT PEPPER ("FALSE" PEPPER)

Another "false" pepper that grows wild in Nepal. It develops citrus notes (lemon and grapefruit), but with a softness and length on the palate. Be careful, this berry is slightly anesthetic on the tongue and the lips! Absolutely divine on poultry and when used to bring freshness to certain sauces.

GREEN PEPPER

Opt for green pepper that is fresh, if you can find it (it's quite rare). Often freeze-dried, green pepper is picked before it's ripe and has fresh flavors that are reminiscent of cloves as well as a very light spiciness. Use just before eating, whole or ground on white meat, peppercorn steak, grilled food, and in certain sauces.

"I'll say it once more: don't cook pepper! Always add the pepper once the dish has been cooked, just before serving, or at the dining table. This way you'll fully benefit from its flavors and aromas."

WHICH BUTTER FOR COOKING?

Butter comes from the fat content in milk. The problem is that it burns when heated on too high a heat. However, there are many ways to get the most out of its flavors and aromas when cooking meat. Let's explore this.

HOW IS IT MADE?

You take cow's milk, skim off the cream, and beat it (or churn it). The fat gathers together to form butter particles that are then removed, washed, and kneaded before being pressed into a mold.

WHY DOES IT BURN?

Butter contains water. As long as there's water it can be heated as much as you want because the temperature will never go past 212°F (the maximum temperature of boiling water). But as soon as there's no water left, the temperature shoots up.

When you heat butter, it first begins to bubble as the water it contains transforms and evaporates. Its temperature then rises to around 266°F and the casein and lactose begin to brown. If you heat it further, the butter starts to burn and char . . . and that's when it goes straight into the trash.

THE SOLUTION

The trick is to remove the casein and the lactose that make the butter burn when hotter than 266°F. Once they're removed, you get a clarified butter that can be heated up to 482°F without burning.

It can be used instead of oil for grilling, roasting, etc. You can even replace oil with clarified butter to fry your fries and it won't burn!

RECIPE FOR CLARIFIED BUTTER

1 Gently melt a stick of butter (in a saucepan or a microwave) without stirring and, most importantly, without burning it. There'll be a foam on top (the casein), a yellowish oil in the center, and a white layer on the bottom (the whey).

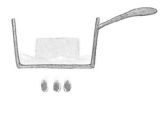

2 Slowly pour the contents of the saucepan through a paper towel over a sieve and catch the clarified butter in a bowl. This clarified butter can be kept for several weeks at room temperature and in the shade.

BROWN BUTTER OR BEURRE NOISETTE

Before burning, butter takes on a pretty, dark beige color that we call "brown butter" or "beurre noisette." It's named for the color of hazelnuts (noisette) but most of all for its flavors. Beurre noisette does indeed taste of hazelnuts.

STOP BUTTER FROM BURNING

~~~~~~~~~~

We know that it's when there's no water left in butter that it burns. The secret of the star chefs is to add a little broth (or water) while the meat browns. Not too much, whatever you do—a tablespoon is more than enough to stop the butter from burning. The second reason for this is to add the flavors of the broth to the cooking juices. Delicious!

BLACK BUTTER

Don't worry, this isn't burnt butter. It's just beurre noisette to which an acid (vinegar, white wine, etc.) is added. Delicious with brains, for example.

THE MYTH OF ADDING OIL

Don't believe those people who tell you to add oil to stop the butter from burning: it'll burn anyway! The burnt color is simply diluted into to oil, so you don't see it.

SOME EXAMPLES OF BUTTER USES

		MAXIMUM °F	FRYING PAN	POT	OVEN
	NORMAL BUTTER	212°F–266°F	Medium temperature	Medium temperature	Up to 302°F
	CLARIFIED BUTTER	482°F	Very high temperature	Very high temperature	Up to 536°F

"The flavor of a good-quality butter varies depending on what the cows have eaten and according to the seasons. The end of spring and the beginning of summer are the best seasons: the prairies are covered in a delicious grass and lots of little flowers that give a lot of flavor to the butter."

WHICH OIL FOR COOKING?

All oils are not equal. Some oils burn faster than others. Some have a lot of flavor. Besides oil, there's also pork fat, duck fat, and beef fat. Here's a little summary of oils and cooking fats.

HOW IS IT MADE?

Cooking oil comes from the seeds or fruits of oleaginous plants. Depending on the nature of these seeds, they can be roasted or made into flour before extracting the oil. As for the fruits, they're put directly into the press. In both cases, the oil is then refined to make it more stable.

Animal fats (lard, duck fat, beef dripping) are melted and purified of all of those "impurities."

WHY DOES IT BURN?

Oil and animal fat decompose and distort from a certain temperature. Smoke escapes from the hot oil, which is what we call the "smoke point."

THE SOLUTION

Unlike butter, there's nothing you can do. You simply mustn't exceed the smoke point.

So, choose your oil or your fat according to what you're going to do with it.

WHY DOES OIL SPLASH AND SPIT?

Actually, it's not the oil that spits, it's the meat juices that explode.

The juices turn from their liquid state into a gaseous state as they turn into steam. This happens in a fraction of a second, so fast that they explode and spit everywhere.

WHY DOES FRENCH FRY OIL OVERFLOW?

When you fry French fries, the water contained inside the potatoes turns into steam (that's the little bubbles you see coming to the surface). The problem is that the steam takes up over 2,000 times more volume than the water.

If there are a lot of fries, a lot of bubbles come to the surface and take up a lot of volume. The result: the fryer overflows. The solution: don't cook too many fries at once.

"**If you can, try to use duck fat or beef dripping,** which result in incredible flavors. Peanut oil is a good oil and corn oil sits nicely on the food after cooking. Avoid sunflower oil as much of possible as it's of average quality."

THE SMOKE POINT

Oils and fats begin to smoke and then burn from a certain temperature depending on the oil, one that mustn't be exceeded. Here's a little review of the smoke points of the most common oils and animal fats.

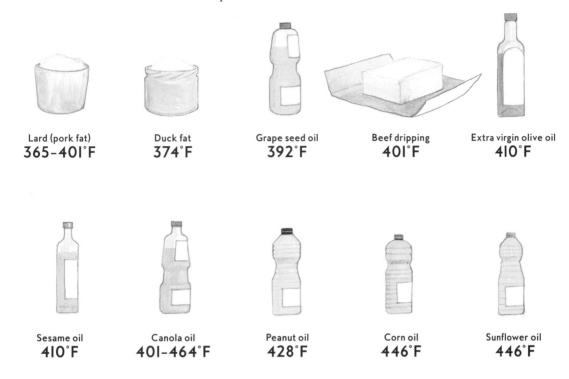

Lard (pork fat)	Duck fat	Grape seed oil	Beef dripping	Extra virgin olive oil
365–401°F	**374°F**	**392°F**	**401°F**	**410°F**

Sesame oil	Canola oil	Peanut oil	Corn oil	Sunflower oil
410°F	**401–464°F**	**428°F**	**446°F**	**446°F**

WHY DO YOU NEED FAT TO BROIL OR ROAST?

Meat doesn't have a completely smooth surface—there are a lot of little holes and textured areas. To cook a piece of meat correctly, the holey and textured areas must be cooked in the same way. The best way to do this is to have a liquid that will cover the whole piece of meat and fill the holes so that they cook at the same speed as the textured parts of the surface.

The other advantage of oil and butter is that they increase the number of Maillard reactions and give a lot more flavor to your meat during the cooking process. Without fat, your meat will brown very little; with fat it will brown a lot more. Don't worry, oil doesn't penetrate the meat at all during cooking.

COOKING MEAT WITHOUT FAT

The air conducts very little heat. There's not a lot of contact between the meat and the heat, so the meat cooks with difficulty and doesn't brown. Very few flavors are created.

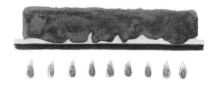

COOKING MEAT WITH FAT

Oil conducts heat very, very well. The meat comes into contact with heat of the pan: it cooks well and browns fast. Many flavors are created.

MEAT MATURATION

Certain butchers like to highlight the fact that their meat was "matured" for a long time, from 90 to 120 days. Does meat maturation really make a difference?

A BRIEF HISTORY

Maturing meat isn't new. In the Middle Ages, meat was already being left to hang to make it more tender and give it more flavor. At the end of the nineteenth century, Frenchman Charles Tellier developed refrigerated cabinets, the temperatures of which could be precisely regulated. He purchased and transformed a boat by installing his cabinets inside. He used the boat to transport beef from Rouen to Buenos Aires in 105 days. The meat, stored at a temperature of between 28.4°F and 32°F, arrived in perfect condition. The maturation of beef could begin.

THE SCIENCE BEHIND MEAT MATURATION

During the course of rigor mortis, the cells in the meat consume the glycogen (a sugar) contained in the muscle and produce a lactic acid that modifies the pH of the meat. This process makes the meat acidic. Then, enzymes called calpains and cathepsins begin to break down the contractile structure of the muscle fibers, a process known as proteolysis. Lipolysis happens next, oxidizing the lipids that will develop flavors. Eighty percent of the meat's tenderness is obtained in two weeks, but the maturation process begins after this to develop even more flavors.

MATURATION VERSUS AGING

The most common maturation method is passive: leaving the meat in a cold room for a number of weeks.

Aging is much more complicated, but develops so many more flavors. A good refiner has sound scientific knowledge of the process. He controls the ventilation of his cold room, knows the hygrometry necessary according to the progression of the meat cuts' aging process, uses the temperature by adjusting it exactly to the correct one-tenth of a degree, places the meat cuts in relation to one another to ensure that they mutually enrich each other, regulates the lighting, etc.

HANGING METHODS AFFECT THE MATURATION

After slaughter, the carcasses are hung from hooks by the Achilles tendon.

HANGING THROUGH THE ACHILLES TENDON

This type of hanging is done to save more space, but means that the back muscles that support the carcass's weight are compressed during the *rigor mortis* process.

Compressed muscles = a slight increase in tenderness during maturation

Other very good and very rare butchers practice pelvic suspension.

PELVIC SUSPENSION

Here, the carcass is hung by the pelvic hip bone. It's the spinal column that holds the carcass to the hook and the back muscles are in a stretching position and become much more tender. With this type of hanging, the back muscles acquire a shape that's different from the one they usually have. For example, the top sirloin is a lot longer and thinner, and so much more delicious.

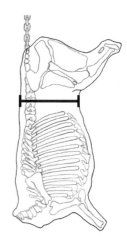

Stretched muscles = a large increase in tenderness during maturation.

"Beef can be matured for long periods of time—but not all beef cuts."

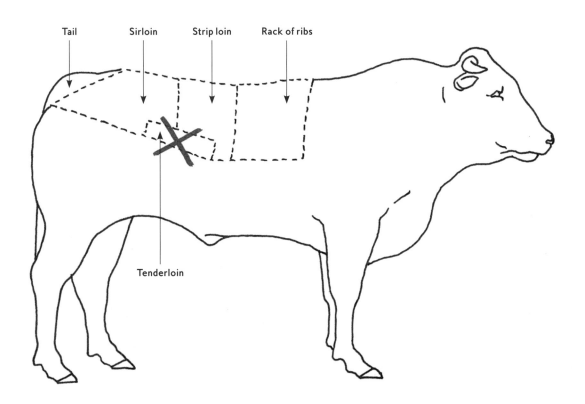

Tail · Sirloin · Strip loin · Rack of ribs

Tenderloin

WHICH MEATS CAN BE MATURED?

VEAL, LAMB, PORK, AND POULTRY

Veal, lamb, pork, and poultry are rarely matured because it has practically no influence on their flavors or tenderness. Generally, these meats aren't matured for any longer than a week.

CERTAIN CUTS OF BEEF

For beef, only certain cuts can be matured for long periods of time. For example, it isn't beneficial to tough meats, but is very much so to the top sirloin, from which the tenderloin is removed and which includes the rack of ribs, the strip loin and the sirloin.

THE INFLUENCE OF BREED, AGE, AND SIZE

The duration of the maturation process depends on the breed of the animal. Old English breeds such as the Hereford and the Angus require quite a short maturation process. The Fin Gras du Mézenc requires longer and Charolais beef even longer than that. The age and the size of the animal also have a part to play.

THE INFLUENCE OF THE ANIMAL'S DIET

The meat of an animal that was fed on corn silage, for example, will spoil very fast and so it isn't possible to mature it for a long period of time.

MATURATION: A USER'S MANUAL

Meat can be matured in two ways: sous vide (in its own humid environment and juices) or dry, in a cold room at a specifically controlled temperature and degree of humidity. The tenderness is the same in both cases, but the flavors of a dry-aged meat are incomparable.

WET AGING

Wet aging (sous vide), a method commonly used for meat sold in big supermarkets, often results in a slightly metallic flavor because the myoglobin that gives beef its red color contains a lot of iron. This type of aging develops very little flavor.

Meat sous vide = wet aging

DRY AGING

Dry aging results in a richer flavor. During this aging process, the sugars concentrate and the fats oxidize. The result is that both delicate and other more intense flavors develop.

Ribs in the open air = dry aging

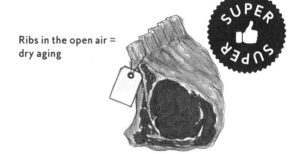

SUPER SUPER

THE STAGES OF DRY AGING

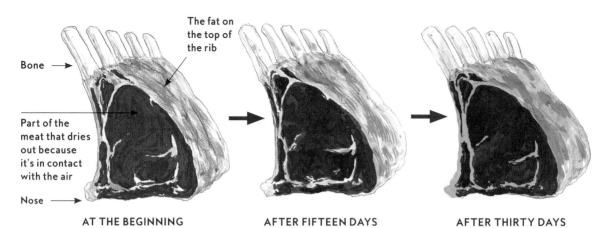

The fat on the top of the rib

Bone →

Part of the meat that dries out because it's in contact with the air

Nose →

AT THE BEGINNING

AFTER FIFTEEN DAYS
The meat begins to dry, a crust forms, the fat starts to change color, and the meat darkens.

AFTER THIRTY DAYS
The meat continues to dry and to concentrate. It's already lost practically 30 percent of its weight.

AGING MEAT AT HOME

LIMITATIONS

There are two challenges with aging meat at home:

The first is the size of the meat at the end of the process. After aging, you have to remove the part that's dried out, which is about ⅓ inch (1 cm) in thickness. On a rack of ribs of more than 19½ inches (50 cm) this doesn't matter much. But on one individual rib, it's too much: you'll be throwing out almost half of your meat!

The second is the space it takes up. The more meat cuts aging together, the better they'll taste because they enhance each other.

But you can still do a good job at home.

INSTRUCTIONS

Take half a rack of ribs, or four ribs, and place them on a grilling rack so the air circulates well all around them then refrigerate them. Place a dripping pan near the ribs and fill it with one glass of water (the humidity of the air is very important). Change the water every day and leave the meat to age for between three and five weeks. Then remove the dried areas from the sides, some of the fat from the top, and you'll be ready to start cooking.

WHY IS IT LIMITING?

~~~

- It requires time.
- It requires space, a lot of space.
- There's a significant loss of weight: some of the water contained in the meat evaporates and the dried areas on the exterior are removed. Basically, you lose between 4 and 50 percent of the original weight, depending on the cut.

WHY IS IT GOOD?

~~~

An aged piece of meat is more tender and more succulent because the broken-down proteins allow the meat to better retain its juices during cooking. This meat has an array of flavors that are so much richer than regular meat; first, because the water inside the meat evaporates, causing the flavors to concentrate, and secondly because new flavors are able to develop.

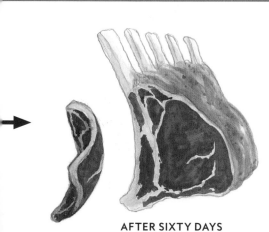

AFTER SIXTY DAYS
The exterior is very dark, almost black. The juices have darkened a lot, too. The meat has lost almost half of its weight. An enormous amount of flavors has developed

A well-aged meat develops a lot of flavors: cherry, hazelnut, butter, cheese, and caramel.

THE IMPORTANCE OF CORRECTLY CUTTING THE MEAT

You can make your meat much more tender and flavorful if you know the secrets to cutting it properly.

THE DIRECTION OF THE CUT AND THE TENDERNESS

You can easily make meat more tender by cutting it into thin slices, perpendicular to the direction of the fibers. Did you know that you need ten times more strength to chew a piece of meat cut in the direction of the fibers than you do for a piece cut perpendicularly?

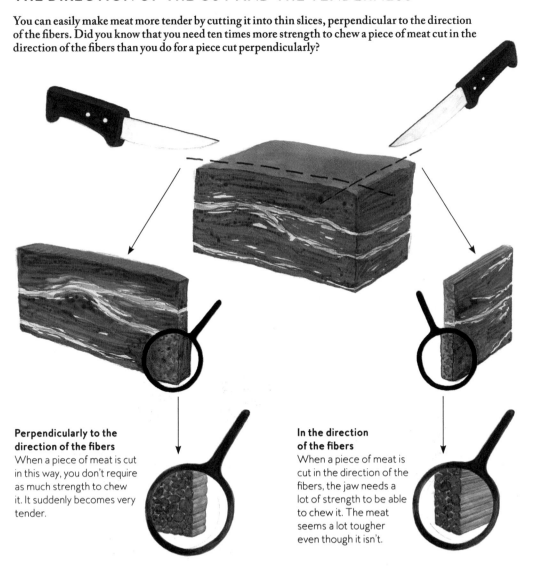

Perpendicularly to the direction of the fibers
When a piece of meat is cut in this way, you don't require as much strength to chew it. It suddenly becomes very tender.

In the direction of the fibers
When a piece of meat is cut in the direction of the fibers, the jaw needs a lot of strength to be able to chew it. The meat seems a lot tougher even though it isn't.

THE CONTACT SURFACE AREA

This seems a bit scientific (it is, let me assure you) but it's also very simple: the larger the contact area between the surface of the meat and the pan, the more the meat browns. This is what we call the contact surface area. And the thinner the piece of meat is, the more of it browns.

If you take two pieces of meat of the same weight, cut one thick and one thin, this is what happens:

With two pieces of meat that weigh the same, the amount of surface area that browns varies according to how the pieces are cut. The one on the left will have fewer flavors created by the Maillard reactions whereas the one on the right will have a lot of them.

When cooking tough meats, braising or in a broth, the principle is the same: the larger the contact surface area, the more the flavors of the meat will infuse the stock.

Surface area in contact with the pan
= **small contact surface area**
= **only a small amount of the meat browns**

Surface area in contact with the pan
= **large contact surface area**
= **a large amount of the meat browns**

THE COOKING TIME AND THE THICKNESS OF THE PIECE OF MEAT

Often we're given a suggested cooking time according to the weight of the piece of meat we want to cook. But it's not the weight of the meat that counts, it's the thickness!

You know very well that a small steak cooks faster than a thick rib-eye steak, which in turn cooks faster than a roast. But how do you calculate the cooking time?

WHY DOESN'T THE WEIGHT COUNT?

Whether it weighs 7 oz or 14 oz, a steak that is ¾ inch (2 cm) thick will cook at the same speed because the thickness is the same. But if you take a slab of meat that's 1½ inches (4 cm) thick and a steak that's ¾ inch (2 cm) thick, the cooking times for each will be very different even though they might weigh the same.

7 oz   **14 oz**
The thickness is the same; the cooking times are identical.

HOW TO CALCULATE COOKING TIME

People tend to think that for a piece of meat that's twice as thick as another, it needs twice as long to cook. But this isn't the way it should be calculated. Actually, the cooking time is proportional to the square of the extra thickness. This means that for a piece that's twice as thick, it needs 2 x 2 = 4 times more cooking time. It's easier to understand with a drawing.

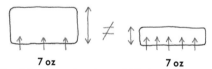

7 oz   **7 oz**
The slab of meat is twice as thick; the cooking times are very different.

AND FOR A ROAST?

It's still the thickness that counts. Whether it weighs 2.2 lb or 4.4 lb, if the diameter is the same, the cooking time is the same.

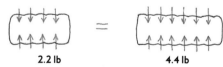

2.2 lb   **4.4 lb**
Both roasts have the same thickness. The heat penetrates the meat at the same speed, regardless of whether the roast is short or long.

ADAPTING THE SIZE OF THE MEAT TO THE COOKING METHOD

Don't simply cut your meat into big or small pieces, but cut them according to your desired cooking method.

CUTTING MEAT FOR GRILLING OR SAUTÉING

THIN SLICES

VEAL OR POULTRY CUTLET ...

The aim is to rapidly cook the meat right through. This is to avoid drying out the exterior while waiting for the center to cook. This method perfectly suits white meats that won't have time to dry out.

1/3 inch (1 cm)

Large contact surface area:
the meat cooks rapidly and evenly.

THICK SLICES

RIB-EYE STEAK, STEAK, TOURNEDOS, PORK CHOP ...

Here there's a good-size contact surface area in relation to the mass of the piece of meat. The aim, however, is to brown the outside of the meat while heating the inside, all the while avoiding overcooking it and keeping the beef medium rare and the pork and the veal pink. Don't do this with poultry, as it will dry out before the middle cooks.

1 1/8 inches (3 cm)

Smaller contact surface area:
the meat cooks slower and the cooking is a little less even.

VERY THICK SLICES

BEEF RIB CHOP, A BIG RIB-EYE STEAK ...

This thickness is better reserved for meats served rare or medium rare, with a big difference between the doneness of the outside and the inside. Avoid if you want a well-done piece of meat, because during the time it takes for the center to cook as much as you want it to, the outside risks overcooking and drying out.

1 1/8 to 2 inches (3 to 5 cm)

Even smaller surface contact area:
the meat cooks even slower and the cooking is uneven.

VERY THIN SLICES (STRIPS)

COOKING IN A WOK ...

The reason for cutting in this way is to have a large surface contact area in relation to the weight of the piece of meat and so to create a lot of juices while cooking it lightning fast. The cut is made perpendicular to the fibers to make it tender.

Maximal surface contact area:
the meat cooks instantly and evenly.

BIG OR SMALL CUBES

RAGOUT, BLANQUETTE OF VEAL...

The size of the cubes has a huge influence on the taste of the meat pieces once they're cooked. The bigger the cubes are cut, the longer the cooking time is but the more the meat will keep its flavors. On the other hand, the smaller the cubes are cut, the faster they'll cook and the more the meat will lose its flavors in the broth or stock. It's your choice.

Big surface contact area: the meat loses some of its flavors.

Smaller surface contact area: the meat loses fewer flavors.

VERY BIG PIECES

STEW, BRAISED HAM...

As with the cube cuts, the bigger the piece of meat is, the better it will retain its flavors during the cooking process. Don't hesitate to cook very big pieces for a long time and on a low temperature. They'll only taste better for it.

Small contact area: the meat loses a lot less flavor.

THIN SLICES

STOCK, SOUP...

This is very beneficial when making a stock or a broth because there's a large surface contact area. The meat will release a lot of its flavors and will therefore quickly make the stock very flavorful. This is the cut used when making stock or soup to which meat is added to give it a savory taste.

Very large surface contact area: the meat loses an enormous amount of flavors.

THICK SLICES

OSSO BUCO...

This is the perfect cut for meats that need to be browned before being slowly braised in a pot. The surface contact area creates a lot of juices that will then be diluted into the sauce. The cooking process generally doesn't take too long.

Smaller surface contact area: the meat retains a large part of its flavors while creating a base for the sauce.

VERY THICK SLICES

ROUND OF PORK, SHANK...

There's a smaller surface contact area than with thick slices so the meat keeps more of its flavors during cooking. And if you brown it first, the pan juices will take on a lot of that grilled flavor.

Smaller surface contact area: the meat retains most of its flavors while releasing its juices through its surface.

BRINING AND SALTING

Salting means putting meat into salt. Brining is putting meat into salt AND water. That's the main difference. Here are the details.

Salting = salt

When it's salted, the meat dries a little and becomes slightly stretchier. This is how duck breast and ham are cured. The meat is left to rest in the salt and some spices and herbs, then it's cleaned, seasoned again, and left to dry.

HOW DOES SALTING WORK?

A piece of meat is put into salt and seasoning and then nature takes its course. For a piece of meat that's not too thick, such as a duck breast, it's generally left to soak between eighteen and twenty-four hours. For a thicker piece of meat, it can go up to forty-eight hours and even two months for a cured ham. During this time, the meat absorbs some of the salt, and as soon as the salt levels surpass 6 percent, it begins to release some of the water it contains.

After the salting, the meat is removed and either cleaned with a brush or rinsed in water and then wiped completely dry. Herbs and spices are added on the top and bottom of the meat and it's left to dry slowly. For duck breast, it should take at least three days for it to dry wrapped in a cloth. For a bigger piece of meat, you should count on it taking up to one week, and for a good quality cured ham, up to three years.

THE DRYING PROCESS

After twenty-four hours, the salt won't have penetrated the whole piece of meat. There's more on the surface than in the center. As the meat dries, the salt continues to move toward the center and, little by little, it will disperse itself evenly throughout the piece of meat. This is the first important thing that happens during the drying process.

The second is that part of the water contained inside the meat evaporates, allowing certain flavors to concentrate and others to develop. Exactly like with beef aging.

THE SCIENTIFIC EXPLANATION

The fibrous proteins are destabilized by the salt levels, so they break down and coagulate. It's this coagulation that gives the meat that familiar, dry texture that we've all experienced in cured ham and Grisons beef.

"Brining and salting seem complicated! Don't worry, these are preparations you should try more often. First, because it's fun and truly easy. And most of all because it will change the taste and texture of your meat and make it even more flavorful!"

Brining = salt + water

With brining, the meat retains more water and stays juicy after cooking. This is how pastrami is prepared: a piece of beef plate is soaked in a mixture of water, salt, sugar, and herbs for several days. It's then rinsed and is ready for cooking.

SALTING VERSUS BRINING

~~~~~~

As soon as the salting process begins, the water contained in the meat is released and evaporates, whereas at the beginning of the brining process, the water is absorbed and then released.

AND WHAT ABOUT BRINING?

Here you need to be a bit more precise with the salt quantity. First the meat is weighed, and then you take the equivalent amount of water. Five percent of the meat's weight is added to the water in salt and 1 percent in sugar (for example, 1.76 oz of salt and 0.35 oz of sugar for 35.2 oz of meat; 3.52 oz of salt and 0.70 oz of sugar for 70.5 oz, and so on) and the water is boiled to destroy any bacteria.

As soon as it's boiling, chopped herbs are added to the water to give it taste and it's left to boil for ten minutes so that it absorbs all the flavors. It's left to cool and the meat is then soaked in it for up to forty-eight hours.

The brine penetrates the meat as it soaks. As soon as the salt levels of the meat surpass 6 percent, it releases the water it absorbed, but the salt levels continue to increase.

It's at this moment that the meat should be removed, rinsed, wiped, and left to dry before being stored in a cool place.

The amount of time the meat should be soaked in the brine depends on the weight and the shape of the meat. The thicker the piece of meat, the longer the soaking time.

THE DRYING PROCESS

This is a lot shorter than with salting. For a piece of meat weighing 35.2 oz, twenty-four hours of drying time is enough for the salt to spread itself evenly through the whole piece of meat.

THE SCIENTIFIC EXPLANATION

The proteins distort and so are more able to retain the water contained in the meat during the cooking process, while resisting against the shrinking of the muscular fibers. The meat will therefore be juicier during and after cooking. This is how cooked ham is prepared.

MARINADES

Everyone knows that the purpose of a marinade is to give the meat flavor, make it juicier, and sometimes more tender. But for that to happen, the marinade needs to penetrate the meat. And that's when things get complicated . . .

ACIDIC MARINADES AND ALCOHOL MARINADES

ACIDITY MAKES THE MEAT MORE TENDER

Lemon juice, vinegar, yogurt, etc. make the meat tender and juicy by modifying the structure of the fibers. Once modified, these fibers will release fewer juices during the cooking process. Thanks to certain enzymes contained in the juice of fresh fruits like pineapple or papaya juice, marinades make meat very, very tender.

MEAT DOESN'T REALLY LIKE ALCOHOL

Certain marinades contain alcohol. It's the acidity of the alcohol that makes the meat tender.

However, if the degree of alcohol is too high, osmosis will cause the meat to dry out and it will become tough.

Pineapple and papaya contain proteolytic enzymes (bromelain in pineapple and papain in papaya) whose properties break down proteins and therefore tenderize the meat.

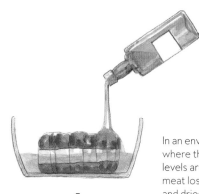

In an environment where the alcohol levels are too high, the meat loses its juices and dries out.

The water contained inside the meat is drawn out by the alcohol.

The meat becomes dry and tough.

THE CORRECT INGREDIENTS FOR A MARINADE

The pieces of meat to be marinated should be no bigger than a mouthful; this is the perfect size for the marinade to work itself deep into the meat. There should also be some acidity to make it juicier. Add herbs, spices, anything you like, really, and let time do the work. Count on at least twenty-four hours for chicken and forty-eight hours for pork or beef.

HOW LONG DOES IT TAKE FOR THE MARINADE TO PENETRATE THE MEAT? THE ANSWER: A VERY, VERY LONG TIME . . .

Marinating meat allows you to change its flavor. To do this, the marinade must penetrate the piece of meat. The problem is that it penetrates very slowly.

FOR A MARINADE TO PENETRATE COMPLETELY, IT TAKES:

For a chicken leg	For a pork chop	For a beef steak
24 HOURS	**3 DAYS**	**1 WEEK**

DO MARINADES PRESERVE MEAT?

In the Middle Ages, pieces of meat were left to marinate for several days. Contrary to common belief, the aim wasn't to make the meat tender but to stop it from spoiling and to preserve it for longer.

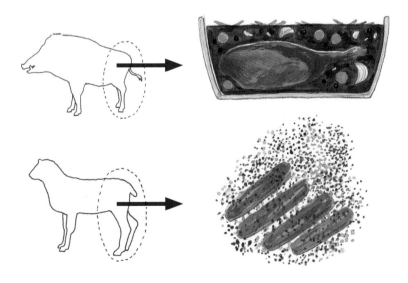

In Europe, meat was marinated with wine and vegetables. This prevented it from being in contact with the air and oxidizing.

In Asia, meat was marinated with spices that had antimicrobial properties to keep it edible for longer.

TIPS FOR SUCCESSFUL MARINADES

Now that we know that marinades barely penetrate meat, here are a few tips to prepare them successfully and make the most of their flavors.

MARINATE SMALL PIECES OF MEAT

When you marinate a thick piece of meat, the marinade remains only on the surface. With each mouthful, you only have a small amount of marinade in your mouth and so very few of its flavors.

On the other hand, if you marinate pieces of meat the size of a mouthful, they'll all be completely coated in marinade and soak up lots of flavors.

Piece of meat covered in marinade	A tiny amount of marinade per mouthful	Piece of meat the size of a mouthful	swimming in marinade	maximum flavors in each mouthful

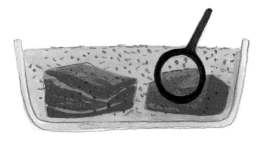

THE BEST MARINADES ARE USED MIDCOOKING

When meat cooks, small crevices form on the surface. The trick here is to allow the marinade to fill in these crevices. Stop cooking halfway or two-thirds through the planned cooking time, let the meat cool, and marinate it. Then finish the cooking. The flavors of the meat will have multiplied a hundred fold.

The marinade penetrates the meat very little but gets stuck in the crevices. With each mouthful, you'll enjoy a large quantity of marinade.

THE METHOD FOR SHOP-MARINATED MEAT

This method consists of directly injecting the marinade into different areas of the meat and allowing it to rest for forty-eight hours. This is how meat bought in commercial stores is marinated.

Each little injection of marinade will spread through the meat only very slightly. But because several areas are injected, the method is very efficient.

You can get big syringes and needles at the drugstore.

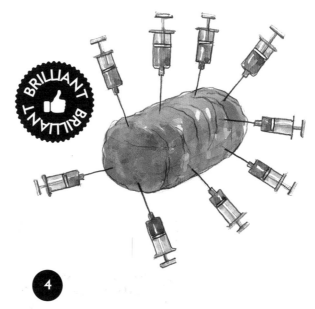

4

MARINADES WORK BEST WHEN PLACED DIRECTLY ON THE GRILL

Don't bother marinating your meat for hours before cooking it on the grill—that would be pointless. Spread the marinade onto the meat and grill immediately.

It's during the cooking process that the magic happens. When your meat cooks on a grill, some of the marinade drips onto the embers. Upon contact, these drips catch fire, burn and make smoke. This smoke rises toward the meat and flavors it. That's why marinades work so well on the grill!

Marinated pork chop

1112°F

Smoke

Embers

> "Marinades work best on the grill because they contribute to the smoking of the meat. Not because they penetrate faster . . ."

COOKING ON THE GRILL

This ancestral cooking method has evolved very little.
The meat cooks above the glowing red embers.
But it's a more complex process than you may think.
Here are the four key points that make all the difference.

1 HEAT, YES, BUT RADIANT HEAT

The thing you need to grill successfully is RADIANT heat. Of course, gas grills heat at almost the same temperature as charcoal grills, but they don't emit radiant heat, or at least they emit very little. And that's what makes the difference, because without radiant heat, the meat won't brown as well. Here lies the limitation of gas grills: gas heats but doesn't brown.

What counts is the strong, radiant heat from the grill that browns the meat rapidly.

Radiant heat is the same heat emitted by the broiling option on your oven, which browns everything so much faster. If you put a slice of bread in an oven at 392°F, it will dry out and will be difficult to brown. But if you switch your oven to broil mode, still at 392°F, that same slice of bread will brown very fast.

2 THE MARINADE GOES UP IN SMOKE

You often read: "Marinate the meat for two to three hours." Don't waste your time on these marinades, they won't penetrate the meat in a mere few hours. A better thing to do is to let the marinade drip off the meat and onto the embers to make smoke.

How does it work?
As it heats, the marinade runs and falls into the embers. Upon contact, the drops of marinade catch fire and create a smoke full of flavors. Cooking the meat creates small fissures on its surface and the smoke penetrates all of these fissures and gives a lot of flavor to the meat.

Embers are odorless
The flavor of a tree's wood is irrelevant to getting that smoky, grilled flavor because embers don't emit any odors.

Herb flavors
Another way to flavor the smoke is to place aromatic herbs like thyme and rosemary directly onto the embers.

3 THE COLOR OF THE GRILL COUNTS, TOO

Grills are generally black to stop you from seeing the scorch marks. The truth is, black is the worst color a grill could be because black absorbs heat but doesn't release it. If your grill is a dark color, the hottest part will be right in the middle. When you cook meat on the whole surface of the grill, the pieces placed around the edges will cook much slower.

The best way to create a more or less equal heat across the entirety of the embers is to cover the sides of the grill in aluminum foil. The shininess will reflect the invisible infrared rays and even out the heat across the surface.

The heat is uneven. The center of the grill is a lot hotter.

The radiant heat is absorbed by the black. The heat isn't as strong along the sides of the grill.

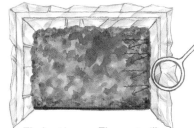

The heat is even. The meat will be perfectly cooked.

The radiant heat is reflected by the aluminum foil. The heat is even across the grill's whole surface.

4 THE TWO HEAT ZONES

Certain thick cuts, such as a big rib of beef or a leg of lamb, need to undergo two cooking stages: the first, on an intense, direct heat to brown them and the second, on a gentler heat to cook the middle.

To achieve this gentler heat you can raise the grilling rack, but that won't change much. To master both temperatures, it's necessary to create two very distinct heat zones: one strong and one weak.

Raise the grilling rack by 4 to 6 inches (10 to 15 cm)
The temperature will be slightly lower, but the radiant heat will be practically the same. The meat will continue to cook vigorously. There will be a small drop in temperature but almost as much radiant heat.

THE BEST · THE BEST

Create two distinct heat zones
The best solution is to move the majority of the embers to a corner, leaving a few strewn across the bottom of the grill and to place the meat above the smaller amount. This will create a big difference in temperature and radiant heat.

LONG LIVE ALUMINUM FOIL!

ON AN OPEN FLAME: ANOTHER SOLUTION

If you can't reduce the strength of the heat from the embers or if they're flaming, remove the piece of meat from the grilling rack, place a sheet of aluminum foil on it, and put the meat on top. The foil will isolate the meat from the flame and reflect the radiant heat.

"Cooking on a grill is browning meat and smoking it at the same time."

SAUTÉING

This is the most common cooking method and the easiest to use. However, there are a few tricks to know to sauté successfully. Here's a hint: The scientific name for this cooking method is "shallow frying."

FOR WHICH MEATS?

A tender meat, not too thick: entrecote, steak, lamb, or pork chop.

WHAT DOES IT MEAN TO SAUTÉ MEAT?

The purpose of sautéing is to cook fast over a very high heat. It's exactly what you need to brown and cook a piece of meat 1⅛ to 1½ inches (3 to 4 cm) thick.

It gives you precisely what you're looking for in a beautiful lamb or veal chop, a hanger steak or an entrecote: crispiness on the outside and warmth on the inside.

TWO KEY ELEMENTS TO SUCCEED

- A strong heat that heats the entire base of the frying pan (or sauté pan), not just one part of it. This is extremely important!
- The fat (butter and/or oil) that allows for the perfect transmission of heat from pan to meat.

BUT WHAT EXACTLY IS SHALLOW FRYING?

Instead of frying food in a large volume of oil like in a deep fryer, you fry it in a shallow pan in a small amount of fat. So it's frying, but in something shallow.

WHERE DOES IT GET ITS NAME?

The term "sauté" comes from the French word for the vessel used to carry out this cooking method: a *sautoir*.

TIPS FOR SAUTÉING WITH SUCCESS

 THE SIZE OF THE PAN

If there's too much meat in the pan, the pan's temperature will drop and the meat will cook in its juices instead of browning.

The steam produced during cooking struggles to escape. Some of the meat is cooked by the steam and doesn't brown very well. The meat cools the surface of the pan. The temperature drops and the delicious crispy layer has difficulty forming on the meat.

The steam escapes with ease and the meat browns very well. The smaller quantity of the meat barely cools the pan at all. A beautifully crispy layer forms.

 THE OIL

The oil should go on the meat and not in the pan. A thin coating of oil is enough.

If you pour the oil directly into the pan, some of it will surround the meat, reach a higher temperature, and burn.

If you put the oil directly onto the meat before placing it in the pan, there won't be any around the sides and so none of it will burn.

3 THE HEAT

Place your meat in the pan as soon as it gets very hot. Can you hear the sizzle and see the white steam rise up around the meat?

The steam lifts the meat intermittently, a bit like how pressure lifts hovercrafts.

The sizzle you hear is the water contained in the meat transforming into steam and rising in the form of a pretty white smoke. As it loses some of its water, the surface becomes crispy.

The pressure beneath the meat is so strong that it's sometimes physically lifted up, so much that it's no longer even touching the pan. It's invisible to the naked eye but evident beneath a microscope. This is why the meat moves a little in the pan.

4 THE STRENGTH OF THE FLAME

We very often have the tendency to turn down the flame when we place a piece of meat in a pan to stop it from burning. This is a huge mistake! On the contrary, the strength of the flame should be kept as it was or even increased.

The size of the gas ring is also very important. If it's too small, the temperature across the pan will be uneven and the meat will cook faster in the middle than on the sides.

When you place a cold piece of meat in a pan, the pan's temperature drops. If, on top of this, you lower the strength of the flame, the pan won't be hot enough to brown your meat.

The whole surface of the pan is at the same temperature. You'll get an evenly cooked piece of meat.

By increasing the strength of the flame you compensate for the drop in temperature caused by the meat. The pan becomes as hot as it was before you added the meat.

ROASTING

Let's get some things straight before we start: roasting meat doesn't mean cooking it in the oven or in a pot. Roasting meat means cooking it on a wood fire. But it's not grilling either. Make sense? No? Let's take a look . . .

FOR WHICH MEATS?

A thick piece of meat that you roast until golden: a beef roast, a fowl, a rack of lamb, a leg of lamb, etc.

ON A SPIT OR IN THE OVEN?

True roasting is done on a wood fire or in the embers, not in the oven. This cooking method has evolved and is still practiced today. So here are two roasting methods: the original method and the modern method.

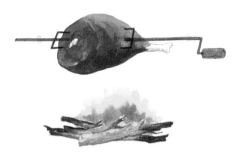

Original roasting method on a spit

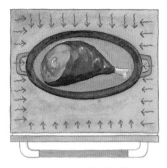

Modern roasting method in the oven

PURE AND SIMPLE ROASTING

The true meaning of roasting is cooking slowly and at a gentle temperature so that the radiant heat has time to deeply penetrate the meat without burning its exterior. It's bit like slow cooking, only you brown the outside of the meat at the same time.

Roasting is pretty simple: as the meat turns it's exposed to waves of heat that slowly penetrate to its center and cook the whole thing without burning the outside.

Each time a piece of the meat is exposed to the heat of the fire or the embers, the heat penetrates very slowly in "little waves." This is why the meat of roasted méchoui, or suckling pig, melts in the mouth.

This part cooks very little

This part doesn't cook

This part cooks

SOME OIL?

You should definitely put a little oil on the meat. This is crucial because the oil increases the transmission of the heat from the surrounding air to the meat. As usual, a thin layer is enough.

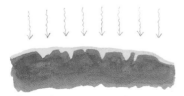

On top: the transmission of heat is good so the meat browns well and flavors are created.

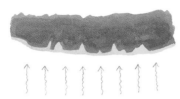

Beneath: the transmission of heat is very good; the meat cooks well and flavors are created.

PREHEATING THE DISH?

If you preheat your oven, the important thing to remember is to preheat your baking dish, too.

WITHOUT A PREHEATED DISH

The dish will have to heat up before transferring its heat to the meat. This can take up to ten minutes. During that time, the surface of the meat cooks.
The result: the top of the meat begins to cook long before the bottom.

WITH A PREHEATED DISH

The dish is already hot when you place the meat inside. The top and bottom begin to cook at the same time.
The result: the top and bottom parts of the piece of meat cook evenly.

OVEN ROASTING

When you cook food in an oven, it dries out a lot, even more so with a fan oven. Contrary to common belief, this type of oven doesn't cook faster but dries food out faster.

When the food cooks, a small layer of humid air sits on the surface. This small layer slows the evaporation of the water contained in the meat. If your oven's fan is on, like it is with a fan oven, it evacuates that humid air and the meat dries out a lot faster.

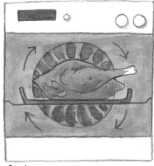

The fan is on
There isn't a small layer of humid air = the roast dries out very rapidly.

The fan is off
There's a small layer of humid air around the meat = the meat dries out slowly.

ROASTING

A TRICK FOR THE BEST ROAST

The best oven-cooked roast is cooked with the broiler on and the oven door half open, so that it can be cooked by radiant heat. The trick is to place the meat quite far from the broiler to prevent it from burning. Put it at the bottom of the oven and turn it over every five minutes. This method will get it as close as can be to the succulence of the traditional roasting method.

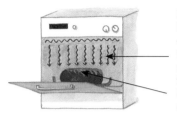

Inside the oven the air isn't very hot and doesn't cook the roast.
Here, the infrared rays are similar to the radiance of a fire and its embers.
Here, the meat roasts slowly.

HOW HIGH SHOULD YOU PLACE THE DISH?

You often read: "Place the dish on the middle oven rack" or "in the middle of the oven." But, for goodness sake, it's not the dish you should be placing in the middle, it's the meat! Place the dish in a way that ensures that the distance between the top of the oven and the top of the meat and the bottom of the oven and the bottom of the dish are equal.

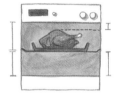

When the dish is in the middle of the oven:
the chicken is too high, the cooking is uneven

When the dish is a little lower:
the chicken is in the middle of the oven, the cooking is even.

SHOULD THE DISH BE AT THE BACK OF THE OVEN?

The back and the corners of the oven are the hottest points. The door is the coolest point, even if you have a fan oven.

For an even cooking, it's imperative that the dish be turned around every 15 minutes.

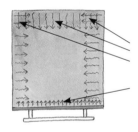

View of the oven from above
This is the hottest part of your oven.

This is the coolest part of your oven.

RESTING THE MEAT

Instead of resting your meat at the end of the cooking process, rest it three-quarters of the way through. Then increase the oven's temperature to its maximum. As soon as the meat is rested, add some oil (never the juices that flowed out as it rested—these are mostly water.) Slip it back into the burning-hot oven to reheat it and crisp up the outside.

As it rests
Three-quarters of the way through its cooking time, the meat rests beneath aluminum foil.

After it has rested
The exterior has absorbed some of the juices contained in the middle and has softened. It's no longer crispy and has cooled down.

The oil
Sprinkle with oil so the surface browns even faster

The last step
Place the meat back in the oven. The whole surface, top and bottom, will brown very quickly. It becomes crispy and hot.

LOW-TEMPERATURE COOKING

This is the thing everyone's been talking about for the last few years even though it's been practiced for centuries.
A cooking method that conserves all the meat's juices and cooks it gently and evenly at below 176°F.

WHY IS THIS COOKING METHOD SO EFFECTIVE?

Because it's carried out at the exact moment when everything comes together to get the best out of the meat.

GOOD

BAD

The collagen, which makes certain meats tough, starts to melt from 131°F.

From 140°F the infectious agents disappear.

Above 149°F the fibers contract more and more strongly and being to lose a lot of water.

The water contained in the meat more or less evaporates from 176°F.

LOW-TEMPERATURE SOUS VIDE COOKING HAS THE EXACT SAME ADVANTAGES.

THE MULTIPLE BENEFITS OF LOW-TEMPERATURE COOKING

A very tender meat because the collagen slowly dissolves.
A meat without bacteria because the temperature and cooking time are high enough and long enough to kill them.
A meat that retains the maximum amount of mineral salts and vitamins because the cooking temperature isn't high enough to expel them.
A very juicy meat because it retains a lot of its water.
A very succulent meat because its exudates don't escape.
An evenly cooked meat without areas that are overcooked or drier than others.

A stress-free cooking method: ten or twenty minutes extra cooking time barely changes a thing. There's nothing to fear if the appetizer goes on longer than planned or if the conversation becomes animated during the starter.

In short, pure happiness!

"**By cooking for longer** at a lower temperature, you consume a lot less energy. It's better for your meat, your wallet and the planet."

SOUS VIDE COOKING

Unlike other cooking methods, this one is very recent and without a doubt one of the most interesting. But remember, the cooking time is very long: from one to seventy-two hours depending on the size of the meat. Yes, you read that correctly—up to seventy-two hours cooking time!

HOW DOES IT WORK?

It's simple. The meat is put into a plastic bag, which is emptied of air and vacuum-sealed. Then it's cooked in a bain-marie or in a steam oven, the temperature adjusted so that the center of the meat heats at the desired degree of temperature. It's left to cook at this temperature for a long time to destroy the majority of the microorganisms.

1. The meat is put into a bag made for sous vide cooking.

2. The bag is placed in a small machine that empties it of the air it contains.

3. A heating rod is placed in a big saucepan of water to heat it and then keep it at the desired temperature.

4. The bag containing the meat is put into the water heated by the heating rod.

"It's a technique that offers very surprising flavors and textures, but you must be equipped with a machine for the vacuum packing and another for the low-temperature cooking."

5. It's left to cook for the desired time according to the chosen temperature and the size of the piece of meat.

> "Honestly, if you care about the flavor of the meat and the flavor only, there's no reason why you shouldn't be an unconditional fan of cooking sous vide!"

THE BENEFITS OF COOKING SOUS VIDE

A TENDER AND JUICY MEAT

By cooking sous vide at low temperatures, you prevent the meat from shrinking and expelling juices. This is why meat cooked sous vide is so tender and so juicy.

Sous vide cooking   Traditional cooking

EVEN COOKING

The meat is cooked evenly inside and out. There are no areas that are more cooked than others, as can be the case with traditional cooking methods.

Sous vide cooking   Traditional cooking

A LIGHT SEASONING

You don't need to add as much salt and pepper as with other cooking methods because the meat fully absorbs all the flavors that are in the cooking bag.

Sous vide cooking   Traditional cooking

MORE EFFICIENT MARINADES

Sous vide marinades work a lot better than the usual marinades. You get the same results in two or three hours of sous vide cooking that you do in several days marinating in the traditional way.

Sous vide cooking   Traditional cooking

BOILING

*Stew and blanquette of veal are
the most well-known examples of the boiling method.
This cooking method is traditionally used for vegetables.
But for meat, the art of boiling is actually to avoid boiling it.*

WATER, THE BASIC INGREDIENT

The first important thing when boiling meat is the quality of the water you cook it in. This water is often used to make a stock or a sauce afterwards. How can your stock be good if the water started off with a bad taste?

If your tap water doesn't taste very nice, buy a filter; it will improve your cooking. And if you don't have a filter yet, don't hesitate to use bottled water— it will make a huge difference.

A FLAVORLESS WATER FOR A MEAT WITHOUT AN AFTERTASTE!

We often use tap water to make broth. But if this water has a slight flavor, that flavor will be intensified in your broth. That would be a shame, wouldn't it?

"Never, ever boil meat, even gently, even on a simmer. It's the best way to make it tough and flavorless."

DO NOT BOIL

In recipes for stew or blanquette, you will often find the words: "Boil gently and skim the stock to remove any impurities." This is problematic.

SUPER SUPER

What actually happens when you heat meat in water or a stock is that the fat it contains detaches and mixes with the liquid. So, if you boil it, even just a little, the fat will be tossed around in every direction and will create a white foam. We're usually told to skim this off because it's bitter and not very appetizing. Incidentally, the "foam" or "impurities" as they're often called aren't foam or impurities at all, but just a mass of fat and proteins mixed with air. It looks like a polluted pond— not very appealing.

To boil correctly, you should only occasionally see a little bubble rise slowly to the surface. Here, the temperature— around 176°F—is high enough to cook the meat and melt the collagen present. No white foam, no bitterness. In short, a colored but translucent stock of very, very high quality.

NEVER BOIL!

The second problem is that when you cook meat in boiling water, the heat transmission is intense—much too intense. Between water that's boiling and water that's on the verge of boiling, there are only a few degrees temperature difference. But even more important than these few degrees is the movement of the water. This changes everything, because moving water heats up much, much more than water that isn't moving.

HOT OR BOILING WATER, WHAT'S THE DIFFERENCE?
It's quite scientific, but still fun to know.

When water is hot but not boiling, the small amount of it in contact with the meat cools slightly because the surface of the meat isn't as hot as the water.

When water is boiling, it moves so much that it doesn't have the time to cool when it comes into contact with the meat.

Here, the water is cooled by the meat. And because this water is barely moving, the part of it surrounding the meat is a little less hot than the rest.

Here, the water is moving so much that the part of it surrounding the meat doesn't cool down.

WHEN TO ADD SALT

Another unavoidable thing that comes with boiling is that the meat loses a lot of its flavors to the stock, due to a phenomenon called osmosis. Therefore, the moment at which you add the salt is of great importance.

1 If you add salt at the beginning of the cooking process, the meat will release few of its flavors, but the stock will be bland.

2 If you add salt halfway through the cooking process, the meat releases a few more flavors and the stock will taste better.

3 If you add salt at the end of the cooking process, the meat will lose many of its flavors and will be quite bland—but the stock will be delicious.

SAVE THE PEPPER FOR LAST!

You should never add pepper to a stock or water as it heats. Like tea that's infused for too long, adding pepper to the stock while it heats will make it bitter and acrid. And, since its flavor won't even penetrate the meat, there's no point adding pepper to a stock before or during cooking. Add pepper just before serving.

BOILING: A USER'S MANUAL

So, how do you make sure that both the meat and the stock are flavorful?

TRICKS OF THE BOILING TRADE

The meat shouldn't be cooked in water, but in a broth that has already been made with another piece of meat (which will be used in a shepherd's pie, for example.)

1

First, brown your broth meat in a little oil. As soon as it's browned on the top and on the bottom, add the vegetables, herbs, and enough water to cover the meat by ¾ to 1⅛ inches (2 to 3 cm).

2

Let it cook without simmering for three hours. During the cooking process, the browned part of the meat will enrich the stock. Whatever you do, don't add salt, because you want the meat to release as many flavors as possible into the stock.

3

After three hours, you'll have a delicious stock. Remove the meat.

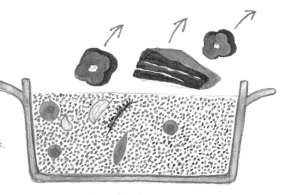

4

Replace the original meat with the meat that you'll serve for your meal. **And now you add the salt.**

5

Let it cook for the necessary time, still without boiling or even simmering.

The flavors of the stock and the meat will begin to balance out. Again, this is the phenomenon called osmosis.

And because the stock is already very rich, the meat will lose very few of its flavors to it. That's the secret to boiling meat!

THE BEST

POULTRY POACHED TO PERFECTION IN A POT

Chicken breast is often dry and that's because it's overcooked. The truth is, it requires less cooking time than the wings and thighs.

 1

To ensure that the breast cooks slower than the wings and thighs, don't cover it with the water or stock. The volume of liquid shouldn't surpass the height of the thighs.

2

Place a cloth over the breast and cover the pot.

3

As it heats, the liquid creates steam. Some of this steam will condense on the lid and drip back down onto the cloth. The breast will cook slowly, will remain humid, and therefore will not dry out. The cloth, hot and damp, cooks the breast at a lower temperature than the rest of the chicken, which cooks at the temperature of the water or stock.

WHY DOES IT TASTE BETTER THE NEXT DAY?

Ideally, dishes such as stew or blanquette should be made the day before. During the cooking process, certain fibers contract and leave little crevices on the surface of the meat. The broth fills these crevices and stays there. Each mouthful will contain not just meat but some of the stock that seeped into the fissures. The meat will seem juicier. This is why it often tastes better the next day.

After cooking, certain fibers contract and leave crevices in the meat. Capillary action will cause the stock to seep into these crevices and stay there.

NEITHER HOT NOR COLD

You often read: "Place the stewing meat in a hot stock so that the meat contracts and retains its juices." Actually, even though meat does contract during cooking, it releases its juices regardless. Hervé This amused himself by cutting a piece of meat in two, placing one half in a hot stock and the other in a cold stock. He removed both halves every fifteen minutes, dried them and weighed them. During the fifteen hours of cooking time, there was never any difference between the piece of meat cooked in hot stock and the one cooked in cold stock.

BRASING

Braising goes all the way back to an era when pots were buried in the embers to cook the meat they contained. Today, things are different.

FOR WHICH MEATS?

All types of meat that require quite a long cooking time and a gentle heat: braised beef, rack of pork, large fowl, etc.

THE TRADITIONAL METHOD

It was the combination of different types of heat that produced exceptional meat: radiation, convection, and conduction. The embers, extremely hot at the beginning of the cooking process, browned the meat. Then, as they cooled little by little, they cooked the meat at a low temperature.

The top of the meat browns at the beginning of the cooking process thanks to the heat transmitted by the lid.

The lid must be airtight to retain the humidity produced by the meat, the vegetables, and the accompanying liquid.

The whole piece of meat cooks in a humid atmosphere, which prevents it from drying out too much and shortens the length of the cooking time.

A small amount of liquid—no more than $1/3$ inch (1 cm)—and vegetables are added. The meat sits on top without steeping in the water or stock. The vegetables also create a lot of steam as they cook.

MODERN BRAISING

Today, braising is commonly done on a gas or electric stove. Unfortunately, these only heat from underneath. The top of the meat cooks in a humid environment like the traditional method, but it doesn't brown. And to avoid overcooking the bottom of the meat, we tend to add a lot of water to the pot, diluting the flavors of the meat. To finish, the water is reduced to enhance the taste of the stock.

NOT GREAT NOT GREAT

Here, it cooks in steam.

Here, it cooks in stock.

THE TWO KEYS TO SUCCESS

THE QUALITY OF THE POT

It should be cast iron and, if possible, black, to better store and release heat from each side. The lid should be as airtight as possible to prevent the steam from escaping and the meat drying out during the cooking process. Another reason for using cast iron is so that it can go in the oven.

A BLACK, CAST IRON POT, PLEASE!

A cast iron pot accumulates heat and diffuses it through the base and the sides. The contents of the pot cook evenly.

A stainless-steel saucepan barely transmits any heat through the sides.

BRAISE IN AN OVEN, BUT NOT JUST ANYWHERE

For a beautifully braised meat, it's preferable to place the pot in the oven rather than on a stove top. It should sit as high as possible in the oven so that the lid transmits the maximum amount of heat.

In an oven, the pot is surrounded by heat and it retransmits this heat all the way through its inside. Something to remember is that the meat is nearer to the bottom of the pot than to the top. To balance out the cooking inside, the lid must be hotter than the base. So, the pot should be placed at the top of the oven.

SUPER SUPER

> ## "The lid is important: it absolutely must seal the pot in a way that makes it airtight."

TRADITIONAL KNOW-HOW: SEALING A POT WITH DOUGH

The simplest way to hermetically seal your pot is to make a dough that you'll place between the pot and the lid. The heat will cause the dough to expand and the seal will be airtight.

Thanks to the sealing dough, there's lot of humidity inside the pot and the pressure increases. In this very humid environment, the meat doesn't dry out and cooks faster.

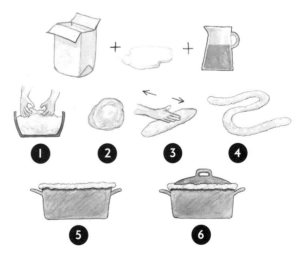

To make a sealing dough, all you need is flour, an egg white, and a little water.

BRAISING

THE ART OF BRAISING

There are two ways to braise meat: brown braising and white braising. So, how do they work?

BROWN BRAISING

Brown braising means that you brown the top and bottom of the meat before cooking it. The point of this is to give it stronger flavors.

As soon as it's been well browned, the meat is removed from the pot and the vegetables and herbs are added until they're at least ¾ to 1⅛ inches (2 to 3 cm) high.

The meat is then placed on top and water (or beef, veal, or poultry stock) is poured in up to the same height as the vegetables. I know, it's very precise, but this is how true braising is done. And then, into the oven!

WHITE BRAISING

It's exactly the same process, but you don't brown the meat. White braising is mainly reserved for poultry and, from time to time, pork, veal, and rabbit.

The cooking liquid absorbs the flavors of the browned meat. The air is so humid that the meat can't dry out. It cooks evenly.

The flavors of the browned meat seep into the liquid. And because there isn't a lot of it, it develops a strong and very flavorful taste. That's the art of braising!

This bed of vegetables will prevent the meat from coming into contact with the bottom of the pot and cooking too fast underneath.

> "**The meat isn't steeping** in the liquid and so it cooks in the steam."

BRAISED OR BOILED?

Never allow the liquid to cover the meat. If you do, it won't cook in hot and humid air but instead in boiling liquid. The difference in flavor and texture is incomparable.

👍 Little liquid = braised meat

👎 Liquid covering the meat = boiled meat

👎 Liquid half covering the meat = half braised, half boiled meat

RAGOUT

*Cooking meat in a ragout is a variant of braising.
Big meat cuts are cut into pieces to accelerate
the cooking process.*

THE METHOD

As with braising, there are
"brown" and "white" ragouts.
But, to make things a bit
more complicated, the meat in
white ragouts is lightly seared.
Basically, it's the same as
browning except you stop before
it begins to color.

Before adding the vegetables and
the stock, you can add some flour
to the meat to make the sauce
slightly thicker.

The great advantage of cooking
meat in a ragout is that the
cooking time is shorter.

A common problem is having too
much liquid, which dilutes the
flavor of the meat. So, don't put
too much in, and definitely do not
cover the meat entirely with water.

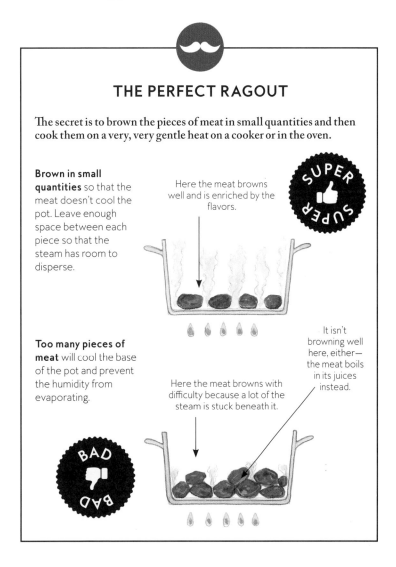

THE PERFECT RAGOUT

The secret is to brown the pieces of meat in small quantities and then
cook them on a very, very gentle heat on a cooker or in the oven.

Brown in small quantities so that the meat doesn't cool the pot. Leave enough space between each piece so that the steam has room to disperse.

Here the meat browns well and is enriched by the flavors.

Too many pieces of meat will cool the base of the pot and prevent the humidity from evaporating.

Here the meat browns with difficulty because a lot of the steam is stuck beneath it.

It isn't browning well here, either—the meat boils in its juices instead.

"To successfully cook a ragout,
think on a small scale and take your time!"

THE COOKING OF A STEAK SEEN FROM THE INSIDE

During the cooking of a steak, a lot of things you can't even imagine occur. Did you know that your meat lifts off the pan? That it swells and then retracts? That a part of the steak is poached in its own juices? Let's zoom in.

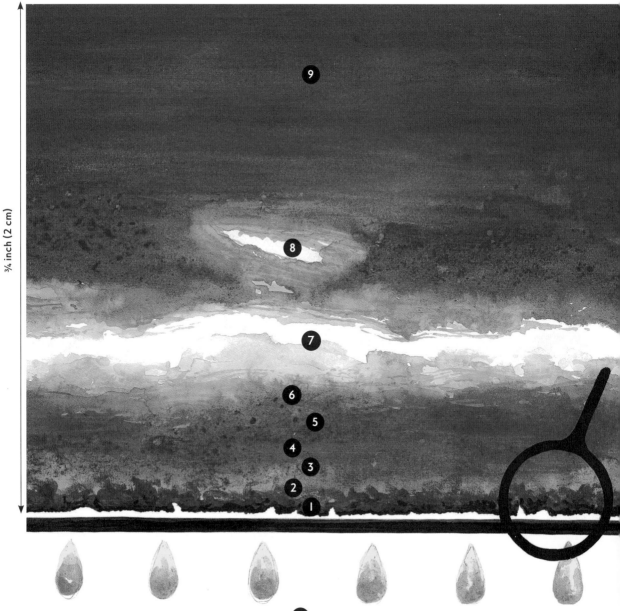

¾ inch (2 cm)

1 The part that browns is very, very thin—.03 inch (1 mm) thick, no more.

2 The color changes from red to a grayish brown because the myoglobin changes color.

3 Maillard reactions occur over a very thin layer: less than half a millimeter.

4 Here, the water contained inside the meat is so hot that it actually starts to boil.

5 Here, the water turns into steam. The meat dries out and its temperature can increase, up to 560 to 640°F—but as long as there's water inside, the temperature doesn't rise higher than 400°F because water cannot surpass this temperature.

6 Here, the fat melts and creates delicious flavors. It's the quality of this fat that gives a different flavor to the meat, depending on the type of animal.

7 The meat appears to turn almost white. There's the impression that it's turning white because the steam coagulates certain proteins, which disperse the light. This part of the meat will look white, even if it's not.

8 The heat rises so slowly that even after an hour of cooking, the top layer of a piece of meat 1½ to 2 inches (4 to 5 cm) thick still won't be hot.

9 Some of the steam dispersed during cooking sneaks between the fibers, rises, and causes the piece of meat to swell and take on a slightly curved shape.

THE CRUST IMPRISONS THE JUICES—TRUE OR FALSE?

Don't be fooled by those who tell you that by browning your meat, you're going to create a crust that will imprison the juices. This crust isn't impermeable, for several reasons:

The white "smoke" that rises is the water in the meat, which comes out through the surface and then passes through the crust before turning into steam.

After cooking, there are still juices stuck to the pan (you deglaze the pan to pick them up). The juices seeped through the crust and dried when they came into contact with the boiling-hot pan.

After the meat has rested, there's a little pool of juice around the meat. This juice came out from the top of the meat and seeped through the crust.

The steam
During the cooking process, some of the water contained in the meat turns into steam. This steam escapes through the top of the meat. As the water turns from its liquid state into steam, its volume expands by almost 1,700 : 1. The pressure beneath the meat is enormous! So huge that it sometimes lifts the meat off the pan in order to escape.

The crust
The crust that forms takes on a pretty, dark color and develops flavors thanks to the Maillard reactions. The more this crust dries and thickens, the more it delays the penetration of the heat into meat. Consequently, the more you cook it, the slower it cooks. So, increasing the temperature to the highest it can go won't cook your meat faster.

The frying pan
The temperature of the frying pan is about 356 to 392°F. The temperature of the steam that escapes is 212°F, so it cools the pan slightly. For this reason, you should never lower the flame after having placed your meat in the pan. The meat and the steam cool the pan down, so don't turn the flame down unless you want a piece of meat that never browns!

SHOULD YOU FLIP MEAT DURING THE COOKING PROCESS?

Answers to this simple question vary. The best thing to do is to observe what happens to two different steaks, one of them flipped one time, the other every thirty seconds.

IF YOU FLIP THE MEAT ONLY ONCE

1

TOP: it doesn't heat up and it doesn't cook.
BOTTOM: it heats up and begins to cook. A crust forms.

2

TOP: it doesn't heat up and it doesn't cook.
BOTTOM: it carries on cooking. The crust continues to form. The heat increases slowly.

3

TOP: it doesn't heat up and it doesn't cook.
BOTTOM: the crust is thick and overcooked and hinders the penetration of the heat. It begins to heat through, but then dries out just beneath the crust.

4

TOP: the browned part has already started to cool even though it's well-cooked just beneath. The heat continues to penetrate toward the center.
BOTTOM: the heat begins to cook the meat. A crust forms.

5

TOP: the surface continues to cool. The heat continues to penetrate toward the bottom.
BOTTOM: it's still cooking and begins to dry out. The crust continues to form and the heat rises slowly.

6

TOP: the surface is almost cold and the meat just beneath is cooling, too.
BOTTOM: the crust is thick and overcooked. The heat rises slowly.

The well-cooked layer, just beneath the crust, is very, very thick. It's a shame because that means that almost one-third of your meat is overcooked, dry, tough, and rough in texture—all that to get the center to the right temperature! You're worth a lot more than that.

The crust is very thick and rough.

The dry, overcooked part is very thick.

The crust is very thick and rough.

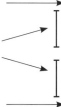

"Flip the meat often so that it cooks evenly." "Flip the meat just once so that it browns nicely . . ." "It's kind of surprising that no one can agree on something that can be so easily checked!"

IF YOU FLIP THE MEAT SEVERAL TIMES

❶

TOP: it doesn't heat up and it doesn't cook.
BOTTOM: it heats up and begins to cook. A crust forms.

❷

TOP: it doesn't heat up and it doesn't cook.
BOTTOM: it continues to cook. The crust continues to form. The heat increases.

❸

TOP: the surface is hot. The heat penetrates the meat but doesn't cook it very much.
BOTTOM: it heats up and begins to cook. A crust forms.

❹

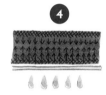

TOP: the heat from the second round of cooking penetrates the meat but doesn't cook it.
BOTTOM: it cooks and the crust continues to form. The heat from the first round of cooking continues to penetrate the inside of the meat, still without cooking it.

❺

TOP: the heat from the first round of cooking continues to penetrate without cooking the meat. The heat from the third round of cooking also penetrates the meat without cooking it.
BOTTOM: it cooks and a thin crust continues to form without preventing the heat from penetrating. The heat from the second round of cooking penetrates the meat without cooking it.

The well-cooked layer, just beneath the crust, is very thin. The entire piece of meat is hot, even in the center. The crust is crispy. Practically all the meat is evenly cooked and remains juicy and very tender. Well done!

The dry crust is very thin and crispy.

The well-cooked and dry area is very, very thin.

The dry crust is very thin and crispy.

CONCLUSION

Flipping a steak every thirty seconds gives a much better result:
a very thin, well-cooked layer and a hot, tender, and juicy piece of meat.

BASTING MEAT

We hear it often:
"To moisten your meat, baste it often as it cooks."
Except that no—that's not how it works at all.

THE MYTH OF BASTING

You've no doubt seen those pictures of cooks who generously baste their meat as it cooks. And how many times have you heard of the rule that meat should be basted during cooking to keep it moist?

This basting can be beneficial for many reasons, but certainly not for "moistening the meat." That's completely wrong.

IT STAYS ON THE OUTSIDE

When you're at home and it rains, your house is all wet and water even drips down in streams from the roof. But inside, you stay dry. The water doesn't go through the roof.

It's exactly the same for a piece of meat. When you baste it, you wet the outside, but not the inside; it doesn't penetrate the meat, not even by one tiny millimeter.

The juice doesn't penetrate the meat any more than rain penetrates the roof of a house.

"**When you baste meat,** the water contained inside spits. When it comes into contact with the fat, which is at the surface and a lot hotter than 212°F, the water transforms into steam and literally explodes."

WHAT ACTUALLY HAPPENS WHEN YOU BASTE MEAT?

IT COOKS THE TOP OF THE MEAT

The cooking fat around the sides of the meat is very, very, very hot. When you baste, this boiling-hot fat continues to heat and cook the upper part of the meat. The top and bottom of the meat will cook more evenly. In fact, it's a bit like cooking in the oven; it heats from above and below.

The boiling-hot cooking fat also cooks the upper part of the meat.

IT MAKES IT CRISPY

The heat of the fat used to baste has another use: by cooking the top of the meat at a high temperature, you prevent the humidity contained in the meat and the air from softening the browned surface. You also create what we call a "humid temperature" inside the meat because the humidity of the meat stays inside it and heats up. It cooks faster and the surface becomes crispy.

The meat stays crispy.

IT ADDS FLAVOR

As the meat cooks, lots of delicious juices form at the bottom of the cooking dish. Each time you baste, you pour some of these juices over the meat. Of course, every time you baste, most of these juices fall back into the pan, but some of them stick to the meat. That's what people call "moistening" the meat. Really, the juices don't moisten the meat but sit on top of it.

The juices are poured onto the meat, adding flavor.

BASTING WITH BUTTER

Here's where it gets interesting. The secret to basting is to add butter as soon as your meat is browned. Lower the flame to avoid burning it and add garlic, thyme, rosemary, or other things you like. Baste the meat continuously until it's finished cooking. As the butter heats it creates flavors so much more delicious than those created with only oil.

As it melts, the butter cooks the meat and creates even more juices and flavors.

RESTING MEAT

*Have you ever cut into a piece of meat and had
lots of juice come out? To avoid this,
the trick is to let it rest in aluminum foil.
But you can do even better than that . . .*

WHY REST MEAT?

Let's set the record straight about a certain widespread belief: resting doesn't "relax" the meat, as we're often told. The animal wasn't tense or stressed!

During cooking, some of the water contained in the meat evaporates. The surface dries out due to the heat, and as it dries, the meat becomes tough.

When you rest it, covered in aluminum foil and away from the flame, the dry areas absorb some of the juices that are still at the center of the meat, a bit like blotting paper absorbs an ink stain. And most of all, as they cool the juices thicken, meaning they don't flow as easily when you cut the meat.

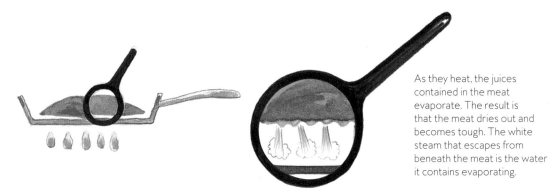

As they heat, the juices contained in the meat evaporate. The result is that the meat dries out and becomes tough. The white steam that escapes from beneath the meat is the water it contains evaporating.

WHAT HAPPENS WHEN MEAT IS RESTING

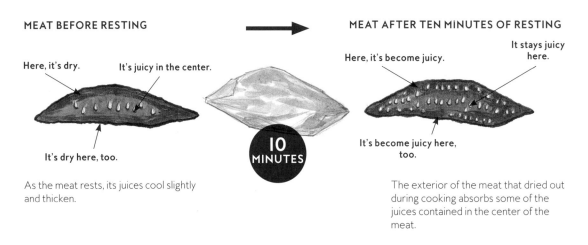

MEAT BEFORE RESTING

Here, it's dry.

It's juicy in the center.

It's dry here, too.

As the meat rests, its juices cool slightly and thicken.

10 MINUTES

MEAT AFTER TEN MINUTES OF RESTING

It stays juicy here.

Here, it's become juicy.

It's become juicy here, too.

The exterior of the meat that dried out during cooking absorbs some of the juices contained in the center of the meat.

HOW TO REST MEAT

It's simple: wrap the piece of meat in aluminum foil and leave it to rest. And don't hesitate to double or even triple the layer of aluminum foil—it will insulate the heat even better.

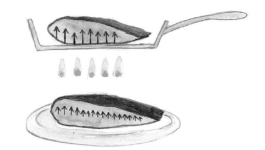

HOW LONG?

The idea that you should "leave the meat to rest for the same amount of time it took to cook it" has no scientific foundation. Make it simple and rest the meat according to its thickness: five minutes for a thin steak, ten minutes for a good-sized rib-eye steak, fifteen minutes for other meat cuts. This is more than enough time.

THERMAL INERTIA

You might think that the meat will be lukewarm by the time you serve it, but that's not quite true.

When you're cycling and you stop pedaling, does the bicycle stop all of a sudden? No, of course not—it continues to move forward.

The heat inside a piece of meat is exactly the same. It disperses itself like a wave through the meat. When you stop cooking, the heat doesn't immediately stop, but continues to move.

THE THICKER, THE WARMER

THE RIGHT MOMENT TO REST MEAT

The most common meat resting method consists of resting it after it's cooked. That's very good. But you can do even better. You can rest your meat BEFORE the end of the cooking process. Don't worry, it's super simple.

If you rest the meat after cooking, the beautiful, crispy skin will slacken and absorb some of the humidity inside the meat.

ROAST CHICKEN

For chicken, it's quite a common process. To make it truly incredible, rest the chicken fifteen minutes before the end of the cooking time. The juices spread nicely through the meat and thicken. The meat doesn't cool down but the skin softens. Once you put it back in a very, very hot oven, at 465°F for ten minutes, the skin will dry out again and become crisp.

THE BEST THE BEST

If you rest the chicken before the end of the cooking process and put it back into a very hot oven, the juices will have thickened and spread through the meat and the skin will become crispy again.

OTHER MEATS

It's exactly the same for other meats. When meat rests at the end of the cooking process, the crispy part humidifies and softens. This is too bad! Instead, try resting your meat before it's completely cooked and apply our little secret: after resting, cook the meat again under a broiler, in a pan, or in a very, very hot oven, just enough to dry the exterior and give it back its crispiness.

MAKING MEAT JUICIER

Apart from seasoning your meat a long time in advance, there's another great way to make meat more tender and, most of all, juicier. Despite what you may have learned, you should prick the meat. Yes, really.

WHY DOES MEAT LOSE ITS JUICES DURING COOKING?

Have you ever washed a wool sweater in a machine switched to the cotton setting at 140°F? Without a doubt, the sweater shrank.

This is precisely what happens when you cook meat. The collagen shrinks during cooking, just like a wool sweater shrinks when you wash it on too high a temperature. As it shrinks, the collagen releases juices contained in the meat, which is in the process of drying out. This is one of the reasons why a "medium rare" piece of meat is firmer than a "rare" piece of meat.

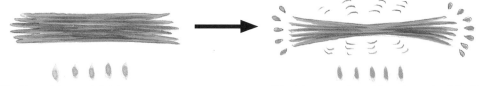

The fibers tighten and shrink.

The juices are released from the ends of the fibers.

WHY SHOULD YOU PRICK THE MEAT?

When, before cooking, you prick a piece of meat with big needles, like those used in syringes, the collagen fibers are cut. As the meat cooks, the cut fibers will contract less and so release fewer juices. The meat will be more tender.

THE BONUS EFFECT

During cooking, one of the meat's proteins is modified. This protein is called myosin. As it mixes with the meat's juices, the myosin thickens them. Because the juices are thicker, they don't flow as easily and the meat is juicier. This works even better when you broil or roast the meat at a high temperature.

Because they're cut in different places, the fibers don't contract very much and so release very few juices.

"**When you grill meat,** all the tiny holes allow the flavors of the smoke to better penetrate the meat and give it more taste. Extraordinary!"

HOW TO PRICK MEAT?

To make the process effective, the meat must be pricked perpendicularly to its fibers. Looking at your piece of meat, you'll be able to see the direction of the fibers very well. They look like little tubes that all go in the same direction. To help you, here are a few examples.

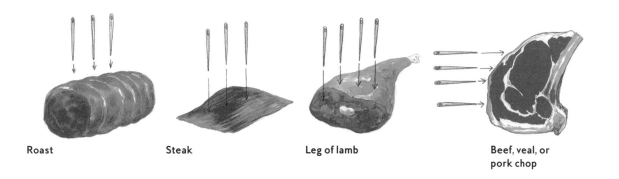

Roast   Steak   Leg of lamb   Beef, veal, or pork chop

ARE THE RED JUICES BLOOD?

ANOTHER MYTH TO DISPEL

How many times have you read that you should avoid pricking the meat so that the blood doesn't leak out?

But there's no blood left in a piece of meat bought from the butcher shop. The animal has been bled and all the blood removed. What's leaking out might be red, but it's not blood.

MYOGLOBIN, ANOTHER PROTEIN

The meat is colored by a red protein called myoglobin. It's this myoglobin that gives the juices their color.

The color of meat depends on the quantity of myoglobin it contains. Bison and wild duck contain a lot of myoglobin, beef a little less, and veal, chicken, and turkey contain very little. That's why the juices in a beef rib chop are dark red, the juices in veal light pink, and the juices in chicken or turkey, transparent. It's got nothing to do with blood.

THE COLOR OF THE JUICES DEPENDS ON THE QUANTITY OF MYOGLOBIN

Myoglobin is just like red dye in a glass of water—the more there is, the redder the water becomes. In meat, the more myoglobin there is, the redder it is.

If you add a small amount of dye, the water turns pale pink
=
a small quantity of myoglobin = the meat and its juices are pale pink, like a veal chop.

If you add a large amount of dye, the water turns dark red.
=
a large quantity of myoglobin = the meat and its juices are dark red, like a beef rib chop.

HOW TO CREATE MORE JUICES

When you cook a piece of meat, juices escape. These are called exudates. As they exit the meat, these exudates take flavor compounds with them. The goal is to lose as little of the juice as possible.

IN A FRYING PAN, IN A SAUTÉ PAN, IN A POT

When meat comes into contact with a burning-hot surface, it expels the juices contained below its surface. The water evaporates and the flavor compounds concentrate and begin to brown; we call this "caramelizing." And when the meat sits on the bottom of the pan, the little pieces of caramelized compounds stuck there also give it lots of flavor.

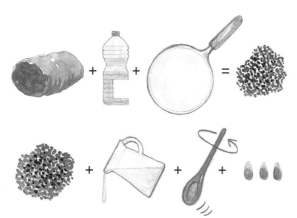

TIPS TO CREATE MORE JUICES

Lightly oil your meat before browning it: you'll multiply the number of Maillard reactions and create more juices. A thin layer is enough, no need to deep-fry it!

Use a frying pan made of a good material: a nonstick pan creates very few caramelized juices because the meat doesn't stick and doesn't heat enough. An iron or stainless steel frying pan will create a lot more juices.

HOW TO COLLECT THEM

Remove the meat, add a little liquid in which the juices will dissolve, and collect all the little pieces attached to the bottom. Cook for two to three minutes, gently scraping the bottom of the pan so as to leave nothing behind.

IN WATER

The meat releases some of its juices into the water as it cooks.

TIPS TO CREATE MORE JUICES

Brown your meat beforehand: the juices created will disperse into the broth and give it a lot more flavor.

Add salt to the cooking water, or don't: if you don't add salt, some of the meat's juices will spread into the cooking liquid and result in a tasty broth.

If, on the contrary, you want a very flavorful piece of meat, add salt at the beginning of the cooking process to hinder the spreading of the juices from the meat into the liquid.

And for a good balance between both, add salt halfway through cooking.

SUPER SUPER

IN THE OVEN

The same principle applies when you cook using the oven. Juices are created on the surface of the meat and drip into the bottom of the dish.

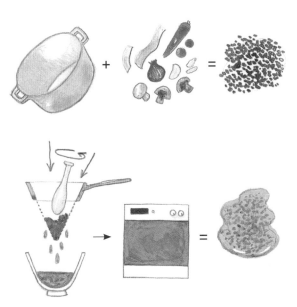

TIPS TO CREATE MORE JUICES

Lightly oil your meat before cooking it: as with pan-fried meat, a thin layer of oil will significantly increase the quantity of juices. When you baste the meat with the juices from the bottom of the dish, you're also covering it in the flavor compounds that escaped to the bottom.

Always ask your butcher for extra meat trimmings: lightly oil them and place them in the cooking dish with the meat; they'll brown, too, and create a lot of juices.

You can also add carrots, onions, mushrooms, garlic, or thyme, for example, which will also create juices.

Choose an oven dish made of the correct material: the material of the pan is crucial. Iron and stainless steel create a lot of juices, and they do it fast; ceramic and glass don't create as many.

HOW TO COLLECT THEM

Remove the meat, add two or three tablespoons of liquid to the oven dish, scrape, and return to the oven for five minutes. Then, pour the herbs and juices through a strainer or a sieve, crushing the mixture with the back of a spoon or a potato masher to extract all the flavors. Use everything and leave nothing at all!

IN A BRAISING LIQUID

The meat will naturally release juices that will seep into the braising liquid. During cooking, this liquid evaporates, condenses on the lid, and drips back down onto the meat, depositing onto it the juices it had lost. The vegetables and herbs you put in the pot will also create flavorful juices.

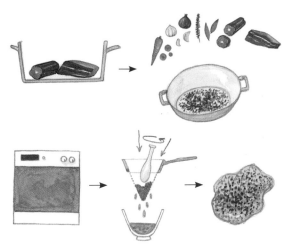

TIPS TO CREATE MORE JUICES

First, brown your meat in the pot: this will create juices that will dissolve into the liquid during the braising process. Then add your vegetables and your herbs and put the pot into the oven.

Use a cast iron pot: it produces more radiant heat and will increase the quantity of juices.

HOW TO COLLECT THEM

Like with oven cooking, when the cooking is finished, pass the braising liquid through a sieve and crush it to collect all of the juices. Then put it back into the pot and reduce it on a medium heat for five or ten minutes to evaporate some of the water and concentrate the flavors.

ALL ABOUT THERMAL SHOCK

You often read that you should "remove the meat from the refrigerator thirty minutes to an hour before cooking it to avoid thermal shock, which will make it tough." That's not correct, and here's why . . .

IT'S NOT THE TEMPERATURE OF THE MEAT THAT'S IMPORTANT

Here are two illustrative examples:

SCENARIO 1

Remove your meat from the refrigerator, leave it at room temperature for one hour, and cook it on a grill at 464°F.
The thermal shock is 464°F–68°F = 396°F.

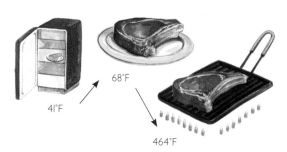

68°F

41°F

464°F

SCENARIO 2

Remove your meat from the refrigerator and immediately place it onto the grill at 392°F.
The thermal shock is 392°F–41°F = 351°F.

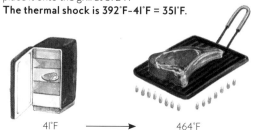

41°F

464°F

When it goes directly from cold to the grill, the meat undergoes a thermal shock that's not as strong as it is when it's been left at room temperature. However, it's still just as tender. It's not the original temperature of the meat that matters, but the cooking temperature.

THERMAL SHOCK HELPS BROWN THE MEAT

In fact, thermal shock is exactly what we want. Here's why:

OPTION 1

When you cook a steak, do you put it in a lukewarm or a hot pan? Hot, of course, or even very hot, so that the steak browns well.

In a burning-hot pan, the meat browns and turns crispy.

Without even realizing, you're looking to create this thermal shock in order to "caramelize" the meat.

OPTION 2

If you cook this same steak in a lukewarm pan, the thermal shock will be a lot less strong.

In a lukewarm pan, the meat cooks but will never be crispy or delicious.

Honestly, would you choose thermal shock and a golden-brown piece of meat or no thermal shock and a limp piece of meat?

It's not thermal shock that toughens meat. Thermal shock is actually necessary and beneficial if you want a browned and juicy piece of meat.

In reality, meat becomes tough due to the fact that its proteins twist in the heat and expel the juices contained inside. This is why well-cooked meat is drier than medium rare meat.

DRY HEAT AND HUMID HEAT

We've all put a hand in a very hot oven for a few seconds and not been burned in the slightest. Try and do the same over a pot of boiling water, albeit much less hot, and tell me how it feels. The difference is the heat transfer coefficient.

HERE ARE TWO EXAMPLES TO HELP YOU UNDERSTAND

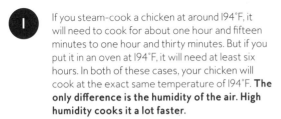

1 If you steam-cook a chicken at around 194°F, it will need to cook for about one hour and fifteen minutes to one hour and thirty minutes. But if you put it in an oven at 194°F, it will need at least six hours. In both of these cases, your chicken will cook at the exact same temperature of 194°F. **The only difference is the humidity of the air. High humidity cooks it a lot faster.**

2 Put a good bottle of rosé wine in the refrigerator: it will need at least one hour before it gets cold. Put it in ice water and it will be cold in only fifteen minutes. **Here, too, the humid water transmits the cold faster than the air.**

HOW DOES IT WORK?

Dry air transmits heat so poorly that it's sometimes even used as insulation in the walls of houses. Humid air, on the other hand, transmits heat very well. The transmission of heat is called the "heat transfer coefficient." It's a dull sort of name for it, I know. All you have to know is that very humid air transmits up to 1,000 times more heat than very dry air.

PUTTING THIS INTO ACTION

This is where it gets interesting! You can oven-cook meat faster by putting a dish of boiling water on the oven floor. This water will create steam that will increase the heat transmission and accelerate the cooking process.

Just before the end of the cooking time, open your oven to evacuate the humidity and turn on the broiler to brown the meat.

STEAM VERSUS CONDENSATION

People often confuse steam with condensation.

The white steam that rises from a pot of boiling water isn't actually steam, it's condensation. It's visible because it's a mixture of air and tiny droplets of water.

Steam, on the other hand, is invisible because it's a mixture of hot air and water in the gas phase.

TELL ME WHERE YOU COOK AND I'LL TELL YOU HOW TO DO IT

Cookbooks give us temperatures and cooking times. That's good, they help. Except that these times and temperatures should be slightly modified according to where you are and to the season.

A LITTLE PHYSICS LESSON

The higher the altitude, the lower the boiling temperature of water is. And once water is boiling, its temperature can't get any higher.

So, the higher up you are, the more the cooking times of boiled or braised meat must be extended. Cooking a stew at just over 6,500 feet (2,000 meters) altitude takes longer than if you were by the sea because the water doesn't get any hotter than 199.4°F, its boiling point.

158°F

Everest
29,000 ft/8,848 m

183.2°F

Mont-Blanc
15,778 ft/4,809 m

199.4°F

6,500 ft/2,000 m

212°F

0 ft/0 m

Boiling temperatures according to altitude

IN THE MOUNTAINS

The air in the mountains is a lot drier than by the sea. This should be taken into account when cooking meat in the oven, because dry air doesn't transmit heat as well as humid air.

Also, because the air is very dry, the surface of the meat dries out and browns quickly, although the time needed to cook the inside doesn't change. This means that when cooking in the mountains you should adjust the temperature so that it's slightly lower than the temperature used at sea level and cook the meat for a little longer to ensure it remains juicy.

Finally, the perception of flavors also changes because the mouth and nose are drier, although each person reacts differently to this. For some, it's necessary to add a lot of salt, whereas for others, a small amount of extra salt is enough. This is why meals served on planes are usually spicy: it's to distract our attention from the possible lack of salt.

IN HUMID AREAS

Humid air transmits heat better than dry air. If you cook your meat in an oven that contains very humid air, it will cook faster but will be difficult to brown.

In New York, for example, the air is very dry in winter and very humid in summer. This difference in humidity has an impact on the length of cooking times. In winter, a leg of lamb or a roast chicken requires around ten minutes of extra cooking time, even if the temperature of the oven is exactly the same.

BONES OR NO BONES IN A STOCK?

You often read that you can add bones to a broth or stock to give them more flavor. But can bones actually do this or is using them just force of habit?

THE PARTS OF THE BONE YOU USE ARE IMPORTANT

Four-fifths of a bone is composed of calcium. This calcium, which doesn't break down in 100 years on a skeleton, isn't going to dissolve in a few hours in some water. So no, the bone itself gives absolutely no flavor to a stock. In that case, which parts of it do?

 What's on it

There are a lot of little pieces of meat stuck to bones. It's almost nothing and the total amount weighs only a couple of grams.

 What's inside it

All bones aren't identical: there are short bones, long ones, rib bones. . . . In the center of the long bones, those belonging to the limbs, and the flat bones, those belonging to the ribs, there is marrow. It's this marrow that can add a lot of flavor.

3 **What's at the end of it**

The ends of the joint bones are rounded and covered in cartilage, which can add flavor and texture, a little like the gelatin that comes from melted collagen.

HOW BONES ARE USED

There's very little point in adding bones, even the best ones, to a stock. The way to truly add flavor is by browning the bones BEFORE adding them to the stock.

Cover the bones in a very, very thin layer of oil and cook them for one hour in an oven at 390°F. At the end of the cooking time the marrow will have begun to melt and create juices; the little pieces of meat on the bones, like the cartilage, will have browned. Now you have bones that will add flavor to your stock.

First in the oven . . .   and then into the stock . . .

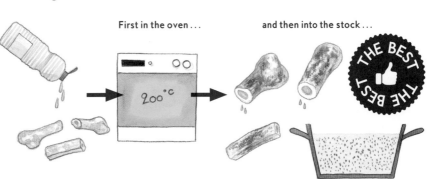

THE BEST THE BEST

MAILLARD REACTIONS

Maillard reactions are reactions between reducing sugars and amino acids. They occur in three stages, but they're really not that complicated to create.

A LITTLE HISTORY

Louis-Camille Maillard was a French doctor born in 1878. After having obtained his high school diploma at the age of sixteen, he obtained his bachelor's degree in economic and social sciences at nineteen. He had nothing to do with the world of cooking; he studied renal pathology! During his research, he studied a reaction that occurred between sugars and amino acids and discovered interesting things from it, to which he gave his name. His research was then forgotten for several decades. During the Second World War the American army sought to understand why certain of its soldiers' dehydrated food rations went brown over time. They discovered that it was due to one of the Maillard reactions, and suddenly Maillard's work was resurrected. It is now used every day in gastronomy as well as the medical and oil industries.

THE SCIENCE

As they heat, the reducing sugars and amino acids contained inside meat link together by creating hundreds of new molecules. They lose some of their water and produce what's known as a Schiff base. As they continue to heat, the link between the sugars and the amino acids degenerates, the loss of water accelerates, and the whole thing leads to what are called Amadori and Heynes rearrangements. The result is something called Strecker degradation, which gives us the very active brown pigment compounds and aroma compounds.

AND IN ENGLISH?

Maillard reactions create the delicious aromas of browned meat, roasted chicken, toasted bread crusts, etc.

A QUESTION OF HEAT

Contrary to what you may hear, Maillard reactions already begin to occur at room temperature, very slowly, without cooking. For example, cured ham turns a dark color when drying in the open air due to, among other causes, the Maillard reactions.

When the heat increases, the reactions multiply. Every time the heat increases by 50°F, the number of reactions is multiplied by 100.

As the heat goes from room temperature at 68°F to the temperature of the surface of the meat at 266°F, the number of reactions is multiplied by ten quintillion, which is 10,000,000,000,000,000,000.

Once the meat has dried out a little and its temperature increases to above 266°F (I'm talking about the temperature of the meat, not of the pan or the oven), the reactions occur very rapidly.

If the temperature of the surface of the meat is increased even further to above 356°F, these reactions make way for another reaction called pyrolysis, which decomposes meat with high temperatures.

THE MAILLARD REACTIONS APPLIED TO A BEEF RIB STEAK

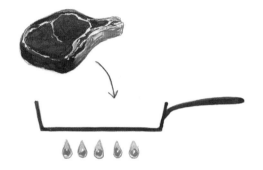

1 Place your rib steak in a burning-hot frying pan.

2 The heat causes the reducing sugars and amino acids to link together (it's invisible to the naked eye). They begin to release water, which appears as white steam that begins to rise from the pan.

3 The water loss and the steam increase. Aromas begin to fill the kitchen. The color of the bottom of the meat begins to change from red to gray.

4 The water loss continues to increase, the surface of the meat dries out and begins to brown. The aromas become more and more delicious. The color changes from gray to a pretty, appetizing dark brown.

MAILLARD REACTIONS

THINGS TO ABSOLUTELY AVOID

1 TOO LOW A HEAT

Of course, if you don't have enough heat, you'll get very few Maillard reactions. Try browning a steak in a pan on a gentle heat. By the time the reactions and browning occur, it'll be overcooked. So, turn up the heat!

212°F
Booo

2 A PROGRESSIVE HEAT

If you start cooking too gently and then increase the flame, the proteins at the surface of the meat will begin to clot. The Maillard reactions won't be able to modify them and the meat won't brown properly. So, keep the flame strong from the beginning!

284°F → 428°F
Shame . . .

3 TOO MUCH WATER

Too much water stops Maillard reactions from occurring. This is why you should never cook a roast or a chicken in liquid (except fat) if you want it to brown in the slightest. It's also why you usually brown meat before braising it.

4 ACIDIC MARINADES

The acidity of the meat hugely hinders the triggering of Maillard reactions. That's why meat that's been marinated in an acid such as red wine doesn't brown during cooking, even if it's been rinsed and dried in between.

"Developing Maillard reactions allows for more flavors and aromas and for the formation of a crispy surface that will contrast with the juiciness of the inside."

WHAT YOU NEED FOR THE BEST MAILLARD REACTIONS

❶ HEAT

First, you need heat, a lot of heat: a frying pan, a skillet, or a grill pan heated to at least 356°F to rapidly trigger the first reactions.

356°F–428°F
Yes!

❷ FAT

You need sugars, amino acids, and water. All of these are already contained inside the meat. But if you add fat, you increase the transmission of heat and so the speed of the reactions. This is why oiled meat browns so much better, faster, and more evenly than meat without oil.

What talent!

❸ WATER, YES, BUT NOT TOO MUCH!

As we've just seen, you need water, yes, but not too much! Meat contains between 70 percent and 80 percent water so Maillard reactions are more effectively produced when there's only 30 percent to 60 percent water.

For this, there are two important things to do:

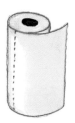

- Dry the meat with a paper towel before browning it;

or

- Remove the meat from the refrigerator and leave it on a grilling rack for two to three hours so that the surface begins to dry out.

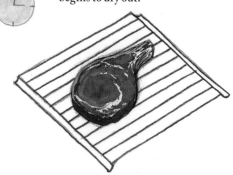

Here, we're verging on perfection.

FAT ISN'T JUST FAT!

When meat cooks, some of its fat melts and develops a lot of flavors. Without this fat, there'd be practically no difference in flavor between pork, beef, and chicken. No fat, no flavor, or very little . . .

DURING COOKING

When, to make fried potatoes, you use duck fat instead of peanut oil, it's to give the potatoes the taste of duck. When you use sesame oil instead of olive oil in a salad, it's to have the flavor of toasted sesame seeds. In both cases, you're using fat, but they don't have the same flavors. It's exactly the same for meat fats. All of the meat's flavor is acquired during cooking, thanks to the fat.

The other major advantage of fat is that when it melts during cooking, its stops the temperature of the inside of the meat from increasing too fast and becoming overcooked and dry. For example, veal or pork chops dry out very fast because they contain very little intramuscular fat.

When you cook your meat, the fat melts, transforms and mixes with sugars, amino acids, and carbohydrates. Together they create an incredible number of new molecules that create chain reactions. These generate thousands of flavors and aromas that give the meat a large part of its flavor.

AFTER COOKING

The true magic happens in your mouth. We're the ones who give even more flavor to the meat.

When you chew, your mouth fills with fat from the meat and its juices. Your salivary glands begin to work like crazy to produce more saliva. And because you have more saliva in your mouth, which mixes with the fat and the meat, you get the impression that this meat is juicier than it actually is.

Basically, our mouths produce a large amount of the meat's juiciness.

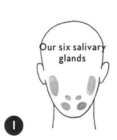

Our six salivary glands

1 Before being chewed, the piece of meat develops few flavors or aromas.

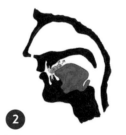

2 When we chew, we cut up and crush the piece of meat, causing it to develop more flavors and aromas.

3 Our six salivary glands (three on each side of the mouth) begin to work like crazy and produce lots of saliva.

4 The saliva mixes with the little pieces of meat. Because there's more liquid, there's a larger contact area between the meat, the saliva, the taste buds, and the nose's olfactory mucus.

There are so many flavors and aromas in the mouth that the flavor of the meat is intensified.

"Fifty years ago, people still often larded big cuts of meat. There was one reason: meat was a lot tougher than it is today. The fat added inside the meat made the brain believe that the meat was more tender and juicy than it really was."

The difference in flavor between beef breeds is mainly linked to fat. Without this difference in fat, there would be no difference in flavor between a Charolais and an Angus or a Hereford and a Normande.

EXPERT DEBATE

Today there are many debates among scientists about whether the "fat" flavor should be added to group of primary flavors, which include salty, sweet, bitter, and sour.

THE CHOICE OF MARBLING

When you choose a piece of meat, there should be fat inside the muscle—the famous marbling—to avoid it tasting bland.

If you choose tenderloin it will be very tender but not very interesting taste-wise, whereas if you choose a marbled rib-eye steak, it will have a lot more flavor.

THE COLOR OF FAT IN BEEF REVEALS ITS DIET: IF IT'S A LITTLE YELLOW, IT MEANS THE ANIMAL WAS FED ON GRASS. IF IT'S VERY WHITE, THEN THE ANIMAL WAS FATTENED ON CORN SILAGE.

THE YELLOW COLOR OF THE FAT COMES FROM THE BETA-CAROTENE IN GRASS, THE SAME ORANGE PIGMENT FOUND IN CARROTS.

SURPRISING FACT!

For animals, fat is an energy reserve used when they need to exert themselves physically or don't have enough food. For a cow, 2.2 lb of fat produces as much energy as 2.2 lb of gas in a car.

"Strictly speaking, the fat surrounding a rib-eye steak isn't animal fat. This white tissue contains fat, but also proteins and collagen. The whole thing is quite tough and difficult to chew. To make it more tender and succulent, it needs to be pricked several times to break down the fatty cells."

WHAT IS COLLAGEN?

You hear about collagen a lot these days, but what exactly is it?

COLLAGEN IS A ROPE...

Collagen is structured like a rope. At its core are three polypeptide strands that wrap around each other. Several groups of additional strands continue to wrap around this core until it forms a solid rope.

...AND A RESTRAINT SHEATH

Once assembled, these ropes form a sheath that surrounds the fibers of the meat to grip them tightly against each other.

This sheath surrounds the fibers, but also the fascicles of muscular fibers and the fascicles of fascicles, etc., until it surrounds the entire muscle.

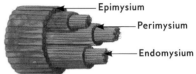

- Epimysium
- Perimysium
- Endomysium

WHY IT SORT OF MAKES LIFE DIFFICULT

As they heat, the collagen sheaths shrink, contract, and expel the juices contained inside the fibers.

140°F

The collagen tightens but doesn't contract yet. It expels very few juices.

154.4°F

The more the temperature increases, the more it contracts.

212°F

The more it contracts, the more juices the fibers expel.

WHAT CAN WE DO ABOUT IT?

When the collagen is thin and not very resistant, a fast-cooking process is enough to make it melt and tenderize the meat.

But, on the other hand, when it's thick and tough, it requires slow cooking in a humid environment to make it melt. It then turns into gelatin, which absorbs the water. The result: the meat becomes juicy once again.

This is why with even a long cooking process, tough meats become juicy.

TENDER MEAT, TOUGH MEAT— WHAT'S THE DIFFERENCE?

There are muscles that work hard and others that work less. They're not all structured in the same way, and this is a big part of what makes a tender meat or a tough meat.

THE GRAIN OF THE MEAT

The pros use the term "grain of the meat" to define the structure and the size of the fibers, also referred to as the thickness of the fibers.

The more a muscle carries out prolonged and/or extensive physical effort, the thicker and shorter its fibers are.

In contrast, the lazier a muscle is, the thinner and longer its fibers are.

The thick fibers of the working muscles are a lot more difficult to chew than the thin fibers of the lazy muscles.

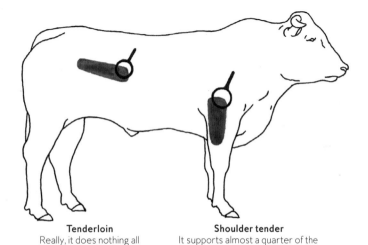

Tenderloin
Really, it does nothing all day, a true slacker!

Shoulder tender
It supports almost a quarter of the cow's weight, and on top of this, it's what allows it to walk.

COLLAGEN, YET AGAIN . . .

The fibers of the lazy muscles are enveloped in a thin, tender collagen, whereas the working muscles are surrounded by a thick, hard collagen. This is why cooking times (fast or slow) are adapted according to whether the meat is tender or tough.

Lazy muscle = fine grain

Working muscle = coarse grain

Fine grain = thin collagen = tender meat

Coarse grain = thick collagen= tough meat

A MATTER OF TASTE

Do we really taste meat with our mouths? Of course!
You don't need to be a genius to understand that.
But you also taste food with your nose. How does this work?

A STUFFY NOSE AND THE FLAVORS DISAPPEAR

Have you ever noticed that you suddenly can't taste what you're eating when you have a cold? This is because a large part of the flavor isn't perceived by the mouth, but by the nose. The mouth perceives tastes and the back of the nose perceives aromas.

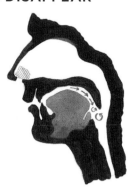

When the nose is blocked, the air doesn't flow; the aromas no longer circulate and don't rise toward the mucus. They stay stuck at the back of the mouth. The result is that the meat doesn't seem to have any flavor.

OTHER VERY IMPORTANT THINGS TO KNOW

FAT

Take a relatively fatty piece of meat. When you chew it, the fat leaves a light film on your taste buds. You won't be able to taste the subtle flavors in the meat, but you'll be able to taste the meat for longer. This is what we call the length on the palate. So, either you drain off the fat from a stewing stock to fully perceive the finesse of its flavors, or you leave the fat for less-precise but longer-lasting flavors.

SOUND

When you chew a piece of meat, the sound is also important. The trigeminal nerve, which runs through the mouth, nose, and forehead, perceives the vibrations of the meat as it's crushed by the teeth. The brain receives these vibrations and signals and determines that you're eating crispy meat at the same time as the mouth and nose distinguish the flavors and aromas. As we grow older, this nerve transmits less information to the brain and food seems blander, even though it actually isn't.

CHEWING

A piece of beef tenderloin has less flavor than a steak because it's very tender and you chew it faster. When you chew, saliva comes into contact with the food. This saliva increases the quantity of the matter that transmits flavors and aromas, so the more saliva there is, the more flavor the meat develops. That's why a tartare chopped with a knife is tastier than one made with ground meat. You chew the slices longer, whereas you swallow the ground meat practically without chewing it.

MULTISENSORIAL!

The perception of flavor encompasses the flavors perceived by the tongue, the aromas sensed by the nose, and the chewing sensations.

"When you chew, the taste buds distinguish part of the flavor while the aromas move toward the back of the mouth and rise toward the olfactory mucosa situated in the nose."

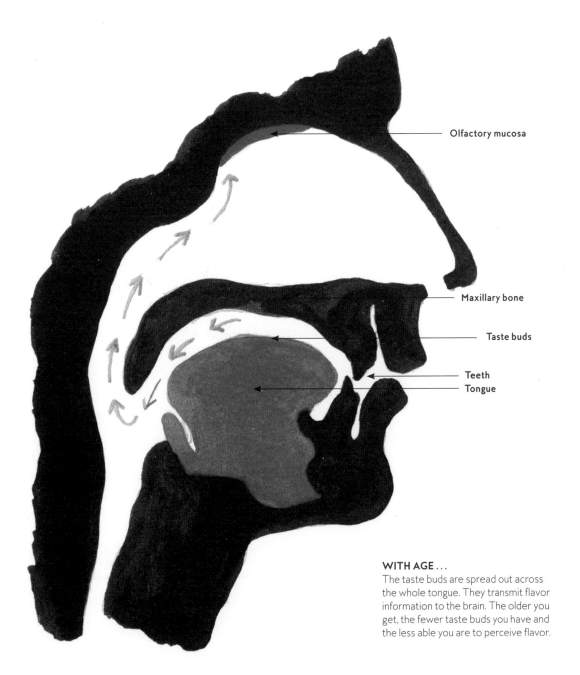

Olfactory mucosa

Maxillary bone

Taste buds

Teeth
Tongue

WITH AGE...
The taste buds are spread out across the whole tongue. They transmit flavor information to the brain. The older you get, the fewer taste buds you have and the less able you are to perceive flavor.

LET'S TALK MEAT

*Here are a few key points to help you determine the qualities
and characteristics of a piece of meat.*

COLOR

FLAVOR

Olfactory
mucosa =
aromas

Taste buds
= flavors

THE SCIENCE

The beautiful red or pink color of meat is directly linked to
the color of a protein called myoglobin. The more myoglobin
there is in the muscle, the more intensely red it is. When
meat is preserved, the myoglobin eventually oxidizes
and turns brown. The meat then becomes a deeper red
color. But the color also depends on the muscle: a steak is
darker than a strip loin because it naturally contains more
myoglobin.

WHY DOES THE COLOR CHANGE DURING
COOKING?

Proteins are modified when heated. This is the case with
myoglobin, whose color changes to gray and then to brown.
That's why a beautiful slice of a roast is brown on the well-
cooked exterior, gray on the medium-cooked areas, and red
on the undercooked areas. Beef is redder than veal or pork
because it contains more myoglobin (not because it contains
more blood).

THE SCIENCE

Flavor means the mixture of flavors and aromas. When
you chew, the nonvolatile molecules create the flavors
perceived by the mouth's taste buds. The volatile molecules,
freed as you chew, make up the aromas and move toward
the olfactory mucosa of the nose. And as if that wasn't
complicated enough, saliva also plays an important role in
developing the flavors and in slightly delaying the movement
of the aromas toward the nose.

WHY DOES IT TASTE GOOD?

The flavor of the meat is essentially linked to the fat
contained in the muscles: the marbling. The bigger the
quantity of intramuscular fat, the more intense the flavor.
  During cooking, some of the fat oxidizes and develops an
incredible amount of flavors and aromas and, most of all, it
retains certain volatile compounds that would have escaped.

"The qualities of a piece of meat come as much from the meat itself as they do from the conditions under which it is tasted."

JUICINESS

TENDERNESS

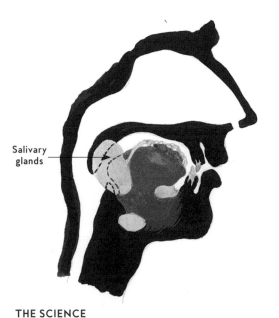

Salivary glands

Tough meat (thick collagen)

Tender meat (thin collagen)

Collagen is a structure that surrounds the fibers, the fascicles of fibers, and eventually the entire muscle.

THE SCIENCE

Juiciness is the quantity of liquid present in your mouth as you chew. The meat, and the quantity of juices that come from it, is the first source of juiciness. The second is salivation, which is directly linked to the intramuscular fat (again, the famous marbling) because it stimulates the production of saliva.

The juiciness of a piece of meat comes as much from our saliva as it does from the meat itself.

HOW CAN YOU MAKE MEAT VERY JUICY?

For tender meat that cooks fast, you should avoid overcooking, which will toughen it and dry it out. So, it's necessary to cook it fast and on a high heat.

On the other hand, tough meat that contains collagen begins by drying out as it cooks and then reabsorbs the water that it released. So it needs slow cooking on a heat just below simmering.

THE SCIENCE

Tenderness of meat is associated with the amount of collagen it contains. The more collagen this muscle contains, the tougher it is.

On the other hand, the less it contains, the more tender it is.

But that's not all. The toughness of the meat depends on the solubility of this collagen—the more liaisons there are between the fibrils and between the fibers, the less the collagen dissolves during the cooking and the tougher the meat will be. Basically, tough meat from an old animal will never become tender, even if you cook it for hours and hours.

HOW CAN YOU KEEP MEAT TENDER?

The tenderness of tender meat increases even more as the meat is matured. But the sworn enemy of tenderness is overcooking.

THE
RECIPES

BEEF STEW

It's really easy to make a stew. It's true that the cooking time is quite long, but what better dish is there to share with friends in the middle of winter? Here's the secret to a perfect stew.

For further information, see:
Which cookware for my beautiful piece of meat? p 106
The size of the cookware p 108
Adapting the size of the meat to the cooking method p 132
Boiling p 150
Boiling, a user's manual p 152
A matter of taste p 182
Stocks and broths p 228

Begin the recipe the day before and finish it the next day.
Preparation time: 30 minutes
Cooking time: 5 hours for the meal and 6 hours for the stock

SERVES 6

- 1 gallon Beef Stock (p 228)
It would be ideal to prepare it when making this recipe, but if you don't have time, prepare it in advance.

- 28 oz tied beef rib tips
- 28 oz tied beef shank
- 28 oz tied beef shoulder chop
- The green leaves of 1 leek, washed and halved lengthwise
- Marrowbones, halved lengthwise
- Coarse salt

For the vegetables:
- 6 carrots, peeled
- 6 small turnips, peeled
- 12 leeks, green leaves removed
- 6 Charlotte, BF-15, or other waxy salad potatoes

For the sauce:
- 2 tbsp whole-grain mustard
- 3 tbsp crème fraîche
- Sea salt and freshly ground black pepper

THE DAY BEFORE

1

In a large pot over medium heat, warm the stock. Lightly season it with salt, then add the rib tips. Heat the stock until it begins to steam, but do not let it boil or simmer; you should only see a little bubble rise to the surface from time to time. Cook for 1 hour, uncovered, then add the shank, shoulder chop, and the leek leaves. Cook for another 3 hours.
→ You don't need to add vegetables because your stock is already made.
→ The rib tips need a slightly longer cooking time than the other cuts of meat.
→ If some of the meat protrudes from the water, add water up to the height of the meat and cover it with the leek leaves.
→ At this cooking temperature, no foam (scum) will form on the surface and the meat will become very tender and juicy.

2

Let cool slightly, then remove the meat and place it on a plate. Remove the leeks and strain the stock through a cloth placed in a sieve .
→ The cloth will catch all the small unpleasant-looking pieces of meat that fall away during cooking. The strained stock will be very clear.

3

Place the meat back in the pot and place the leeks onto the parts of the meat that are protruding from the water to prevent them from drying out; let rest until the next day.

4

Meanwhile, place the marrowbones in a large bowl of water along with 4 tablespoons of coarse salt.
→ By leaving the bones to disgorge in the water, you'll ensure that the small, unappetizing traces of blood disappear during the cooking process.

ON THE DAY

5

With the help of a skimmer or large spoon, remove two-thirds of the layer of fat that has solidified across the surface of the stock.
→ During the night, the fat, which is lighter than water, will have risen to the surface of the stock and solidified. Although it gives flavor to the stock, the fat also coats your taste buds with a thin film, preventing you from tasting all the other flavors.

6

Pour 2 pints of the stock into a saucepan (this will be used to make the sauce).

7

Prepare the vegetables. About 1 hour before serving, gently heat the pot containing the meat and remaining stock; do not let it simmer. As soon as the contents of the pot are hot, add the carrots. After 30 minutes, add the turnips. After 10 more minutes, add the leeks. Cook the peeled potatoes separately in a large saucepan of boiling water for 20 to 25 minutes, depending on their size, or until tender when pierced with a fork.

8

Make the sauce. While the vegetables are cooking, reduce the reserved stock until it thickens and is reduced to about ½ cup.
→ When the stock reduces, the water it contains evaporates, allowing all the flavors to concentrate until it becomes as thick as syrup.

9

Stir in the mustard and cook for another 2 minutes over gentle heat, stirring to remove some of its acidity. Add the crème fraîche and cook for another 5 minutes, stirring occasionally. Season with salt and pepper.

10

Preheat the broiler to 475°F and place an oven-safe dish full of coarse salt in the middle of the oven.

11

Place the marrowbones in the dish of salt, pushing them down slightly, with the marrow facing up. Roast for 15 minutes, or until browned.
→ By cooking the bones in hot salt, the bottom will heat as fast as the top, cooking the bones evenly—this is world-class cooking!

12

Remove the meat and carve it into attractive slices before plating it on a warmed serving dish. Arrange the vegetables and marrowbones around the meat. Serve the stock and coarse salt on the side and the sauce in a gravy boat. Bring everything to the table with a big smile!

This dish takes a long time to prepare, but your friends will be impressed by this legendary stew.

THE ORIGINAL RECIPE

In the past, stew was a vegetable broth that was left to cook on a fire and to which was added a small piece of meat to add more flavor. This meat would typically be from an old cow that had worked all its life and whose meat therefore was as tough as old boots. The goal wasn't to eat the meat, but instead to allow it to release as many of its flavors as possible into the cooking water to make a tasty broth.

Today, we continue to cook stewing meat in the same way so that it releases the maximum amount of flavor into the water. But there's a better way.

A MORE INTELLIGENT METHOD

When making a stew, the meat cooks in the water and enriches it with good flavors, turning the water into a delicious broth. But done in this way, the meat loses flavor; the result is a very tasty broth and a not-so-tasty piece of meat. A better approach to stew is to cook the meat not in water, but in a stock that is already so full of flavors that the meat will retain more of its own flavors.

RIB ROAST
FOR 4 FRIENDS

A cut fit for a king and one to be shared. Remember to season the meat with salt at least one day before and stand it upright in the oven to cook it.

For further information, see:
Temperatures and cooking thermometers p 110
How to season your meat with salt p 112
The cooking of a steak seen from the inside p 158
Basting meat p 162
Resting meat p 164
Making meat juicier p 166
How to create more juices p 168
Maillard reactions p 174

Season the meat with salt up to two days before
Preparation time: 10 minutes
Refrigeration time: 24 to 48 hours
Cooking time: 20 minutes
Resting time: 10 minutes

SERVES 4

- I good-sized rib roast
- 2 marrowbones
- A few drops white vinegar
- Peanut oil, for coating
- 5 or 6 cloves garlic, crushed
- 10 sprigs thyme
- 2 sprigs rosemary
- 7 tbsp unsalted butter
- Fleur de sel fine sea salt and freshly ground black pepper

THE DAY BEFORE OR TWO DAYS BEFORE

I
Remove the rib roast from its packaging and prick it about twenty times with a large needle.
→ When you pierce a piece of meat through its fibers, the fibers are cut and therefore expel less juice during cooking, making the meat juicer.

2
Generously season the top, bottom, and sides of the rib roast with the salt, place it on a grilling rack, and refrigerate it for at least 24 hours and up to 48 hours.
→ This step will also help keep the meat juicy. The salt will slowly penetrate the meat and change the structure of its proteins, causing the meat to expel less juice during the cooking process.
→ The surface of the meat will dry out slightly, but this will increase the amount of Maillard reactions and result in a more flavorful meat.

3
Using a skewer, remove the marrow from the marrow-bones and leave the marrow to disgorge for 24 hours in a bowl of water containing I teaspoon of salt and a few drops of white vinegar.
→ To remove the marrow, insert the skewer between the bone and the marrow and turn slowly; the marrow will detach on its own.

ON THE DAY

4
One hour before cooking, remove the grilling rack with the rib roast from the refrigerator so that it warms to room temperature. Preheat the oven to 475°F.

5
Take your best cast iron pot (or a large, heavy frying pan, but cast iron produces more juices) and place it over high heat. Cut the marrow into very small cubes. Using a brush or your fingers, coat the entire surface of the rib roast with the oil.

6
As soon as the pot begins to smoke, add the cubes of marrow and let them melt for 2 minutes, stirring. Add the rib roast, fat side down, and cook on all sides for 2 minutes, or until browned on the top, bottom, and sides.
→ The marrow and the fat from the ribs will melt, creating an exceptional fat in which to brown the meat.

7
As soon as it's well browned, remove the rib roast and stand it vertically, with the bone on top, in a large oven-safe dish and place it in the oven for 15 minutes, no more. If you have a meat thermometer, let the meat cook until its center reaches 125°F. Leave any remaining browned bits (the fond) in the pot as you'll use them later to finish cooking.

→ People usually lay a rib roast flat to cook it. This is a mistake because the bottom and top don't cook in the same way. The rib will cook much more evenly if it is stood vertically. Plus, the juices that form on the bone drip toward the meat, giving it lots of flavor.

8

Once the rib roast is cooked, remove it from the oven, wrap it in three layers of foil, and let it rest for 10 minutes on a carving board.
→ As it rests, three things happen:
1) The dry exterior absorbs some of the juices from the center and it becomes juicy again;
2) As the meat cools, the juices thicken and therefore won't trickle out as much when you carve it;
3) The heat continues to spread toward the center and heats it so that it's the perfect temperature.

9

Meanwhile, in the same pot with the reserved fond over medium heat, place the garlic, thyme, and rosemary. Scrape up any fond from the bottom of the pot to collect all the flavor.
→ The garlic should sizzle very gently so that it doesn't burn.

10

After the resting time, remove the rib roast from the foil and place it flat in a large pot along with the juices that leaked out onto the carving board and those left in the baking dish. Add the butter and cook the meat for 2 minutes on each side, basting it continuously and rapidly. If the butter begins to brown, add 1 tablespoon of water.
→ The more often you baste the meat with the delicious juices, the tastier it will be. Be generous!

11

As soon as it's heated through, remove the rib roast and carve it. Place the slices on a warmed serving dish, pour the juices from the pot on top, and season with salt and pepper.
→ Be sure to carve the rib roast properly: slice it at an angle to cut through the length of the fibers. The shorter the fibers, the more tender the meat will be.

Serve this splendid dish at the dining table to make a grand impression.

BEEF BOURGUIGNON

The meat is usually marinated in red wine overnight before browning it and cooking it with a little flour. But you can make it even better by browning the meat before marinating it and by cooking the flour before adding it to the pot.

For more information, see:
Adapting the size of the meat to the cooking method
p 132
Tips for successful marinades p 174
Ragout p 157
How to create more juices p 168

Begin the recipe two days before and finish on the day of serving.
Preparation time: 30 minutes
Marinating time: 1 night
Cooking time: 5 hours 30 minutes

Serves 8

- 4 lb 6½ oz beef shoulder, cut into 2–2½-oz pieces, central nerve removed
- 4 tbsp peanut oil
- 7 oz fresh tender carrots, peeled and diced
- 2 onions, peeled and diced
- 1 bottle Burgundy wine
- 2 cloves garlic, peeled and crushed
- 1 bouquet garni (5 sprigs parsley, 5 to 6 sprigs thyme, 2 bay leaves cut in half) wrapped in leek leaves and firmly tied
- 7 tbsp all-purpose flour
- 1 tbsp port
- 1 quart Beef Stock (p 228)
- 2 (5½-oz) slices lightly salted brisket, diced
- 1 tbsp chopped flat-leaf parsley
- Fine sea salt and freshly ground black pepper

For the side vegetables:
- 2 tbsp unsalted butter
- 1½ tsp granulated sugar
- 24 small pearl onions, peeled
- 1 tbsp balsamic vinegar
- 10½ oz button mushrooms, the smallest you can find

TWO DAYS BEFORE

1
Put the pieces of shoulder in a large bowl and coat them with 2 tablespoons of the oil. Heat a large cast iron pot over high heat. Brown 5 or 6 pieces of the shoulder at a time on every side for 5 minutes then transfer them to a large bowl.
→ If you put too many pieces in the pot at the same time, they won't brown but instead will boil in their juices, which won't evaporate.

2
Once all the meat is browned and set aside, add the carrots and onions to the pot and sweat for 5 minutes over gentle heat; transfer them to a separate bowl. Add the red wine to the pot and heat over medium heat, scraping up the browned bits (the fond) stuck to the bottom of the pot. As soon as the wine is simmering, flambé it by setting it alight with a long match. Let it reduce by about one-third; let cool.
→ The vegetables and the wine collect all the juices that the meat left in the pan. This creates a great stock!

3
Return the meat to the pot with the reduced wine, then add the carrots and onions, garlic, bouquet garni, and the remaining oil. Refrigerate overnight to marinate.

THE DAY BEFORE

4
Preheat the oven to 300°F. While the oven is preheating, place the flour in a skillet over medium heat and toast it until it becomes a light amber color, stirring constantly. As soon as it's toasted (this will take about 5 minutes), sift it through a sieve to remove any lumps that might have formed.
→ When you toast flour it takes on nutty flavors that will reinforce the flavors of the cooking juices.

5
Place the pot containing the meat and the marinade over medium heat until it's steaming; do not let it simmer. Meanwhile, heat 1 cup of beef stock in a saucepan, and as soon as it begins to steam, throw in all the toasted flour at once, stirring with a whisk to avoid lumps. Cook for 5 minutes while stirring constantly, then pour this mixture into the pot with three-quarters of the remaining beef stock; if necessary, add water until it's level with the meat. Cover the pot and place it in the middle of the oven for 5 hours, stirring occasionally and checking throughout the cooking process that there's enough liquid to cover the meat. If not, add a little water.

→ It's the pot that should be in the middle of the oven, not the rack on which it sits.

6

At the end of the cooking time, you should be able to easily cut through the meat with the tip of a knife. If not, cook a little longer. Remove the pot from the oven and let it cool until the next day.

ON THE DAY

7

Make the sauce. Transfer the meat to a large bowl and cover it with foil. Discard the bouquet garni and drain the vegetables through a colander set over the pot, pressing down on the vegetables to extract all the juices.
→ By pressing on the vegetables, you collect most of their own flavor as well as those they absorbed during the cooking process.

8

Place half the pressed vegetables in a blender with all the cooking liquid from the pot and blend for 3 minutes. Strain this sauce through a sieve into the pot.
→ This vegetable puree will thicken your sauce. This is a much better approach than adding too much flour.

9

The sauce should be thick enough to coat the back of a spoon. If it's too thick, add some of the remaining beef stock. If it's not thick enough, let it reduce, uncovered, for several minutes. Add the meat and gradually heat the contents of the pot.

10

Prepare the side vegetables. Melt 1 tablespoon of the butter in a saucepan over gentle heat. Add the sugar and the onions, then add water until it's level with the mixture and cover. Cook for about 15 minutes. Just before the onions are cooked, remove the lid and let the water evaporate. Pour in the balsamic vinegar and let it reduce by half. Remove the onions and set them aside in a warmed bowl.
For the mushrooms, brown them in the remaining butter over medium heat for 5 to 10 minutes, depending on their size, then set aside in a bowl.

11

Meanwhile, brown the diced brisket over medium heat for 7 to 8 minutes.

12

Present the meat in a serving dish with the brisket on top and the sauce all around. Place the mushrooms and the onions along the edges and sprinkle with a few chopped parsley leaves to add freshness. Season very lightly with salt, add a good amount of pepper, and serve.

You know you've just made something crazy delicious!

WHY BEGIN COOKING BEFORE MARINATING?

We often think that marinades add flavor and tenderize meat. The problem is that it takes a long time for a marinade to penetrate the meat. For a thick cut weighing about 3½ oz, the marinade would need a week. So, in one night, practically nothing happens; the marinade won't penetrate the meat, not even by one tiny millimeter. But if you cook the meat first, everything changes: as it browns, lots of small fissures are created across the surface of the meat, which will allow the marinade not to "penetrate," in the true sense of the word, but to sit inside the fissures. In this way, the strength of the marinade is multiplied tenfold.

WHY NOT COOK THE FLOUR IN THE USUAL WAY?

Because you can do so much better! After the meat has browned, people usually then incorporate the flour, then cook the meat in the oven. But treated this way, the flour becomes soaked in meat juices, so it's difficult for it to cook and brown. Now you know that toasting the flour before you incorporate it into the dish will yield a much better result.

WHY IN THE OVEN AND NOT ON THE STOVE TOP?

When you heat food on the stove top, the heat comes only from underneath, but in the oven the heat comes from the bottom, sides, and top. As a result, the food cooks more evenly, resulting in a better-quality dish.

PASTRAMI

I know, this is a recipe that needs to be prepared 4 days in advance, but it's completely worth it, I promise—slightly crunchy on the outside, melt-in-the-mouth on the inside. The cooking method is similar to low-temperature cooking and the result is mind-blowing!

For more information, see:
Brining and salting p 134

Begin the recipe 4 days in advance
Preparation time: 30 minutes + 6 hours for the brine
Brining time: 4 days
Cooking time: 6 hours

SERVES 8

For the pastrami:
- 4 lb 6½ oz beef brisket
- 3 tbsp coriander seeds
- 2 tbsp black peppercorns
- 2 tbsp smoked paprika
- ½ tbsp red pepper flakes
- I tsp garlic powder
- I½ tsp brown sugar

For the brine:
- I tsp coriander seeds
- I tsp black peppercorns
- 4 tsp allspice
- I tsp powdered mustard
- 2 cloves
- I tsp juniper berries
- 4 cloves garlic, peeled and crushed
- I bay leaf
- 7 oz sel gris (gray sea salt, untreated and without additives. Check the packet, as this is important)
- 3½ oz brown sugar
- 2 tsp honey

4 DAYS BEFORE

1
Prepare the brine. Gently toast the coriander seeds and the peppercorns in a skillet over a high heat for 2 to 3 minutes, stirring constantly to avoid burning them. Let cool, then place them in a mortar with the remaining spices, the garlic, and the bay leaf, and grind everything into a powder.

2
Bring 3 quarts of water to a boil in a large pot with a lid and let it boil for 10 minutes to destroy any bacteria it might contain. Add the sel gris, brown sugar, and honey. Stir so that the salt and sugar dissolve and the honey melts, then add the powdered spices. Let cool to room temperature before refrigerating for 5 to 6 hours, or at least enough time to reduce the temperature of the brine to the same temperature as the fridge.
→ If you place the meat into the brine before the brine has completely cooled, you risk ruining the brining process. The hardest part is now done—well, almost.

3
Add the meat to the brine once the brine has cooled, place a small plate on top to ensure the meat stays completely submerged, and place the lid on the pot. Return to the refrigerator for 4 days. Stir the brine twice a day. The hardest part is now over!
→ Only a small part of the meat should be exposed to the open air, otherwise it could spoil.
→ The brine needs time to penetrate the meat. After 4 days, the meat will be entirely brined.

ON THE DAY

4
Remove the meat from the refrigerator and preheat the oven to exactly 250°F. Rinse the meat in cold water to get rid of the remaining brine and dry it with paper towels.

5
Toast the coriander seeds and the black peppercorns in a skillet over high heat, stirring constantly to avoid burning them. Transfer them to a mortar, add the paprika, pepper flakes, garlic powder, and brown sugar and grind everything together. Coat the entire brisket in this mixture, gently rubbing the spices into it to make them stick.
→ The flavors of the spices will barely penetrate the meat during the cooking. It will be interesting to see the difference between the taste and texture of the outside compared to the inside.

6

Wrap the meat in a triple layer of foil so that it's airtight. Place it fat side up in the oven for 6 hours.

→ The fat will melt slightly during the cooking process. If the fat side is facing up, it will drip down into the meat's fibers. If it's facing down, it will, sadly, drip away into the pan.

→ It's imperative that the meat be wrapped airtight so that the moisture released while cooking is confined inside. The will create a very humid cooking environment and the meat will remain very juicy.

7

Remove the meat from the oven and set the oven broiler to 535°F. Remove the foil and place the brisket on a grilling rack. Once the oven reaches full temperature, insert the grilling rack so that the meat is positioned in the middle of the oven, with an oven-safe dish placed beneath it to catch the juices that may drip down. Broil for 5 to 7 minutes, or until browned; do not let it burn.

Now it's done! It was a long process but the sublime taste makes it worth it, don't you agree?

WHY SHOULDN'T YOU USE NITRITE SALT?

I deliberately chose not to use a nitrite (pink) salt, which is usually the salt used for pastrami, ham, and charcuterie. Although it gives the meat a good color, this salt is suspected of causing severe health problems including cancer.

WHY DO YOU SOAK THE MEAT?

This salty, sweet, and spiced water in which you submerge the meat is called a brine. As the brine penetrates the meat, the salt modifies the structure of the proteins, preventing them from contracting during the cooking process and expelling any juices. The other advantage is that the flavors of the brine will also penetrate the meat much faster than a simple marinade.

BREADED VEAL CUTLET WITH ARUGULA, TOMATO, LEMON, AND PARMESAN SALAD

This dish is not really Veal Milanese because you add Parmesan to the bread crumbs, but it's not Veal Parmigiana either—but it's still a delicious dish. Crunchy, juicy, a touch of acidity, and a touch of pepper—total bliss!

For more information, see:
The size of the cookware p 108
Which butter for cooking? p 122

Preparation time: 15 minutes
Cooking time: 15 minutes

SERVES 4

- 4 (5¼-oz) veal cutlets, cut from the cushion of veal and lightly flattened by the butcher
- 3½ oz all-purpose flour
- 2 large eggs, beaten with 2 tbsp water
- 3½ oz Panko (p 197) or homemade bread crumbs
- 10½ oz Clarified Butter (p 122)
- 1⅔ oz freshly grated Parmesan cheese

For the salad:
- The juice of ½ lemon
- 1 tbsp olive oil
- 8 cherry tomatoes, quartered
- 2 handfuls arugula, washed and dried
- A few fresh shavings Parmesan cheese
- Sea salt and freshly ground white pepper

1
Remove the cutlets from the refrigerator 1 hour before cooking and space them out in a baking dish so that they're not overlapping.
→ If the cutlets overlap each other it will take a long time for their centers to reach room temperature—at least 3 hours.

2
Preheat the oven to 320°F. Place the flour, eggs, and panko in three separate shallow bowls.

3
Heat the clarified butter over medium heat in a frying pan large enough to hold 2 cutlets without touching each other.
→ This is very important: if you use a frying pan that's too small, you'll struggle to brown the cutlets, and the bread crumbs will soak up the fat from the butter. The result will be greasy breaded cutlets!

4
Check the temperature of the butter by placing a small piece of bread in it. If it browns in 15 seconds, the butter is the right temperature.
→ When you cook your cutlets at a high temperature, the humidity contained inside the meat and inside the bread crumbs releases and repels the oil. As a result, your cutlet will be light and delicate. But if the heat isn't high enough, the opposite happens: the bread crumbs absorb the oil and your cutlet will be heavy and greasy.

5
Coat the first 2 cutlets in the flour and brush off any the excess using your fingers. Then dip them in the beaten egg, let the excess drip off, then roll them in the panko.
→ Without the flour, the egg wouldn't stick to the meat and without the egg, the bread crumbs wouldn't either. So the order in which to coat the cutlets is very important.

6
Cook the 2 cutlets for 2 minutes, just enough time to brown the exterior, then flip them and cook them again for 2 minutes.
→ Whatever you do, don't flip the cutlets too early or the panko coating could fall off.

7
Gently dab the cooked cutlets with a paper towel to remove the excess fat. Place them on a grilling rack in the middle of a hot oven with an oven-safe dish placed underneath to catch any small pieces of panko that might fall off.
→ By placing your cutlets on a grilling rack, you're allowing the humidity to escape the bread crumbs; this way they'll stay crunchy. If, on the other hand, you place the cutlets in a baking dish, some of the humidity will get trapped under the cutlets and the bread crumbs will soften.

8

Repeat the same steps with the last 2 cutlets.

9

Prepare the salad. Gently combine half the lemon juice, the oil, tomatoes, and arugula in a large salad bowl.

10

Place the cutlets in a big dish, add the salad on top, sprinkle with the Parmesan shavings and a few drops of the remaining lemon juice. Season with salt and pepper and serve.

Look at those colors, textures, and flavors. It's insanely good, yet so simple. Well done!

VEAL CHOP OR MILANESE VEAL CUTLET?

The original recipe calls for a veal chop that's ¾ inch (2 cm) thick, breaded with clarified butter without flour or Parmesan. (Parmesan comes from Parma, and Parma is miles away from Milan.) The cutlet is more common but not as traditional.

THICKNESS, THICKNESS, THICKNESS!

Forget those cutlets that your butcher flattens so much that they're almost transparent. Those are good for piccata, but we need a piece of meat that's ⅓ inch (1 cm) thick—if not, there will be too many bread crumbs.

PANKO?

Panko is Japanese bread crumbs, a lot lighter than those found in the West. Here's the recipe in case you can't find any at your grocery store. Don't buy commercial, ready-made bread crumbs, as these are full of additives and tend to absorb all the cooking fat.

WHAT IS CLARIFIED BUTTER?

Clarified butter is butter from which the water and milk solids (which can burn over high heat) have been removed. Using clarified butter allows you to brown the cutlets without burning the butter so you can take advantage of the butter's many flavors.

SIMPLY BROWNED VEAL CHOP

Forget the dry veal chop often served in restaurants. I'm talking about a chop that's tender, juicy, soft, and golden brown, accompanied by a wine sauce. What makes the difference? Soaking the meat in brine for 2 hours.

For more information, see:
The size of the cookware p 108
Brining and salting p 134
Marinades p 136
Should you flip meat during the cooking process? p 160
Basting meat p 162
Resting meat p 164

Preparation time: 10 minutes + 3 hours for the brine
Brining time: 2 hours
Marinating time: 1 hour
Cooking time: 40 minutes

SERVES 2

- 2 veal chops, ¾ inch thick or weighing 12 oz
- 1 tbsp Clarified Butter (p 122) or olive oil

For the brine:
- 3 level tsp fine sel gris (gray sea salt)
- ½ tsp granulated sugar

For the marinade:
- ½ clove garlic, peeled and diced
- ½ tsp finely chopped fresh thyme
- 4 tbsp olive oil

For the sauce:
- 1 large shallot, diced
- 2 tbsp bold red wine, such as Cabernet Sauvignon
- 2 tbsp unsalted butter
- Sea salt and freshly ground black pepper

1
Prepare the brine. Bring 3 quarts of water to a boil with the sel gris and the sugar and boil for 5 minutes. Let cool to room temperature. Pour the brine into a large bowl and place it in the refrigerator for 2 to 3 hours to chill.

2
Submerge the veal chops in the brine for 2 hours. Turn them over every half hour to ensure that every part of the meat is in contact with the liquid. Remove them, rinse them under cold running water, and dry them well with paper towels.

3
Prepare the marinade. Combine all the ingredients in a large bowl. Add the veal chops and coat them in the marinade. Place some plastic wrap directly onto the chops and keep them at room temperature for 1 hour.
→The marinade won't penetrate the meat, but it will give flavor to the exterior. This is more than enough, as with each mouthful you'll be able to taste light notes of thyme and garlic.

4
Prepare the sauce. In a saucepan over medium heat, reduce the beef stock to three-quarters its volume to obtain a slightly syrupy consistency. Place the shallot and the red wine in another saucepan over medium heat and reduce again to three-quarters its volume, without boiling; this takes about 30 minutes. Season with salt and pepper.
→The water contained in the stock and the wine will evaporate: you'll retain all the flavors which will no longer be diluted by the water.
→You can make the sauce in advance.

5
Remove all the bits of garlic from your veal chops before you cook them. Its flavors have already begun to penetrate the meat.
→Garlic burns and becomes bitter and acrid when overcooked. This is why you should remove it before cooking.

6
Over high heat, heat a frying pan large enough to hold both veal chops at the same time. Place the clarified butter in the hot pan and let it sizzle for a few seconds. Stack one chop on top of the other, take both in one hand, and hold them to brown the edges, about 1 minute.
→If you place the chops directly in the pan to begin cooking, the edges will never brown, which would be a shame. By browning the edges in this way, the entire piece of meat will be browned.

7

Place the chops face down and let them brown for 5 minutes, flipping them every 30 seconds and basting constantly with the butter. Reduce the heat to very low and cook for another 5 or 6 minutes, still flipping every 30 seconds.

→By flipping the meat every 30 seconds you'll ensure that it's more evenly cooked and juicier.

8

Remove the chops from the pan, wrap them in a triple layer of foil, and let them rest on a platter for 5 minutes.

→As the meat rests, the juices contained inside thicken and rise to the surface, which has slightly dried out but will now be moistened from absorbing some of the juices from the center.

9

Meanwhile, combine the reduced red wine and shallot with the beef stock. Add the 2 tablespoons of butter to make it richer, season with salt and pepper, and keep warm.

10

Place the frying pan over high heat and reheat the meat for 30 seconds on each side to make the surface a little crispy before serving.

→As the meat rests, the surface moistens and softens. By heating it over high heat, you'll dry the surface out again and make it crispy.

11

Place each chop on a plate and pour the sauce in an attractive way on the side.

You're about to eat a world-class veal chop. Well done!

WHY BRINE THE MEAT?

Don't worry, the flavors of the meat won't dilute into the water. This is an ancient practice called brining and it's how you prepare ham to keep it very tender after cooking. The mixture of water + salt + sugar will slightly penetrate the meat, modifying the structure of the proteins and preventing them from releasing juices during the cooking process. Your brined veal chop will be a lot juicier than one that is not brined.

BLANQUETTE OF VEAL

Blanquette is a recipe that goes back to the eighteenth century and used to be made with leftover pieces of veal roast and served as a starter with mushrooms and pearl onions. The recipe has evolved, and today people make it without knowing the original recipe.

For more information, see:
Which cookware for my beautiful piece of meat? p 106
The size of the cookware p 108
Which oil for cooking? p 124
Boiling p 150
Stocks and broths p 228

Preparation time: 20 minutes
Cooking time: 3 hours

SERVES 6

- 1⅓ lb veal shoulder, diced into 1½-inch cubes
- 1⅓ lb brisket, diced into 1½-inch cubes
- 2 tbsp olive oil
- 3 quarts fresh Beef Stock (p 228) or use frozen
- Sea salt

For the side:
- 4 tbsp unsalted butter
- 10½ oz wild black rice, rinsed in cold water
- 24 pearl onions, peeled
- 2 tbsp granulated sugar
- 2 bunches baby carrots, peeled
- 7 oz button mushrooms, washed

For the sauce:
- Scant 1½ cups crème fraîche
- 4 large egg yolks
- Pinch of nutmeg

1
Place the meat in a large bowl and thoroughly coat all the pieces with the oil. Heat a large pot over medium heat. Once it's hot, lightly brown the cubes of meat.
→ When you put oil directly into a pot, it sits between the pieces of meat, burns, and takes on a bad flavor. But if you coat the meat with the oil first, the oil doesn't burn.

2
Once the meat has browned, pour in the stock until it's 1 to 1½ inches above the pieces of meat. Lightly season with salt only (not pepper). Reduce the heat and let it cook for 2½ hours without letting it boil or simmer; you should only occasionally see a bubble rise to the surface.
→ When the cooking liquid is at a temperature that's just beneath simmering, the meat cooks slowly and keeps all its juiciness. But if it reaches the boiling point, the air bubbles that rise will cook the meat too quickly and dry it out.

3
Remove the meat from the pot. Set it aside in a bowl covered with foil. Place a moistened cloth over a colander and pour the stock through it into a large bowl.
→The cloth will catch all the little pieces of meat that fell away during cooking. The result is a very clear stock.

4
Wipe out the pot, pour the filtered stock back into the pot, and reduce it to two-thirds its volume over medium heat.
→ By reducing the stock you're allowing some of the tasteless water it contains to evaporate. You'll have the same amount of flavor but a lot less liquid. The reduced stock will be a lot more concentrated and, as a result, a lot tastier.

5
Prepare the side. While the stock is reducing, melt 1 tablespoon of the butter in a frying pan. As soon as the pan is hot, add the rice and heat it for 3 to 4 minutes, stirring constantly. Add twice the rice's volume in water, cover, and let simmer for 40 minutes.

6
Heat 1 tablespoon of the butter in a small frying pan, add the onions, 1 tablespoon of the sugar, and enough water to fill the pan halfway. Cover and let cook for 20 minutes on very gentle heat, stirring from time to time.

7
Heat 1 tablespoon of the butter in a small frying pan, add the carrots, the remaining sugar, and enough water to fill the pan halfway. Cover and let cook for 20 minutes over a very gentle heat, stirring from time to time.

8

Heat the remaining butter in a small frying pan, add the mushrooms and enough water to fill the pan halfway. Cook for 5 minutes over very gentle heat, stirring from time to time.

9

Make the sauce. Once the stock has reduced, lower the heat so that it keeps the stock warm but doesn't cook it. In a large bowl, combine the crème fraîche, egg yolks, and nutmeg. Incorporate a small ladle of the broth. Pour this mixture into the reduced stock and let it cook over very low heat, stirring constantly, so that the sauce thickens. Put the meat into the thickened sauce and reheat it for 10 minutes.

10

Now everything is cooked, and you can take it all to the table. Arrange the meat and the sauce on an attractive serving dish, the vegetables on a second platter, and the rice on a third: the guests will fill their own plates at the table.

Aren't all those colors beautiful? The off-white, the orange, and the black of the wild rice?

WHY DON'T YOU BLANCH THE MEAT BEFORE COOKING IT?

In the past, people used to blanch meat for reasons related to hygiene, but these reasons are no longer valid. When you discard the water in which you blanched your meat, you're also throwing out all of the flavors it released— what a waste!

WHY SUCH A WHITE SAUCE?

In the past, the sauce was white to show that the meat was neither spoiled nor green. It had nothing to do with taste, only with hygiene: the whiter the sauce, the fresher the meat.

DON'T COOK THE MEAT IN CLEAR WATER!

If you cook your meat in clear water, it will become a broth by absorbing the flavors released by the meat. The result will be bland meat. However, if you cook the meat in a preprepared broth, the meat won't lose any flavor and will taste much better.

MILANESE OSSO BUCO AND GREMOLATA

Never put tomato in osso buco! The flavors, texture, and amount of water a tomato has will only dilute the sauce. Instead, you can make a real osso buco and an authentic gremolata.

For more information, see:
Which cookware for my beautiful piece of meat? p 106
The size of the cookware p 108
Braising p 154
How to create more juices p 168
Stocks and broths p 228

Preparation time: 30 minutes
Cooking time: 2 hours 10 minutes

SERVES 6

- 6 (10½-oz) slices veal shank
all the same size, if possible
- 2 quarts fresh Beef Stock (p 228) or use frozen
- 2 tbsp unsalted butter
- 1 large onion, diced
- 2 carrots, peeled and diced
- 1 celery stalk, washed and diced
- 1 cup dry white wine
- Sea salt and freshly ground black pepper

For the gremolata:
- 1 clove garlic, peeled and finely chopped
- 3 sprigs parsley, stems removed, leaves finely chopped
- Zest and juice of 1 lemon
- Zest and juice of ½ orange (optional)

1
In a large saucepan, reduce the beef stock by half over medium heat.
→ When you reduce beef stock, most of the tasteless water it contains evaporates and the stock retains all the flavor. The result is a much tastier stock.

2
Preheat the oven to 320°F. Remove the shanks from the refrigerator, either in advance or just before cooking—it doesn't matter for this recipe. Make a few small incisions in the membrane that surrounds the perimeter of the shanks.
→ The membrane that encases the shanks contracts during cooking, tugging on the meat and deforming it. If you make some small incisions in the membrane, the meat won't be deformed and will cook more evenly.

3
Over medium heat, heat a cast iron pot large enough to hold the 6 shanks without stacking them on top of each other. When the pot is hot, add 1 tablespoon of the butter, and as soon as the butter begins to foam, place 3 of the shanks in the pot without touching or over-lapping them. Brown for 3 to 4 minutes on each side, then transfer them to a warm platter. Repeat with the 3 remaining shanks.
→ When pieces of meat are touching each other while cooking, the water they release due to the heat gets trapped underneath them. The meat therefore boils in its own water and can't brown.

4
Reduce the heat slightly and add the remaining butter as well as the diced vegetables. Season with salt and sweat for 5 minutes without browning them, stirring occasionally.
→ Seasoning your vegetables with salt will help evaporate the water they contain while preserving the best part: the flavors.

5
Pour in the white wine and let it reduce to three-quarters its volume.
→ Reducing the wine evaporates most of the alcohol it contains and concentrates its flavors.

6
Gently place the shanks on top of the vegetables and pour on the reduced stock so that it sits just beneath the meat. Whatever you do, don't add any more stock than this—you want to braise the meat, not boil it!
  Cover the pot, position the oven rack so that the pot sits in the middle of the oven, and cook for 1 hour 45 minutes. Turn the shanks over halfway through the

cooking process and check that there's enough liquid left in the bottom of the pot. If there isn't, add some more reduced stock so that it sits just below the shanks. Check the doneness of the meat by piercing it with a knife; it should go through with ease.

→ Osso buco should be braised in the oven and definitely not in a liquid as you often see it done. When braised, the meat loses very few of its flavors, whereas boiling it in a large quantity of water causes it to lose much of its taste and deteriorate.

7

Prepare the gremolata. In a bowl, combine the garlic and the parley with the zest and juice of the lemon and orange, if using. Spread this mixture onto the meat, cover it again, and let it cook for 5 minutes. It's almost finished.

8

Remove the shanks, arrange them attractively on a large platter, add the vegetables, and pour the cooking liquid around it. Season with salt and pepper. It's ready!

Look at the color of that magnificent sauce! Have you tasted its flavors? Have you smelled its aromas? This is a true osso buco alla milanese!

SHOULDN'T YOU FLOUR THE MEAT?

People generally flour pieces of meat before browning them. The flour is used to thicken a cooking stock that's too liquid or that contains the water released from tomatoes (them again!). Basically, when the sauce is diluted, people thicken it with flour so that you can't tell. It's a poor solution... Boo!

A LITTLE BONUS

You can add 1 or 2 veal marrowbones to this dish. Serve the marrow as a side, sliced, and sprinkled with a little chopped parsley.

If, like me, you're a fan, don't hesitate to add 2 rinsed, crushed anchovies to the gremolata; it'll add a bit of umami to the dish. And to be even more fitting, make a risotto alla milanese.

WHAT ABOUT THE ORIGINAL RECIPE?

There are no tomatoes in the original recipe for the simple reason that in eighteenth-century Italy, tomatoes were rarely consumed: people thought them poisonous. It was most likely the French cook Henri-Paul Pellaprat who added them for the first time in his recipe book *L'Arte Culinaire Moderne*, published in 1932. And since then, everyone has followed his recipe without questioning it.

PORCHETTA

This recipe comes from Italy and is usually made with a whole or half boned pig. For a small number of guests, pork belly, a meltingly delicious cut, is generally used instead. The most renowned porchetta is the one from Ariccia in Rome. That's the recipe we're using!

For more information, see:
The size of the cookware p 108
Basting meat p 162

It's preferable to begin the recipe the day before
Preparation time: 20 minutes
Cooking time: 4 hours 15 minutes

SERVES 8

- 1 (8¾-lb) pork belly, boned and rind intact
- 1½ tbsp fennel pollen, or 2 heaping tbsp fennel seeds
- 2 tbsp finely chopped rosemary
- 1½ tbsp black peppercorns, freshly ground
- 8 cloves garlic, peeled and crushed
- 2 tbsp olive oil
- 9 feet butcher's twine
(ask your favorite butcher for it)

THE DAY BEFORE

1
If you don't have any fennel pollen (this would be a shame, fennel pollen is truly delicious!), lightly toast the fennel seeds for 2 minutes in a hot pan, stirring constantly to avoid burning them. Put the seeds in a mortar and grind them to a fine powder.

2
Place the pork belly flat. Trim 1⅛ inches of meat from around the edges, but only the meat: leave the rind.
→ This will allow you to close the porchetta without directly exposing the meat to the oven's heat.

3
With a sharp knife, make around thirty incisions, ⅓ inch deep, on the flesh side. Season with the herbs and spices, pressing them down to make them stick.
→ The seasoning will penetrate the incisions and give up to twenty times more flavor to the pork belly.

4
Firmly roll the pork belly toward you and close it with the butcher's twine, tying the pieces of twine at a maximum of 1⅛-inch intervals, always gripping the pork belly with the same strength for a uniform roast and even cooking. Wind the twine twice around the length of the pork belly, tying the rind to the flesh to cover the meat on the ends of the roast.

5
Place overnight on a rack in the refrigerator, uncovered.
→ The rind will dry slightly which will make the formation of a super-crispy crust during cooking easier. The flavors of the herbs and spices will slowly start to penetrate the meat.

ON THE DAY

6
Preheat the oven to 285°F. Place the pork belly in a roasting pan just big enough to hold it, with the slightly open side facing downward. Drizzle with the olive oil.
→ The cooking process will take a long time if the pan is too big, and the juices that flow from the meat will be at risk of burning. With the correct size pan, there will be no burned juices.

7

Put the pork belly in the oven for 4 hours. Baste it every half hour with the juices that spill into the pan.

→ When you baste, you're coating the rind with some of the delicious juices that form on the bottom of the pan, making it even more divine.

8

Check the doneness: you should be able to easily stick a skewer into the meat without meeting any resistance. Remove the pan from the oven. Increase the temperature of the oven to 500°F and, once it's reached full temperature, return the pan to the oven to brown the rind for 10 to 15 minutes.

→ The rind will expand, fill with air, and turn crispy. Perfect!

9

Remove the pan from the oven and let the meat rest for about 15 minutes; it's been working hard!

This meal is fit for a king and can be served hot or warm in thick slices, or cold in very, very thin slices to pick at with your fingers.

WHAT IS PORCHETTA?

This recipe is made with a side of pork, spanning from the back to the belly, between the third dorsal vertebra and the last lumbar vertebra. The meat is boned, laid flat, and seasoned with herbs and spices, then rolled before being cooked for about 8 hours in an oven that's not very hot, or even better, next to a wood fire. It can also be made with a stuffed suckling pig.

ROLLING AND TYING THE PORCHETTA

To ensure that the porchetta is evenly cooked, it needs to be prepared with great care: After having boned and seasoned it, roll it firmly on itself, starting from the side farthest from you; make sure that it's evenly rolled because if it isn't, some sections may cook faster than others.

Wind the twine once around the roll about every 1 1/8 inch (3 cm); this must also be even, both by tying at regular intervals and in the tightness of the knots. Tie the two ends of the twine around the roll lengthwise to grip the rind to the roll.

PULLED PORK

Pulled pork is a pork shoulder that is slowly braised for a long time until it can be pulled apart with two forks. This is a perfect meal with good friends.

For more information, see:
Marinades p 136
Braising p 154
What is collagen? p 180

Depending on your preference, you can marinate it up to 2 days in advance.
Preparation time: 15 minutes
Cooking time: 6 hours

SERVES 8

- 1 (5½-lb) pork shoulder, bone in
- 2 large onions, peeled and large diced
- 2 carrots, peeled and large diced
- 4 cloves garlic, peeled and crushed
- 2 cloves
- 1 small piece onion (stick the cloves into the onion)
- 1²/₃ cups apple cider
- 5 cups chicken broth
- Sea salt and freshly ground black pepper

For the marinade:
- 4 cloves garlic, peeled and crushed into a paste
- 2 tsp honey
- 2 tsp Worcestershire sauce
- 1 tsp Dijon mustard
- 1 tbsp smoked paprika
- 1 tbsp olive oil
- 1 tsp salt

2 DAYS BEFORE OR ON THE DAY, DEPENDING ON YOUR PREFERENCE

1
Prepare the marinade. Combine all the ingredients. Coat the shoulder in the marinade using your fingers. You have two options: refrigerate the shoulder for up to 2 days to marinate it, allowing the flavors to penetrate the inside, or cook it immediately, which will allow only the exterior to benefit from the marinade. Personally, I let it marinate for 2 days.
→ Marinades take a long time to penetrate meat, but make a big difference in the final result.

2
Preheat the oven to 500°F. Take the shoulder out of the refrigerator several minutes before cooking.

3
Place the onions, carrots, and garlic, and the onion with the cloves into a pot. Add the cider and 3 cups of the chicken broth, place the shoulder on top with the curved side facing upward.
→ The meat sits on a bed of vegetables and so is not in direct contact with the heat of the pot. Therefore, it cooks slowly in the moisture produced by the vegetables, the cider, and the broth.

4
Cover and heat for 5 minutes until the liquid is hot, then place it in the middle of the oven and reduce the temperature to 285°F.
→ By preheating the oven to 500°F then reducing the temperature to 285°F, the top of the pot will become very hot and in turn will lightly brown the top of the meat.
→ If you place the pot at the top of the oven, the heat concentrates at the top; just as if you chose to place it on a fire or a stove top, the heat would concentrate on the bottom. By placing the pot in the middle of the oven, you'll ensure the meat cooks evenly.

5
Let cook gently for 6 hours. This amount of time is necessary for the collagen to turn to gelatin, the fat to melt, and the whole thing to cook in the steam released by the vegetables and liquid. Check regularly that there's enough water in the bottom of the pot. If not, add a little chicken broth.
→ During the cooking process the liquid turns into steam, condenses on the bottom of the lid, then retransforms into liquid droplets that drop down onto the meat. This means that the shoulder is being constantly basted.

6

Did you have the will power to wait 6 hours? You're patient! Remove the pot from the oven, transfer the shoulder to a platter, and let it cool slightly. While the shoulder is cooling, strain the remaining juices through a sieve, pressing down on the vegetables to extract everything they have.

→ There's flavor left in the vegetables. By pressing them through a sieve, you'll be able to capture all of it.

7

Pull the shoulder apart with 2 forks, pour some of the cooking juices over it, stirring the pork to make it even juicier. Season with salt and pepper and serve.

Say hi to your friends for me, they look nice.

WHY A SHOULDER AND NOT A ROASTING JOINT?

During the cooking process, the cartilaginous part at the end of the bone adds its own flavors to the flavors of the sauce and gives it a shininess, too. Capillary action causes the flavors to spread down the length of the bone, providing even more flavor to the meat. Don't use just any piece of meat, not even a roast—it will be a lot less flavorful.

THE MEAT COOKS ON A BED OF VEGETABLES

Placed like this, the meat cooks without being in direct contact with the heat of the pot. It cooks in the moisture produced by the vegetables and the broth and will be extremely tender and juicy.

SUBLIME PORK CHOP

This uses a simple but devilishly effective cooking process. You'll need two pork chops from a pig that was fed well and loved by the people that raised it. Only four ingredients and less than 10 minutes of cooking time create one incredible result.

For more information, see:
Which cookware for my beautiful piece of meat? p 106
Sauteing p 142
Should you flip meat during the cooking process? p 160
Basting meat p 162
Resting meat p 164
How to create more juices p 168

Preparation time: 10 minutes
Resting time: 2 hours 10 minutes
Cooking time: 10 minutes

SERVES 2

- 2 (¾-inch-thick) pork chops with a good amount of fat around each
- 1 tbsp Clarified Butter (p 122) or olive oil
- 20 sprigs thyme
- 2 cloves garlic, peeled and crushed
- 1½ tbsp unsalted butter, cubed
- Sea salt and freshly ground black pepper

Have you found a butcher that sells real pork? Great, now you're ready to cook!

1
Make several incisions in the fat of the pork chops. Place the chops on a grilling rack so that the exterior dries out a little and browns more easily. Let rest for 2 hours at room temperature.
→ During the cooking process the rind will contract and deform the meat, causing it not to cook evenly. By making incisions, you'll prevent the contraction of the rind.

2
Get out your biggest and most beautiful frying pan or pot, made either of cast iron or stainless steel. Place it over high heat. Once hot, melt the clarified butter and let it sizzle; it should steam slightly.
→ Don't use a nonstick pan, or I'll be angry! Those nonstick things don't brown meat and don't create juices. And we want juices! Choose the biggest pan possible so that the meat browns perfectly.

3
Don't season with salt and pepper before the cooking process because it's pointless. You can do it after. Place one chop on top of the other, pick them both up by their sides, and brown the edges for 1 minute.
→ If you put them immediately into the pan, the edges will never brown.

4
Space the chops out in the pan. Add the thyme and the garlic. Cook for 30 seconds to brown, then flip them to brown the other side, then add the butter. Reduce the heat slightly and flip the chops every 30 seconds, basting them often with the quickly melting butter.
→ When you baste meat, three things happen: 1) The boiling hot butter heats and cooks the top of the meat, cooking the top and bottom more evenly; 2) You're constantly covering the meat in the sticky, flavorful juices that the butter picks up from the bottom of the pan, and 3) The fat in the butter hinders the evaporation of the juices contained inside the meat.

5
Cook the chops for 3 minutes 30 seconds on each side but no more, and a little less if you like your meat pink. Don't hesitate to place the chops on top of the thyme and the garlic from time to time and to move them around in the pan. Mix it all up to intensify the flavors.
→ By flipping your meat often, it will cook more evenly and, most of all, you'll avoid overcooking the area just beneath the crispy surface. The result is a moister and more tender meat.

→ As the thyme and the garlic cook, some of their flavors disappear with the steam. If you place the meat on top of them, it will absorb those flavors and be even tastier. It's the same principle for meat as it is for smoked fish.

6

Remove the chops from the pan and let rest for 5 to 10 minutes wrapped in foil so that the juices inside spread and thicken as they cool. Keep the pan over very low heat.
→ As the chops rest, the crust softens a little as it soaks up the juices from the center of the chop.

7

Put the chops back in the pan over high heat and reheat them for 20 seconds on each side.
→ By placing the chops over high heat just before serving them, you dry out the crust and make it crispy again.

8

It's ready! Season generously with salt and pepper and serve immediately.

You've made something incredible with just four ingredients. Cooking is magical, don't you think?

IS A GOOD PIG A FATTY PIG?

A good pork chop is a chop with fat. The fat provides a lot of flavor to the meat and it's also a sign that it comes from a good-quality animal and not one raised on a "factory" farm.

WHY FLIP THE MEAT?

If you flip your pork chop only once, the well-cooked and dry surface layer will be too thick. But if you flip it every 30 seconds, this overcooked part stays very thin while allowing the heat to penetrate and cook the center of the meat. Perfect!

SLOWLY BRAISED PORK CHEEK

This is pure French pub food, cooked slowly and for a long time. But there are a few tips you should know to make this dish even more flavorful. Don't hesitate to make it the day before, it will only taste better for it.

For more information, see:
Braising p 168
How to create more juices p 168
What is collagen? p 180
Tender meat, tough meat—what's the difference? p 181

Begin this recipe a little in advance or even the day before
Preparation time: 20 minutes
Cooking time: 3 hours 30 minutes

SERVES 6

- 18 pork cheeks
- 3 tbsp olive oil
- 2 carrots, diced
- 1 large onion, diced
- 1 clove
- 1 small piece onion (stick the clove into the onion)
- 4 cloves garlic, peeled and crushed
- 5 sprigs thyme
- 1 bay leaf, halved lengthwise
- 1 cup dry white wine
- 2⅛ cups fresh Pork or Veal Broth (p 230) or use frozen
- 1 tbsp unsalted butter
- Sea salt and freshly ground black pepper

1
Preheat the oven to 285°F. Heat a cast iron pot over medium heat.

2
Place the pork cheeks in a large bowl and drizzle them with the olive oil. Stir to coat using a large spoon or (even better) your fingers so that each cheek is covered in a thin layer of oil.

3
Place some of the cheeks flat in the hot pot and brown them on each side. Transfer them to a large platter. Brown the other cheeks.
→ Whatever you do, don't put too many cheeks into the pot at the same time; they won't brown.

4
In the same pot (don't clean it!) and over low heat, add the carrots, onion, piece of onion, garlic, thyme, and the bay leaf. Season lightly with salt and let sweat for 5 or 6 minutes, or until the onions are translucent. Increase the heat, add the wine, and let simmer for 5 minutes, or until reduced by half. Add 1 cup of the broth and bring to a simmer before adding the cheeks side by side and flat against the bottom of the pan. You've just created the base for your sauce.
→ As it browns, the meat creates juices that stick to the bottom of the pot. The water from the vegetables as well as the wine and broth loosen these juices and create a base for the sauce.
→ When you sweat vegetables, you also cause some of the water they contain to evaporate. By adding a little salt, you accelerate this evaporation and concentrate the flavors of the vegetables. That's great!

5
Cover the pot and place it in the middle of the oven for 3 hours.
→ During the cooking process the liquid heats and turns into steam, which condenses on the bottom of the lid before turning back into liquid droplets and dripping down onto the meat. This means that the cheeks are being constantly basted.

6
Remove the cooked cheeks and put them in a large dish. Pour the sauce through a sieve set over a large bowl, pressing the herbs and spices to extract all the flavors. Pour the sauce into the pot and place it over low heat. Add the butter, stir well, and allow the sauce to thicken for 2 to 3 minutes, if necessary.
→ The butter will make the sauce rounder and give it length on the palate. "Round" means that the sauce's flavors are softer and "length" means that they linger longer in the mouth.

7

Place the cheeks in the pot and ladle the sauce on top. Cover the pot and let rest for at least 1 hour or even until the next day, if you can resist.

→ During the resting time the sauce infiltrates the meat's fibers. Each mouthful of meat will contain some sauce, and this will give you the impression that the meat is juicier than it actually is. The sauce will also very slightly penetrate the meat; this is why saucy dishes prepared the day before taste even better the next day.

8

Reheat the cheeks and the sauce for about 15 minutes over very low heat. Season with salt and pepper. Serve this dish with homemade mashed potatoes, a scattering of green cabbage, or a lentil salad.

You can boast about it because your dish is beautiful!

WHY THREE HOURS OF COOKING FOR SUCH SMALL PIECES OF MEAT?

The cheek is classed as a "tough" meat because it contains collagen. To turn this tough meat into a tender meat, you need to slowly melt the collagen in a moist environment and over a low temperature. The melted collagen turns into gelatin, providing a lot of benefit to the meat and the sauce.

PORK CHEEK?

Yes! It's a lean, soft, very slightly gelatinous cut, and delicious when cooked slowly and for a long time. Traditionally, it used to be a tripe product, but do you know many tripe butchers? Luckily, regular butchers sell them too, or they can order them.

CAN'T YOU USE WATER INSTEAD OR BROTH TO MAKE A SAUCE BASE?

Yes, of course you can. But it's not as good. When meat is cooked in water, the flavors balance out, causing the flavors of the meat to dilute a little into the water. When it's cooked in a broth that's already full of flavor, the meat doesn't have to make up for the lack of flavors in the water and so loses very little of its taste.

HERBY RACK OF LAMB EN CROÛTE

This is a really simple recipe and one that will amaze your guests when you bring it to the table.

For more information, see:
How to season your meat with salt p 112
Roasting p 144
How to create more juices p 168

Preparation time: 20 minutes
Salting time: 3 hours
Cooking time: 30 minutes

SERVES 6

- 2 racks of lamb, formed from the front ribs and 2 rib chops
(separate the ribs from the chine bone to facilitate carving)
- 1 tbsp olive oil
- Salt

For the jus:
- 1 tbsp olive oil
- 1 lb trimmings and crushed lamb bones
- ½ onion, peeled and diced
- ½ carrot, peeled and diced
- 1 clove garlic, peeled and diced
- 1 bouquet garni (2 sprigs parsley, 3 to 4 sprigs thyme) wrapped in leek leaves and firmly tied
- 1 tbsp unsalted butter
- 3 sprigs tarragon, stems removed, leaves finely chopped
- Fine sea salt

For the herby crust:
- 10 slices bread, dried, without the crusts
- 1 anchovy, rinsed
- 2 cloves garlic, peeled
- 1 bunch parsley, leaves removed
- 1 bunch tarragon, leaves removed
- 4¼ oz butter, half salted, half unsalted, at room temperature
- 1 tbsp unsalted butter, melted

1
Make incisions in the fat of the lamb racks.
→ Make the incisions without cutting into the flesh! These incisions will allow the herby crust to stick to the meat instead of slipping off into the cooking dish.

2
Season the top and bottom of the racks with salt and let rest for 3 hours at room temperature.
→ I know it's repetitive, but I'm going to repeat this: salt penetrates meat very, very slowly. For it to be effective, it needs to be added hours before.

3
Prepare the jus. Heat a pot over medium heat, add the oil, and brown the bones and the trimmings. Reduce to low heat and add the onion, carrot, garlic, and bouquet garni. Lightly season with salt and let sweat for 5 minutes, or until the onion is translucent. Pour in 1 cup of water and reduce it, uncovered, by three-quarters its volume, about 20 minutes.

4
Prepare the herby crust. In a food processor, process the dried bread (crumbling it into pieces), anchovy, garlic, parsley, and tarragon with the room-temperature butter until you obtain a relatively coarse mixture. Pour this mixture into a bowl and set 1 tablespoon of it aside for the "grand finale." Add the melted butter to the bowl and mix well with a fork until it makes a paste.

5
Preheat the oven to 350°F. Place the meat in a dish and drizzle it with the olive oil, making sure that it's entirely covered in a light coating of the oil. Over high heat, heat a frying pan or a pot large enough to easily hold both racks and brown them for 1 minute on the cap side, then for 1 minute on the other.
→ The cap side (fat side) should be browned first; the fat will melt slightly and create flavors in which the other parts will cook, causing them to create even more flavors themselves. Next, brown the other side, which will turn golden brown in the fat juices.

6
Place the lamb on a serving platter. See all those juices begging to be unstuck from the bottom of the pan? You're not going to leave them there, are you? Up they come! Collect them with a spoon and baste the racks with them.
→ Baste the top, bottom, and sides of the racks. These juices will give flavor to the meat and the sauce.

7

Place the racks, bone down, in the middle of the hot oven for 10 minutes.
→ By placing your racks bone down, the cap side and the curved interior side will cook evenly.

8

Remove the racks, baste them with the remaining fat in the pot, and let rest for 10 minutes under a triple layer of foil. Switch your oven to broil at the highest temperature.

THE GRAND FINALE

9

Pour the juices from the pot through a cheesecloth without pressing the vegetables down. Add the 1 tablespoon of butter and reheat over low temperature, stirring gently.

10

Remove the foil and lay out your racks, cap side facing upward. Lightly baste them with the melted butter, which will help adhere the herby crust to the meat. Then, with a spoon, evenly spread the parsley paste across the meat and add the 1 tablespoon of the coarse mixture that you kept aside. Use the back of the spoon to press it down, and place the meat in the middle of the oven beneath the hot broiler for 2 to 3 minutes, just enough time for it to turn golden brown.

11

Place the racks on a serving platter. Add the tarragon to the jus, pour into a gravy boat, and serve.

You'll cut the rack into separate ribs.

AN ANCHOVY? HEY, YOU'RE INSANE!

Hey, calm down! First of all, the meat won't taste of fish at all. The interesting thing is that this anchovy contains lots of glutamic and inosinic acids. These two acids, along with guanylic acid, are at the base of "umami," the fifth flavor. This isn't really new; Brillat-Savarin had already spoken of it back in 1825, calling it "osmazome" in his book *The Physiology of Taste*. It's unknowingly used in France in many recipes. For example, in a veal stock, onions, and carrots, rich in glutamic acid, are paired with veal, rich in inosinic acid. And then, when these two acids are combined, we get even more flavors than both their flavors together. Basically, it's 1 + 1 = 3. All this to tell you that that tiny little anchovy will give a huge boost to your herby crust and make it even tastier.

AND THE SIDES?

With such an explosively tasty lamb rack, you need a mixture of barely cooked vegetables warmed in a pan, such as asparagus, a few fresh mushrooms, or green beans.

5-HOUR LAMB SHOULDER

This dish is usually made with a leg of lamb and cooked for 7 hours, but shoulder has so much more to offer. It's a tastier, more meltingly delicious meat, and the fat it contains brings roundness to the dish. Use the shoulder!

For more information, see:
Which cookware for my beautiful piece of meat? p 106
The size of the cookware p 108
Braising p 154
How to create more juices p 168

Preparation time: 20 minutes
Cooking time: 6 hours

SERVES 4

- 1 lamb shoulder, boned and tied + the bone, crushed
- 1 tbsp olive oil
- 2 slices lamb neck
- 7 oz lamb trimmings
- 1 large onion, peeled and large diced
- 2 carrots, peeled and large diced
- 20 cloves garlic, unpeeled
- 1 bouquet garni (10 sprigs parsley, 5 to 6 sprigs thyme, 1 sprig rosemary) wrapped in leek leaves and firmly tied
- 1 cup dry white wine
- Fine sea salt
- 1 clean cloth
(ensure it hasn't been washed with softener, otherwise your dish will smell like a flowery meadow)

For the sealing dough:
- 10½ oz all-purpose flour
- 1 large egg
- 1 tsp fine salt

1
Heat a pan barely larger than the shoulder over high heat. Coat the shoulder in the oil on all sides. Brown the shoulder on the top, bottom, and sides. Set it aside on a plate and wrap it in plastic wrap.
→ By browning the meat you're giving it more flavor and creating juices that you'll use to make the cooking stock.

2
In the same pot (do not wash it), brown the lamb neck, the shoulder bone, and the trimmings. Reduce the heat and add the onion, carrots, garlic, and bouquet garni. Lightly season with salt and let sweat for several minutes until the onions are translucent. Add the white wine and let it evaporate almost completely. Then pour in 1 quart of water, cover, and let cook slowly, without simmering, for 1 hour.
→ You're infusing all these lovely ingredients to make a proper sauce base.

3
Make the sealing dough. In a large bowl, combine the flour, egg, and salt with 1 scant cup of water to make a dough with an elastic consistency (you can also do this in a food processor). Cover with plastic wrap and set aside.

4
Preheat the oven to 250°F. Pour the sauce base into a bowl.

5
Here's the secret to easily removing the meat from the pan after cooking: place the clean cloth in the bottom of the pot. Put the neck, the bone, the trimmings, the vegetables, and the herbs in the middle of the cloth and place the shoulder on top.
→ The meat shouldn't be in contact with the juices because you want it to steam cook. We're braising this according to classic culinary practice: not boiling it or, worse, something in between the two!

6
Prepare the sealing dough. Lightly flour a work surface, place the dough on top, and roll it into a sausage shape, long enough to wrap around the pot. Place the lid on the pot and apply the dough over the gap between the two, pressing down firmly so that it sticks and makes the pot airtight.

7

Place in the middle of the oven for 5 hours.
→ Here's what happens inside the pot: the meat doesn't boil in the stock, it cooks in a flavorful steam. The vegetables and the neck release some of their flavors, enriching the cooking stock that slowly evaporates. The steam, confined inside the pot, comes into contact with the lid, condenses, liquefies, and drips down on to the meat. This continues during the whole cooking process and is what makes the meat so tasty.

8

Break the sealing dough and gently remove the shoulder by picking up the cloth on each side. Transfer the shoulder to a warmed platter before covering it with a triple layer of foil.

9

Discard the slices of neck and the crushed bones (They've given all they had, the poor things.) Pour everything that remains in the pot and in the cloth through a conical strainer above a large bowl, pressing down on the vegetables to capture all their juices. Put the collected liquid back into the pot over medium heat for a few minutes to reduce it slightly and to give it some consistency.

10

Pour the sauce into a gravy boat and take it to the table with the shoulder and serve. Your friends will be truly impressed!

A DOUGH COVERING THE POT AND THE LID?

This is called "sealing the pot." Thanks to this dough, your pot will be airtight and nothing will escape, not even the smallest wisp of steam. And it makes such a difference! Your lamb shoulder will cook in a very humid environment and become so tender. This type of dough is called "dead dough" because you don't eat it.

A RADICAL APPROACH

If, like me, you're pretty crazy, you can put the vegetables, the neck slices, and the bones in a large muslin cloth at the bottom of the pot. Then place the shoulder, also rolled in muslin cloth, on top. You'll make removing the lamb easier and you can simply strain the muslin containing the vegetables to extract all the juices.

WHY THIS PARTICULAR COOKING METHOD?

This recipe dates back to a time when people didn't eat lamb but instead ate old, tough mutton. The meat was so tough and so strong that it had to be cooked for a long time to make it edible.

WHAT IS THE CLOTH AT THE BOTTOM OF THE POT FOR?

By placing your cloth at the bottom of the pot and picking it up by its sides, you'll be able to remove the meat easily without it falling apart.

ROLLED LEG
OF LAMB

A typical approach when preparing leg of lamb is to rub the herbs and spices onto the lamb leg and roast it at 355°F. But there is a more cunning approach for a better result while using the same ingredients!

For more information, see:
The size of the cookware p 108
How to season your meat with salt p 112
Marinades p 136
Basting meat p 162
Resting meat p 164

Begin the recipe the day before
Preparation time: 20 minutes
Salting time: 2 hours
Marinating time: 2 hours
Cooking time: 3 hours 30 minutes
Resting time: 20 minutes

SERVES 6

- 1 (4 lb 6½-oz) leg of lamb, boned (ask your butcher for the crushed bone and the trimmings)
- 5 cloves garlic, unpeeled
- ⅓ cup dry white wine
- 2 tbsp unsalted butter
- Butcher's twine
- Fine sea salt and freshly ground black pepper

For the marinade
- 1 tbsp olive oil
- 3 cloves garlic, peeled and crushed
- 1 sprig rosemary, stems removed, leaves finely chopped

THE DAY BEFORE

1
Place the lamb leg face down on a work surface with the boned side up. Lightly season with salt, spreading the salt with your fingers to get it into all the little crevices. Turn the leg over and do the same on the other side. Roll up the leg and place it in the refrigerator for 3 hours, enough time for the salt to dissolve and begin to slightly penetrate the meat.
➔ When salt penetrates meat, it modifies the structure of certain proteins. Once modified, these proteins won't expel any juices; the meat will stay much more tender during the cooking process as a result. But salt needs a long time to penetrate deeply into the meat. This is why you salt it 24 hours before cooking.

2
Prepare the marinade. Heat the olive oil in a saucepan over gentle heat. Add the garlic and the rosemary and let cook slowly for 5 minutes. Turn off the heat and let cool.
➔ This is very important. When you cook the lamb leg, the temperature of its center won't surpass 130°F for a pink meat or 150°F for a medium-rare meat. The garlic doesn't cook at these temperatures and remains raw. Therefore, you cook the garlic before adding it to the leg.

3
Remove the leg from the refrigerator and place it flat again on a work surface with the boned side up. Spread half the marinade over it with your fingers so that the meat is completely covered. Roll the leg up again with the boned side on the inside, ensuring the thickness is even so that it cooks evenly.

4
Now tie up the beast. Tie the leg evenly at ¾-inch intervals, pulling the twine relatively tight because the meat expands a little as it cooks. Make a knot at every interval. Spread the remaining marinade on top.
➔ By putting marinade on the inside and the outside of the lamb leg, this will make it considerably more flavorful.

5
Wrap the meat tightly in plastic wrap to make it airtight and place it in the refrigerator for 24 hours.
➔ The less air around the meat, the more effective the marinade.

ON THE DAY

6

Preheat the oven to 285°F. Remove the leg from the refrigerator, remove the plastic wrap, and choose a baking dish that's slightly larger than the leg—but only slightly!

7

Place the leg in the baking dish, spread the crushed bone, trimmings, and garlic around it, and place it in the middle of the oven. Cook for 3 hours, basting 4 or 5 times throughout.
→ During the cooking process, juices form on the meat and the bones and drip down into the dish. When you baste, you pick these juices up and pour them onto the meat.

8

Remove the leg from the oven, transfer it to a plate, and let rest for about 20 minutes under a triple layer of foil.
→ It's not true when people say that the meat "relaxes" as it rests! Here's what really happens: the exterior, which dries out a little as it cooks, absorbs some of the juices contained in the center of the meat, and as they cool, these juices thicken. That's it! The meat was never tense, poor thing.

9

Increase the temperature of the oven to its maximum. Discard the trimmings and the crushed bone and crush the garlic cloves. Combine the crushed garlic with the juices from the bottom of the baking dish. Pour in the white wine and scrape up the sticky juices before pouring all of this into a saucepan. Heat over gentle heat and add the butter. Let it melt, stirring slowly; set aside in a warm place.

10

Once the oven is very hot, place the leg in the baking dish and place it in the oven for about 10 minutes. Don't let it burn (that would be such a shame!). When the leg is golden brown, remove it from the oven and remove the twine. Cut it into thin slices and season with salt and pepper. Pour the sauce into a gravy boat and off you go, dinner is served!

You're about to serve an incredibly tender piece of meat.

WHY NOT COOK THE LEG AT 350°F AS USUAL?

The higher the temperature at which you cook the meat, the more it dries out and the bigger the difference between the doneness of the exterior and of the center. With a low temperature and a longer cooking time, you get a juicier and more tender piece of meat that's cooked evenly on the inside and outside.

WHY DON'T YOU PUT SALT IN THE MARINADE?

It's simple: salt dissolves in water but not in oil. If the grains of salt are covered in oil, the oil will form a protective layer, which will stop the grains of salt from coming into contact with the moisture of the meat. As a result, they won't be able to dissolve!

SOME GOOD, HOMEMADE MASHED POTATOES AS A SIDE?

For such a simple dish, you need a simple side. So why not some good old homemade mashed potatoes? You can make a little well in them and fill it with the meat juices.

NAVARIN OF LAMB

A great French culinary classic to celebrate the return of spring: a magnificent, braised lamb dish, light and colorful with orange (carrots), green (peas and greens), purple (turnips and radishes), and white (spring onions). This dish will fill people with joy!

For more information, see:
Adapting the size of the meat to the cooking method
p 132
Braising p 154
Ragout p 157
How to create more juices p 158
Stocks and broths p 228

Preparation time: 20 minutes
Cooking time: 2 hours 20 minutes

SERVES 6

- 1⅓ lb lamb shoulder, cut into 6 identically sized pieces
- 1⅓ lb lamb saddle, cut into 6 identically sized pieces
- ⅓ cup fresh Lamb Stock (p 230) or use frozen
- 2 tbsp olive oil
- 1 bouquet garni (5 sprigs parsley, 5 to 6 sprigs thyme, 2 sprigs rosemary) wrapped in leek leaves and firmly tied
- 3 cloves garlic, peeled and crushed
- 1 onion, peeled and small diced
- 1 carrot, peeled and small diced
- Fine sea salt

For the vegetables:
- 8 tbsp unsalted butter
- 1 tbsp confectioners' sugar
- 1 bunch baby carrots, peeled, with greens cut down to ¾ inch
- 1 bunch small spring onions
- ¼ bunch radishes, rinsed, roots removed, with greens cut down to ⅓ inch
- 14 oz new potatoes, rinsed in water
- 7 oz peas
- 1 large sheet parchment paper

1
Reduce the lamb stock by two-thirds in a large saucepan over medium heat.
→ Stock reduces a lot faster in a large saucepan because the surface area through which the steam can escape is larger.

2
Preheat the oven to 285°F. Heat a cast iron pot over medium-high heat. Place the lamb pieces in a large bowl, drizzle with the oil, and toss well so that all the pieces are covered in a thin layer of oil.
→ The meat, less hot than the oil, cools the oil during the cooking process. If there's no meat to cool it, the oil burns. This is why you put the oil on the meat and not directly in the pot.

3
Once the pot is hot, add 4 or 5 pieces of lamb, spacing them out so that they're not touching.
→ Meat releases water as it browns. If this water gets trapped beneath the meat, the meat will boil in its own juices and won't brown.

4
Let the meat brown for 1 to 2 minutes, then flip it and brown the other side. Set aside on a plate.

5
Reduce the heat to low. Add the bouquet garni, garlic, onion, and the carrot. Season lightly with salt and let sweat for a few minutes until the onions are translucent.
→ The salt will absorb some of the water contained inside the vegetables. Once this tasteless water has evaporated, you get vegetables that are a lot tastier and that you can use to make a broth.

6
Add the reduced lamb stock, scraping up all the cooking juices that are stuck to the bottom of the pot. Place the meat on top, cover, and place in the oven for 1 hour 30 minutes.

7
Prepare the vegetables. Heat a large frying pan over gentle heat. Add the butter, confectioners' sugar, and 2 tablespoons of water. Bring to a simmer, then add the carrots, onions, and radishes. Place a sheet of parchment paper on top and cut around it using the edges of the pan as a guide. Make a hole in the center to allow steam to escape. Cook over gentle heat for about 20 minutes.
→ The vegetables will release very little water because there's no room for steam between them and the parchment paper.

8

Put the potatoes in a small saucepan, cover with water, and boil for about 15 minutes.

9

Heat a large saucepan of water. Once boiling, add the peas and cook for 1 to 2 minutes, then transfer them to a large bowl of ice-cold water to stop the cooking.

10

Check the doneness of the vegetables in the pan. If there's still some liquid in the pan, remove the parchment paper to allow it to evaporate. Add the cooked peas and stir gently for another 2 to 3 minutes to glaze the vegetables.
→ During the cooking process, the mixture of butter, sugar, vegetable juices, and water form a syrup that envelops the vegetables and gives them a shiny glaze.

11

Check the doneness of the meat and place it in a large, warmed dish. If you find that the sauce isn't thick enough, reduce it for 2 minutes over high heat. If, however, you prefer a more liquid consistency, add a little lamb stock. Pour the sauce onto the meat and arrange the vegetables attractively around it.

Look at that meat with its silky sauce and the slightly sweet and crunchy vegetables. Aren't all those springtime colors beautiful? Quick, sit down at the table for the magnificent dish you've just prepared. What talent!!

SHOULDER AND LEG AT THE SAME TIME?

The two cuts are different and have different textures and flavors to offer. The leg of lamb is drier than the shoulder, which is a little fattier. These characteristics enrich the navarin, just like when you use several different meats in a stew.

DOES THE SIZE OF THE MEAT PIECES MATTER?

It matters very much! Specify with your butcher that the pieces of meat must be of the same size. If not, the small pieces will cook faster than the big pieces and, as a result, some will be overcooked and some undercooked.

WHY IS IT CALLED "NAVARIN"?

People often say that it's the French word for one of the ingredients, the turnip, that gave its name to this dish: *navet* → "navarin." So why not call it "carrot" or "onion of lamb," in that case? It was actually the naval Battle of Navarino (1827). Admiral de Rigny asked that the usual rice be replaced by vegetables to improve the diet of his crew. This recipe was first called a "Navarin Ragout" and then "Navarin of Lamb." It has nothing to do with turnips.

ROAST CHICKEN WITH THE CRISPIEST SKIN IN THE WORLD

Have you ever walked past a Chinese restaurant with roasted Peking duck hanging in the window? They're suspended like that so that their skin dries out and they're extra crispy when cooked. We're going to do the same with the chicken skin to make it scandalously crunchy.

For more information, see:
Brining and salting p 134
Roasting p 144
Resting meat p 164

Begin the recipe 3 days before cooking (yes, 3 days!)
Preparation time: 20 minutes
Brining time: 12 hours
Drying time: 48 hours
Resting time: 20 minutes
Cooking time: 3 hours 15 minutes

SERVES 4

-1 chicken weighing between 4¼ to 4¾ lb, with the giblets set aside
(ideally you need a prize chicken, such as a Bresse or one of the ancient breeds)

For the brine:
-1½ gallons mineral water
-Salt (6 percent of the weight of the mineral water)

For the sauce:
- 1 (16-oz) can beer
- 1 onion, peeled and diced
- 1 carrot, peeled and diced
- 2 button mushrooms, washed and diced
- 1 clove garlic, peeled and crushed
- About 15 sprigs thyme
- 5 tbsp unsalted butter, room temperature
- 3 tbsp good-quality dry white wine
- 1 cup chicken stock
- 1 sprig tarragon, stems removed, leaves finely chopped
- Fine sea salt and freshly ground black pepper

3 DAYS BEFORE

1
Remove any twine from around the chicken, if necessary. Pull on the legs to separate them a little from the breast.
→ When the thighs are stuck to the body, the cooking time is longer, causing the breast meat to overcook. If you pull the thighs away from the body, the thighs and breast meat cook evenly.

2
Gently slide your fingers beneath the chicken skin to detach it from the flesh, being careful not to pierce it. Start with the breast and slowly move down toward the thighs and the tops of the wings.
→ During cooking, the flesh releases a lot of water. If the skin is separated from this water, it will dry out more easily and be a lot crispier.

3
Prepare the brine. Place the chicken in a large pot and pour in the mineral water until it's 2 inches above the chicken. Measure the quantity of water you've just used and add 6 percent of its weight in salt. Stir to dissolve the salt, incline the chicken to release any air stuck in its cavity, and place it back down so that it's flat on the bottom of the pot. Cover and refrigerate for 12 hours.
-Inclining the chicken will allow the chicken to be completely submerged and full of the brine on the inside as well.

TWO DAYS BEFORE

4
Rinse the chicken under cold water. Bring a large pot of water to a boil. Fill a large bowl with ice-cold water. Drop the chicken into the pot, boil it for 30 seconds, then submerge it in the ice-cold water. Repeat this once more, then dry the inside and outside of the chicken.
→ The bad-quality fat will liquefy and release from the chicken. By cooling the meat immediately, you'll prevent the flesh from starting to cook.

5
Clean the beer can thoroughly all over. Insert it into the chicken's cavity, and stand the chicken up on the can, set the chicken down into a baking dish, and refrigerate it for 2 days without covering.
→ The moisture inside the skin will evaporate little by little. Protected by the skin, the flesh won't dry out.

ON THE DAY

6

Preheat the oven to 250°F. Remove the can from the chicken. Pour out half the beer. With a bottle opener, make some holes in the top of the can and place it back inside the chicken's cavity. Place the chicken, upright on its can, in a baking dish. Arrange the diced onion, carrot, mushrooms, garlic, and thyme around it. Spread 1½ tablespoons of the butter across the whole surface of the chicken. Position the grilling rack at the bottom of the oven so that the chicken will sit mid-height, then place the chicken on the rack, the breast turned toward the oven window and as close to it as possible. Cook for 3 hours.

→ The oven window emits a lot less radiant heat than the rest of the oven. Even if the breast is the same temperature as the thighs, it cooks slower.

→ During cooking, the beer produces steam that condenses on the walls of the chicken's cavity, absorbing its flavors before dripping down into the baking dish to make the sauce even more delectable.

7

Remove the chicken from the oven and let rest with the can still inside for 20 minutes. Strain everything from the baking dish through a sieve and reserve; this will be the base for the sauce.

8

Increase the temperature of the oven to its maximum. Once hot, place the chicken back in the oven, still on its can and in a baking dish, but on the middle rack this time. Let it brown without burning; this should take about 10 minutes.

9

In a saucepan, heat the cooking juices over medium heat, then add the white wine and chicken stock. Cook to reduce by half. Just before serving, add the remaining butter, then add the tarragon leaves. Season with salt and pepper and pour it into a gravy boat.

10

Take the chicken to the table, still on its can. Remove the can and carve the chicken in front of your guests.

Can you hear the crackling of the skin when you slice through it with your knife? Can you imagine how succulent this thing is? See the flesh beneath it, shining with all the juices it contains? This recipe is insane!

HOW DOES LEAVING THE CHICKEN TO DRY MAKE A DIFFERENCE?

Three-fourths of a chicken's skin is made of water. As long as there's water, the skin will be moist and therefore won't crisp. When you leave the chicken to dry in the refrigerator, most of this moisture evaporates. Once the skin has dried out, it will be able to become extremely crisp.

WHAT DOES BRINING ACHIEVE?

When meat is brined it stays juicier. Depending on which type and cut of meat you're using, brining can make meat up to 20 percent more juicy as it cooks. That's a lot, don't you think?

WHY A CAN?

A can, yes, but a big one, such as 16 oz. This is important! It needs to be half empty, and, above all, very clean: when we're ready to begin cooking, we'll slide the can into the chicken's cavity. Standing upright on its can inside the oven, no part of the chicken sits on the baking dish so every bit of its skin will be crispy.

DUCK BREASTS

Of course, you could cook your duck breasts in a pan, like everyone else. But look closely and you'll see that breast has two very different sides: flesh on one and fat and skin on the other. It pays to cook each of these sides using the temperature and technique that will enhance their differences.

For more information, see:
Temperatures and cooking thermometers p 110
Brining and salting p 134
Sauteing p 142

Preparation time: 5 minutes
Salting time: 1 hour
Cooking time: 5 minutes + 1 hour

SERVES 4

- 2 duck breasts, from the best possible source
- Fine sea salt and freshly ground black pepper
- 1 sewing needle

1
Pour 4 tablespoons of salt on a plate and place the breasts on top, skin side down. Leave at room temperature for 1 hour.
→ As the salt dissolves it absorbs the water contained inside the skin. The skin dries out and will become super crispy when cooked.

2
Brush off the excess undissolved salt, then dry the breasts with a cloth. Preheat the oven to 175°F.
→ I advise you to use a thermometer to check that the oven is at the correct temperature and not at 140°F or 210°F, as some oven thermostats can be inaccurate.

3
Take the sewing needle and wash it with water. Prick the skin through the fat under the skin without penetrating the flesh beneath it. Make about fifty little holes in each breast.
→ Don't worry, the holes will be so small that you won't see them once the meat is cooked.

4
Heat a large frying pan over medium heat and add the breasts, skin side down, ensuring that there's space between them. Cook for 5 minutes, spooning the melted fat out of the pan several times.
→ It's not visible to the naked eye, but a lot of the fat beneath the skin will come out through the little holes you made.

5
Press down gently on the excess skin to brown it. Once browned, flip the breasts and sear the flesh side for 2 minutes. Place the breasts in a baking dish with the skin side on top and cook them in the middle of the oven for 45 minutes.
→ The low cooking temperature prevents the meat from contracting and expelling juices: the meat cooks while remaining tender and juicy. At this temperature, the meat will also cook more evenly.

6
Check the temperature at the center of the breasts, it should be between 130°F and 140°F for rare to medium rare.

7
Just before the end of the cooking time, reheat the frying pan over high heat. Take the breasts out of the oven and add them to the pan for 2 minutes, skin side down, to make them crispy again.

8

Remove the excess skin from the sides and cut the breasts at an angle into slices.

→ An angled cut allows you to cut through the length of the fibers. Shorter fibers make the meat easier to chew and your meat will be a lot more tender.

9

Season with salt and pepper and serve.

Two breasts, salt and pepper, 5 minutes of work, and such a different result. Cooking is magical, isn't it?

WHY NOT REMOVE THE EXCESS FAT BEFORE COOKING?

Absolutely not! We've just seen that the skin will retract under the effect of the heat; the extra skin will contract and shrink, too. By a great deal or by very little, we don't know—it varies from breast to breast. So, we remove the excess skin after cooking for a perfectly cooked breast and a clean cut, but never before.

AND WHY FINISH THE COOKING IN THE OVEN?

Cooking duck breasts presents a major difficulty: their two sides are different and call for opposite cooking times and temperatures. For a good result, a hot pan is needed for the skin side and a much cooler pan for the flesh side. The solution is to pan-fry only the skin side and then very quickly sear the flesh side, before finishing the breasts slowly in the oven at a low temperature. This will ensure the breasts are cooked and hot all the way through and avoids overcooking the flesh side, as is commonly done.

WHAT ABOUT INCISIONS?

We generally make incisions in the skin, and people say that it's to prevent the meat from retracting as it cooks. This is not true! The proof is in the cooking: once cooked, there's a lot of space between the incisions. The skin retracts with or without them.

WHY DO YOU SALT THE SKIN IN ADVANCE?

The skin is full of water. And to make it super crispy, it needs to contain as little of this water as possible. When you add salt before cooking, the salt absorbs some of the moisture the skin contains and dries it out. The skin will turn crispy a lot faster and you'll avoid overcooking the flesh.

PRICKING THE SKIN WITH A NEEDLE?

It's funny how this happens: during the cooking process, the fat beneath the skin heats and melts slightly. The tiny invisible holes allow the fat to drip out and into the pan, avoiding an overly thick layer of fat beneath the skin after cooking.

FRIED CHICKEN FOR LITTLE RASCALS

Forget KFC, here's a recipe for real fried chicken—light, super crispy, juicy, and flavorful—that the kids, and everyone else, will love!

For more information, see:
Marinades p 136

Begin the recipe in the morning or the day before
Preparation time: 20 minutes
Marinating time: 2 to 24 hours
Resting time: 2 hours
Cooking time: 15 minutes

SERVES 6

6 boneless and skinless free-range chicken thighs

For the spice mix and the marinade:
- 2 tsp paprika
- 2 tsp dried oregano
- I tsp ground coriander
- Pinch of grated nutmeg
- ¼ tsp cayenne pepper
- I tsp freshly ground black pepper
- 2 tsp garlic powder
- ½ tsp fine sea salt
- 1¼ cups buttermilk, or I scant cup milk plus ½ cup Greek yogurt, combined

For the sauce:
- 2 tbsp unsalted butter
- I onion, peeled and very finely diced
- 3 cloves garlic, peeled and finely diced
- I tsp cornstarch
- Scant cup milk
- Scant cup crème fraîche
- Fine sea salt and freshly ground black pepper

To fry:
- 6 cups peanut oil
- I egg, beaten
- ¼ tsp salt

- 3½ oz all-purpose flour
- 1¾ oz cornstarch
- 1¼ tsp baking powder

THE MORNING OR THE DAY BEFORE

I
Place one of the thighs in a freezer bag and pound it with a saucepan to flatten it until it's ⅓ inch thick. Repeat with the other thighs.

2
Prepare the spice mix and the marinade. Mix all the spices with the garlic powder and salt; set aside two-thirds of this mixture for cooking. Combine the buttermilk with the remaining one-third to create a marinade.

3
Coat each thigh in the marinade and cover them with plastic wrap. Refrigerate for 2 hours or, even better, until the next day.

ON THE DAY

4
Remove the chicken from the refrigerator, reserve the excess marinade, and leave the meat at room temperature for 2 hours to warm up.

5
Prepare the sauce. Melt the butter in a large sauté pan over gentle heat, then add the onion, lightly season with salt, and sweat for 3 to 4 minutes until the onion is translucent. Add the garlic and cook for another 2 minutes. Add the cornstarch and cook for another I or 2 minutes until the cornstarch has been absorbed by the butter. Add the milk and crème fraîche. Reduce for a few minutes to thicken it. Taste and season with salt and pepper.

6
Prepare to fry. Heat the oil in a large pan to 320°F.
→ The secret to nongreasy fried food is to keep the oil very hot during the cooking process. This way, the moisture contained in the chicken and in the coating turns into steam and repels the oil. However, if the oil isn't hot enough, there'll be no steam to repel it; it will penetrate the coating and make it greasy. Opt for a large sauté or frying pan because the heated surface area is a lot bigger.

7

Preheat the oven to 285°F. In a large bowl, combine the reserved spices with the beaten egg, salt, flour, cornstarch, and baking powder. Incorporate 3 tablespoons of the marinade with a fork.

→ When the flour in this mixture comes into contact with the marinade, small moist clumps will form and explode during the cooking process, becoming super crispy.

8

Place the chicken pieces one by one into the mixture, pressing down firmly so that they're completely coated.

9

Check the temperature of the oil: Toss a piece of bread into it; it should brown in 30 seconds. Gently place the chicken pieces in the pan. Don't touch them and don't turn them over until the coating is golden brown. This will take about 2 minutes. Flip and brown the other side.

10

Place the fried chicken pieces on a double layer of paper towels. Gently pat the top with more paper towels.

→ You'll remove more than 90 percent of the excess oil by doing this.

11

Put the chicken pieces on a grilling rack in the middle of a hot oven and place a large baking dish on the floor of the oven to catch all the bits that might fall.

→ The chicken pieces stay hot and the steam continues to escape, preventing the little remaining oil from penetrating the coating. Magic!

→ Don't put place the chicken pieces in a baking dish, the steam will be trapped underneath the meat and will soften the coating. That would be too bad!

12

Reheat the sauce before pouring it into a gravy boat. Remove the fried chicken from the oven and bring it to the table accompanied by its sauce.

Begin by serving the children, give them a little bit of sauce and . . . oh! They've already started without you. Isn't it great seeing them so happy?

WHAT EXACTLY IS BUTTERMILK?

Buttermilk is like milk with a slightly lumpy consistency, and tastes like a yogurt drink with its acidic flavors. When you churn cream to make butter, a whitish liquid appears. This is the whey, also called buttermilk. This milk, slightly acidic, is commonly used in marinades for poultry.

BAKING POWDER?

Yes! As it mixes with the moisture of the marinade, the baking powder releases a gas that causes the coating to expand, making it very light and airy. Crazy!

WHY NOT USE CHICKEN BREAST?

Think of a roast chicken. Which part is the tastiest, the juiciest? Is it the breast or the thighs? It's the thighs, of course! So they're what we use for this recipe.

STUFFED GOOSE

Be careful, the goose is a real trickster. It's fatty but its meat is lean. It has a lot less flesh to eat on it than you would think. The secret to a perfect goose is a long, slow cooking process to stop the meat from drying out.

For more information, see:
Brining and salting p 134
Roasting p 144
Stocks and broths p 228

Begin the recipe the day before or two days before
Preparation time: 45 minutes
Drying time: 24 to 48 hours
Resting time: 30 minutes
Cooking time: 5 hours 30 minutes

SERVES 10

- 1 (8¾-10-lb) free-range goose with its liver and giblets
- 1 tsp fine sea salt
- Freshly ground black pepper
- 1 sewing needle

For the sauce:
- The goose's liver and giblets, finely diced
- 1 tbsp goose fat
- 3½ oz poultry liver, finely diced
- 1 large onion, peeled and finely diced
- 2 carrots, peeled and finely diced
- 4 cloves garlic, peeled and crushed
- 1 bouquet garni (5 sprigs flat-leaf parsley, 2 sprigs thyme) wrapped in leek leaves and firmly tied
- ¼ cup port
- 1⅔ cups red wine
- 4¼ cups fresh Chicken or Duck Stock (p 230)
- 4 tbsp unsalted butter, cubed
- Fine sea salt

For the stuffing:
- 14 oz foie gras, diced into ¾-inch cubes
- 14 oz ground veal
- 3 cloves garlic, peeled and finely diced
- 3 large shallots, peeled and finely diced
- 10 sprigs flat-leaf parsley, stems removed, leaves finely chopped
- 4 tbsp Panko (p 197) or homemade bread crumbs
- 2 large eggs

- 2 tbsp crème fraîche
- About 20 croutons
- Fine sea salt and freshly ground black pepper
- Butcher's twine

THE DAY BEFORE OR TWO DAYS BEFORE

1
Gently detach and discard the two lobes of fat from either side of the opening of the goose's cavity.
→ These lobes of fat would give a bad taste to the meat.

2
With the clean needle, make little holes ¾ inches apart across the surface of the bird, without penetrating the flesh beneath.
→ Geese have a thick layer of fat, which protects them from the cold when they swim. There's more of this fat around the breasts. The little holes will allow the fat to drip out through the skin once it's hot.

3
Fill a pot halfway with water and bring to a boil. Take the goose by the legs and immerse it in the boiling water for 2 to 3 minutes. Let cool for 5 minutes then immerse it again from the other end, holding it by the wings. Let it cool before drying it thoroughly inside and out.
→ When you soak the goose in the boiling water, some of the fat beneath the skin will heat, liquefy, and leak out through the holes made by the needle.

4
Salt the goose with the 1 teaspoon of salt across its entire surface. Press down gently so that the salt sticks, and place the goose on a grilling rack in the refrigerator to dry for 24 to 48 hours.
→ The salt acts as a drying accelerator and will make the skin so much crispier once it's cooked.

5
Prepare the sauce. Brown the giblets in a frying pan with the goose fat for 7 or 8 minutes. Set aside in a bowl. Brown the goose and poultry livers for 1 minute. Set aside in a bowl. Reduce the heat and add the diced vegetables, garlic, and the bouquet garni. Lightly season with salt and let cook slowly until the onion is translucent. Add the port and let it reduce slightly, scraping up the sticky juices from the bottom of the pan. Add the red wine and let it reduce by half before adding enough water to just cover the vegetables. Add the giblets, then cover and let cook for 1 hour over very low heat. Add the stock and let it reduce, uncovered, by half.

6

Pour the sauce base through a conical strainer, pressing down on the vegetables. Let the sauce cool slightly before incorporating the livers. Cover with plastic wrap and refrigerate overnight.
→ The flavors develop and are enriched overnight.

ON THE DAY

7

Prepare the stuffing. In a hot dry pan, fry the diced foie gras for I minute. In a bowl, gently combine all the stuffing ingredients and incorporate the foie gras along with the fat it released in the pan. Stuff the goose with this mixture and close the bird's cavity with the butcher's twine.
→ To tie up the goose, thread the twine through your biggest sewing needle and pierce the flesh ¾ inch (2 cm) above the cavity, pulling the thread across the opening and back again. Don't pull it too tight to avoid ripping the skin.

8

Preheat the oven to 285°F. Lay the goose on one thigh in a large baking dish and place it in the middle of the oven, positioning the breast as close as possible to the oven window. Cook for I hour 30 minutes, basting from time to time with the fat released by the bird. Flip it over onto the other thigh and baste again. Remove the fat from the bottom of the baking dish if there's too much of it. After I hour 30 minutes (3 hours after the beginning of the cooking process), put the goose back on its back, baste it, place the baking dish in the middle of the oven, and cook for I more hour.
→ It's important to position the breast meat near the window. This surface emits very little radiant heat so the meat will cook a lot more gently in this position than in other areas of the oven. It's perfect for slowly cooking breast meat and stopping it from drying out.

9

After 4 hours of cooking, take the goose out of the oven and collect all of the fat into a bowl; it will be perfect for frying potatoes another day. Let the goose rest at room temperature for 20 minutes before increasing the oven's heat to its maximum.

10

Brown the goose in the hot oven for about 10 minutes, making sure it doesn't burn. Heat the sauce over gentle heat and add the butter little by little, whisking constantly.

II

Carve the goose, lightly season with salt and pepper, and pour the sauce into a gravy boat.

Quick, hurry up taking this dish to the table. Everyone's waiting impatiently!

YOU ADD SALT TO THE SKIN THE DAY BEFORE?

Yes, yes, yes! This salt will absorb some of the moisture in the skin and, by leaving the bird in the open air of the refrigerator, the skin will continue to dry so that it becomes diabolically crispy when cooked.

THE STUFFING

Don't believe those who frequently tell you that the stuffing will give flavors to the meat. That's untrue, for not one but three very precise reasons:
I) Marinades take hours and hours to penetrate the meat. And you think the flavors of the stuffing could penetrate faster than that? Ridiculous!
2) There's a membrane inside the cavity whose purpose is to protect the flesh from the digestive system. This membrane is impermeable, so the flavors of the stuffing won't be able to get through; and 3) Between this membrane and the flesh is the rib cage, which is made of bones. Do you think the flavors are likely to get through bones in only a few hours?

STOCKS AND BROTHS

Of course, you could cook your stew, your blanquette, and your boiled chicken in water with vegetables. Of course, you could make a sauce by deglazing your cooking dish with water. But you can do better, and here's how.

For more information, see:
Which cookware for my beautiful piece of meat? p 106
Boiling p 150
Boiling, a user's manual p 152
Maillard reactions p 174
A matter of taste p 182

BEEF STOCK

Preparation time: 10 minutes
Cooking time: At least 6 hours
Resting time: 1 hour

MAKES 4¼ QUARTS

- 4½ lb beef (oxtail, thick rib, or shin)
- 2 marrowbones
- 2¼ lb ox bones, crushed by your butcher
- 2 tbsp olive oil
- 2 large onions, halved
- 3½ oz button mushrooms, washed and diced
- 3 carrots, peeled and diced
- 2 leeks (green leaves removed), washed and diced
- 6 cloves garlic, peeled and crushed
- 5 cloves
- 1 bouquet garni (10 sprigs parsley, 5 to 6 sprigs thyme, 2 bay leaves, cut in half) wrapped in leek leaves and firmly tied

1
Preheat the oven to 390°F. In a cast iron pot, coat the bones in the olive oil, place them in the pot, and brown them in the oven for 30 minutes, turning them over from time to time. Once well browned, remove the pot from the oven.

→ It doesn't look like much, but this is the base for our stock. The little pieces of meat stuck to the bones have browned and the cartilage on the ends of the bones has turned a golden color, too. The marrow melts and creates sticky juices at the bottom of the pot. All of this together develops an incredible quantity of flavors.

2
Set the bones aside in a dish. Heat the pot over very high heat. Place the meat in the pot and add the onions flat side down. Brown for 5 to 6 minutes, turning the meat over only after 3 minutes.
→ To our greatest delight, more juices are created here and numerous Maillard reactions occur on the meat, developing its flavor. The onions will turn the stock a nice amber color.

3
Take the meat out of the pot and set it aside in a dish. Add the mushrooms, carrots, leeks, garlic, cloves, and bouquet garni. Cook the vegetables for 5 minutes over low heat until softened.

4
Place the meat and the bones back into the pot, add water up to 2 inches above them, and heat slowly without letting it boil or even simmer.
→ You should only be able to see some steam and a little bubble float to the surface from time to time. You're infusing the meat to extract as many of its flavors as possible.
→ As this temperature, no foam or scum forms on the water.

5
Don't add salt, don't add pepper, don't stir it, don't cover it. Let it infuse for at least 6 hours over gentle heat.
→ Meanwhile, the flavors of everything you put in the pot creep slowly into the liquid. The tasteless water evaporates and the flavors of the stock intensify little by little. Just add a little water if the meat or the bones begin to peek out of the surface. Again, let time do its work because we are making an infusion.

6
After cooking, let cool for 1 hour before pouring your stock through a conical strainer or a cloth-covered colander over a large bowl.
→ The cloth will collect lots of tiny, useless pieces of meat that fell off the bone during the cooking process. Your stock will be a lot clearer and tastier.

And now you have an insanely delicious stock!

A STOCK IS AN INFUSION

When you make a broth or a stock, you're not cooking the meat but infusing it so that it releases as many of its flavors as possible. It's exactly the same as making a herbal infusion. That's the idea you should have in mind: an infusion.

IT'S EASY TO FREEZE

Once your stock is cooked, pour it through a cloth and store it in closed containers in the freezer. You can take them out when you need them, for a stew or for boiling a chicken, for example.

SCUM AND IMPURITIES

You often hear "remove the scum and impurities that float to the surface." Don't be fooled by this! First of all, the definition of the word "scum" is a mixture of liquid and impurities. There are impurities in our meat? Really? What do you do about the impurities when you're grilling a rib of beef or cooking vegetables? Well, nothing, because there are none. There's meat and there's vegetables. That's it! The white foam that forms is a mix of clotted proteins, fat, and air. Don't worry about impurities; there aren't any. But you should remove this foam if it forms because it might give a bitter taste to the stock.

HOW CAN I AVOID GETTING THIS FOAM?

It's funny that all the cookbooks tell you to "skim it off." But what if, instead of skimming, we make sure that there isn't any scum (or foam) at all? The secret to no scum, or very little of it, is to cook the stock just below the simmering point.

IT'S VERY FAST TO MAKE

The preparation time for a stock or a broth is very brief: 10 minutes, no more! It's the cooking time that's long. But we don't mind that because it cooks on its own. And as it does, we can read or chat to a friend on the phone.

STOCK, BROTH, CONSOMMÉ, AND VELOUTÉ

Stock is cooked for a long time with bones, to extract as many flavors as possible. Broth isn't cooked for as long and doesn't usually contain bones. A consommé is a stock or a broth that's been clarified with egg white and ground meat to make it translucent. A velouté is made with broth and thickened with a roux (butter + flour). And if you add cream, a velouté will become a cream sauce. An egg yolk is sometimes added.

SHOULD I DRAIN OFF THE FAT OR NOT?

As the stock cools, the fat rises and forms a layer across the surface. You can leave it, remove some of it, or remove all of it. If you leave the fat, the flavors of the stock will be less distinct but will linger for longer on the palate. If you remove part of it, the flavors will be more refined. If you remove all the fat, the flavors will be very refined. In any case, don't throw out the fat; it's perfect for replacing oil in a vinaigrette or for basting vegetables.

VEAL STOCK

Preparation time: 10 minutes
Cooking time: at least 6 hours
Resting time: 1 hour

MAKE 4 ¼ QUARTS

- 4½ lb cheap veal cuts, such as veal tail or short rib
- 2 marrowbones
- 4½ lb ox bones, crushed by your butcher
- 2 tbsp olive oil
- 1 large onion, halved
- 3½ oz button mushrooms, washed and diced
- 3 carrots, peeled and diced
- 2 leeks (green leaves removed), washed and diced
- 4 cloves garlic, peeled and crushed
- 2 cloves
- 1 bouquet garni (10 sprigs parsley, 5 to 6 sprigs thyme, 2 bay leaves cut in half) wrapped in leek leaves and firmly tied

It's the same principle as for the beef stock: brown the bones in the oven, then the meat, then soften the vegetables and mushrooms, and finally, pour in the water to cook everything for at least 6 hours.

PORK STOCK

Preparation time: 10 minutes
Cooking time: at least 6 hours
Resting time: 1 hour

MAKES 4 ¼ QUARTS

- 4½ lb cheap pork cuts (cheek, rib tips, shank)
- 7 oz pork rind
- 2¼ lb pork bones, crushed by your butcher
- 2 tbsp olive oil
- 1 large onion, halved
- 3½ oz button mushrooms, washed and diced
- 3 carrots, peeled and diced
- 2 leeks (green leaves removed), washed and diced
- 5 cloves
- 1 bouquet garni (10 sprigs parsley, 5 or 6 sprigs thyme, 2 bay leaves cut in half) wrapped in leek leaves and firmly tied

It's the same principle as for the beef stock: brown the bones in the oven, then the meat, then soften the vegetables and mushrooms, and finally, pour in the water to cook everything for at least 6 hours.

LAMB STOCK

Preparation time: 10 minutes
Cooking time: 4 hours
Resting time: 1 hour

MAKES 3 QUARTS

- 2¼ lb cheap lamb cuts, such as the breast or neck
- 2¼ lb lamb bones, crushed by your butcher
- 2 tbsp unsalted butter
- 3½ oz button mushrooms, washed and diced
- 3 carrots, peeled and diced
- 2 leeks (green leaves removed), washed and diced
- 2 large onions, halved
- 6 cloves garlic, peeled and crushed
- 1 celery stalk, washed
- 1 bouquet garni (4 to 6 sprigs parsley, 5 to 6 sprigs thyme) wrapped in leek leaves and firmly tied

It's the same principle as for the beef stock: brown the bones in the oven, then the meat, then soften the vegetables and mushrooms, and finally, pour in the water to cook everything for 4 hours.

POULTRY STOCK

Preparation time: 10 minutes
Cooking time: 2 hours
Resting time: 1 hour

MAKES 3 ⅛ QUARTS

- 2¼ lb poultry giblets (wings and drumsticks)
- 3 poultry carcasses, cut into small pieces
- 2 tbsp unsalted butter
- 3 carrots, peeled and diced
- 2 leeks (green leaves removed), washed and diced
- 2 large onions, halved
- 3½ oz button mushrooms, washed and diced
- 6 cloves garlic, peeled and crushed
- 2 cloves
- 1 celery stalk, washed
- 1 bouquet garni (5 to 6 sprigs parsley, 5 to 6 sprigs thyme) wrapped in leek leaves and firmly tied

It's the same principle as for the beef stock but without browning the bones or the meat or the onions. Soften the vegetables, the herbs, and the mushrooms in the butter, then add the giblets and the carcasses. Add water and cook everything for 2 hours.

THE GOLDEN RULES FOR A GOOD STOCK

THE QUALITY OF THE WATER

This is fun-da-mental! Water is the main ingredient in stock. Don't hesitate to use a few bottles of mineral water if your tap water has an aftertaste. It will cost very little and will make a huge difference.

NO SALT OR PEPPER

Salt slows down the transfer of the meat juices to the stock. The pepper infuses and becomes bitter and acrid when cooked in liquid. You can add them at the end. In the past, pepper was used not for its flavors but solely for its antiseptic properties.

THE COOKING TIME

It takes time for the meat to infuse and release the most flavors possible into the water, at least 2 hours for a poultry stock and 6 or 7 for a beef stock.

THE COOKING MATERIAL

You don't make stock in just any saucepan. Nope! The type of material the saucepan or the pot is made of is of huge importance: it should be cast iron or stainless steel. Whatever you do, don't use a simple iron saucepan.

THE COOKING TEMPERATURE

For heaven's sake, no boiling or even simmering! As the ingredients infuse, the collagen in the meat melts and turns into a delicious gelatin. The water should only be steaming and you should see a little bubble rise to the surface from time to time, nothing more.

CHECK THE QUALITY OF THE STOCK

After a night in the refrigerator, your stock should have turned into a delicious gelatin, just like red-currant jelly. This is the proof that the collagen in the meat transformed into a flavorful gelatin. A world-class stock!

THE APPENDICES

SCIENTIFIC BIBLIOGRAPHY

Alberti P., Panea B., Sanudo C., Olleta J.-L., Ripoli G., Ertbjerg P., Christensen M., Gigli S., Failla S., Concetti S., Hocquette J.-F., Jailler R., Rudel S., Renand G., Nute G.-R., Richardson R.-I., Williams J.-L., « Live weight, body size and carcass characteristics of young bulls of fifteen European breeds », *Livesock Science*, 2008.

Allen P., « Test du système MSA pour prédire la qualité de la viande bovine irlandaise », *Viandes & produits carnés*, 2015.

Barnes K. K., Collins T. A., Dion S., Reynolds H., Riess S. M., *Importance of cattle biodiversity and its influence on the nutrient composition of beef*, Iowa State University, 2012.

Bastien D., « Suspension pelvienne, un impact important sur la tendreté des gros bovins », *Viandes & produits carnés, n°24*, 2005.

Bernard C., Cassar-Malek I., Gentes G., Delavaud A., Dunoyer N., Micol D., Renand G., Hocquette J.-F., « Qualité sensorielle de la viande bovine : identification de marqueurs génomiques », *Viandes & produits carnés n°26*, 2007.

Christensen M., Ertbjerg P., Failla S., Sañudo C., Richardson R.-I., Nute G. R., Olleta J.-L., Panea B., Albertí P., Juárez M., Hocquette J.-F., Williams J.-L., « Relationship between collagen characteristics, lipid content and raw and cooked texture of meat from young bulls of fifteen European breeds », *Meat Science*, 2011.

Collectif, *Les qualités organoleptiques de la viande bovine, bases scientifiques pour une bonne utilisation culinaire*, Centre d'information des viandes, 2004.

Contreras J., *L'alimentation carnée à travers les âges et la culture*, 12ᵉ Journée des sciences du muscle et technologies des viandes, 2008.

Cornu A., Kondjoyan N., Frencia J.P., Berdagué J.-L., « Tracer l'alimentation des bovins : déchiffrer le message des composés volatils des tissus adipeux », *Viandes & produits carnés n°22*, 2001.

Cuvelier C., Clinquart A., Cabaraux J.-F., Istasse L., Hornick J.-L., « Races bovines bouchères, stratégies d'orientation des viandes par analyse factorielle », *Viandes & produits carnés n°24*, 2005.

De Smet S., « Meat, poultry and fish composition; Strategies for optimizing human intake of essential nutrients », *Animal Frontiers*, 2012.

Dolle J.-B., Gac A., Le Gall A., *L'empreinte carbone du lait et de la viande bovine*, Rencontre Recherches Ruminants, 2009.

Durand D., Gatelier P., Parafita É., « Stabilité oxydative et qualités des viandes », *Inra Productions Animales*, 2010

Ellies-Oury M.-P., Durand Y., Delavigne A.-E, Picard B., Micol D., Dumont R., « Objectivation de la notion de grain de viande et perspectives d'utilisation pour évaluer la tendreté des viandes de bovins charolais », *Inra Productions Animales*, 2015.

Escalon S., *Ne dites plus goût mais flaveur, Inra Productions Animale*s, 2015.

Gandemer G., Duchène C., *Valeurs nutritionnelles des viandes cuites*, Centre d'information des viandes, 2015.

Geay Y., Beauchart D., Hocquette J.-F., Culioli J., *Valeur diététique et qualités sensorielles des viandes de ruminants. Incidence de l'alimentation des animaux, Inra Productions Animales*, 2002.

Guillemin N., Cassar-Mallek I., Hocquette J.-F., Jurie C., Micol D., Listrat A., Leveziel H., Renand G., Picard B., « La maîtrise de la tendreté de la viande bovine : identification de marqueurs biologiques », *Inra Productions Animales*, 2009.

Hall J.-B., Hunt M.-C., « Collagen solubility of A-maturity bovine longissimus muscle as affected by nutrinional regimen », *Journal of animal science*, 1982.

Hocquette J.-F., « Les lipides dans la viande : mythe ou réalité ? », *Cahiers Agriculture*, 2004.

Hocquette J.-F., Botreazu R., Legrand I., Polkinghome R., Pethick D. W., Lherm M., Picard B., Doreau M., Terlouw E.-M.-C., « Win-win strategies for high beef quality, consumer satisfaction, and farm efficiency, low environmental impacts and improved animal welfare », *Animal Production Science*, 2014.

Hocquette J.-F., Gigli S., *Indicators of milk and beef quality*, European Association for Animal Production, 2005.

Hocquette J.-F., Ortigues-Marty I., Picard B., Doreau M., Bauchart D., Micol D., « La viande des ruminants, de nouvelles approches pour améliorer et maîtriser la qualité », *Viandes & produits carnés n°24*, 2005.

Hocquette J.-F., Van Wezemael L., Chriki S., Legrand I., Verbeke W., Farmer L., Scollan N.-D., Polkinghorne R., Rodbotten R., Allen P., Pethick D. W., « Modelling of beef sensory quality for a better prediction of palatability », *Meat Science*, 2014.

Jurie C., Martin J.-F., Listrat A., Jailler R., Culioli J., Picard B., « Carcass and muscle characteristics of bull cull cows between 4 and 9 years of age », *Animal Science*, 2006.

Kondjoyan A., Oillic S., Portanguen S., Gros J.-B., « Combined Heat Transfer and Kinetic Models to Predict Cooking Loss During Heat Treatment of Beef Meat », *Meat Science*, 2013.

Manuel Juarez J., Larsen I. L., Klassen M., Aalhus J. L., « Évolution de la tendreté du bœuf canadien entre 2001 et 2011 », *Viandes & produits carnés*, 2013.

Martineau C., « Viande de veau, importance de l'évolution de la couleur après 24 heures post mortem », *Viandes & produits carnés n°26*, 2006.

Matthews K., « Le standard de qualité EBLEX : un exemple de démarche qualité en Angleterre », *Viandes & produits carnés*, 2015.

Micol D., Jurie C., Hocquette J.-F., « Muscle et viande de ruminant – Qualités sensorielles de la viande bovine. Impacts des facteurs d'élevage », *Quæ*, 2010.

Normand J., Rubat É., Évrat-Georgel C., Turin F., Denoyelle C., « Les Français sont-ils satisfaits de la tendreté de la viande bovine ? », *Viandes & produits carnés*, 2014.

Normand J., Rubat E., Evrat-Georgel C., Turin F., Denoyelle C., *Enquête nationale sur la tendreté de la viande bovine proposée au consommateur français*, Rencontre Recherches Ruminants, 2009.

Ouali A., Herrera-Mendez C. H., Coulis G., Becila S., Boudjellal A., Aubry L., Sentandreu M. A., « Revisiting the conversion of muscle into meat and the underlying mechanisms », *Meat Science*, 2006.

Ouali A., Herrera-Mendez C.-H., Becila S., Boudkellal A., « Maturation des viandes, une nouvelle donne pour la compréhension de la maturation des viandes », *Viandes & produits carnés n°24*, 2005.

Oury M.-P., Agabriel C., Agabriel J., Blanquet J., Micol D., Picard B., Roux M., Dumont R., « Viande de génisse charolaise, différenciation de la qualité sensorielle liée aux pratiques d'élevage », *Viandes & produits carnés n°26*, 2007.

Parafita É., « Les viandes marinées, que savons-nous sur le marinage des viandes ? », *Viandes & produits carnés n°28*, 2011.

Parafita É., « L'instabilité de couleur des UVCI de bœuf », *Viandes & produits carnés n°27*, 2009.

Pethick D.-W., Harper G.-S., Hocquette J.-F., Wang Y.-H., *Marbling biology – what do we know about getting fat into muscle ?*, Australian beef – The leader conference – « The impact of science on the beef industry », 2006.

Picard B., Bauchard D., « Muscle et viande de ruminant », *Quæ*, 2010.

Piccigirard L., « Cuisson industrielle des viandes, mécanismes et contraintes », *Viandes & produits carnés n°27*, 2009.

Polkinghorne R.-J., Breton J., « Qualité des carcasses et des viandes bovines pour le consommateur », *Viandes & produits carnés*, 2013.

Richard H., Giampaoli P., Toulemonde B., Duquenoy A., *Flaveurs et procédés de cuisson*, École nationale supérieure des Industries agricoles et alimentaires.

Thomas E., « État d'engraissement des carcasses », *Viandes & produits carnés n°23*, 2003.

Thompson J.-M, « The effects of marbling on flavour and juiciness scores of cooked beef, after adjusting to a constant tenderness », *Australian Journal of Experimental Agriculture*, 2004.

Thornberg E., « Effects of heat on meat proteins – Implication on structure and quality of meat products », *Meat Science*, 2005.

Tribot Laspière P., Chatelin Y.-M., « Le procédé « Tendercut », un impact non négligeable sur la tendreté de la viande de gros bovins », *Viandes & produits carnés n°25*, 2006.

ACKNOWLEDGMENTS

"So, firstly, thank you, or THANK YOU to my wife, Marine, for having left me so much time to work on this book. Thank you for supporting me during this long project. Darling, you're the coolest. I love you!

A huge thank you to the whole team at Marabout; honestly, I didn't know that such hard-working people existed.

Thank you to Emmanuel Le Vallois and to Raphaële Wauquiez for giving me free rein to do my research. Thank you also for having verified this mass of information.

Thank you to Alexandre Livonnet who created the mock-up of this book to make all the information digestible.

Thank you to Agathe Legué who oversaw and coordinated the progress of this project from one day to the next.

Thank you to Marion Pipart for positioning and reorganizing all the texts and drawings—there were a lot of them!

Thank you to Sophie Villette who did an incredible job on the page layouts.

And thank you to Anne Bonvoisin and to Alizé Bouttier who are now taking charge of this baby.

A very, very big thank you to Jean Grosson for his magnificent drawings and for the unbelievable amount of time you spent on them. A crazy amount of hard work! We thought we'd never get there, but we did. Thank you, so much of this book exists because of you.

Among those who lent me a hand by giving me time, knowledge, explanations and information:

A big thank you to Hervé This for his research, his writings, and the time he spent answering my questions.

Thank you also to Jean-François Hocquette who manages the meat department within the National Institute of Agricultural Research, who sent me hundreds and hundreds of pages of hugely helpful scientific research. Thank you to the institute's Émilie Parafita, too.

Finally, thank you to all those people who set aside their time to answer particular questions whose answers were difficult to find. In no particular order: Charles Dufraisse, Éléonore Sauvageot, Patrick Duler, Éric Ospital, Joris Pfaff, Gérard Vives, Stéphanie Maubé, Alessandra Pierini, Chihiro Masui, Jean-François Ravault, Jacques Reder, Cédric Landais, Sylvie Horn, Xavier Épain and his sidekick Jean-Charles Cuxac aka "The Cube," Francis Fauchère, Jacques Appert, Thomas S.B., Claude Élissade, Vincent Pousson, Vincent Giroud. and last but not least, Anne Etorre.

This isn't the Star Wars end credits, but it's pretty close ;-)